A CENTURY
of INNOVATION

3M *Innovation*

This book is dedicated to the thousands of 3M employees who have made 3M a strong, vibrant, growing, diversified technology company with innovative products and services in markets throughout the world.

About the cover:
Shortly after the Century of Innovation began, 3M introduced Wetordry sandpaper, shown in the background, giving the company its first entry into the important automotive market. Inventor Francis Okie often scribbled notes on scraps of the sandpaper as he worked. Today, 3M optical films, shown in the foreground, are among the company's newest products. These innovative films enhance the performance of electronic displays from the smallest hand held devices, such as cell phones, to large liquid crystal display monitors and televisions.

First Edition: 2002

International Standard Book Number
ISBN 0-9722302-0-3 (cloth)
ISBN 0-9722302-1-1 (paper)

from the CEO . . .

It is exciting to celebrate 3M's first Century of Innovation with the extended 3M family.

There are many reasons for 3M's hundred years of progress: the unique ability to create new-to-the-world product categories, market leadership achieved by serving customers better than anyone else and a global network of unequalled international resources.

The primary reason for 3M's success, however, is the people of 3M. This company has been blessed with generations of imaginative, industrious employees in all parts of the enterprise, all around the world. I hope you'll join us in celebrating not only a Century of Innovation but also a century of talented and innovative individuals.

W. James McNerney, Jr.

Chairman of the Board and Chief Executive Officer

Contents

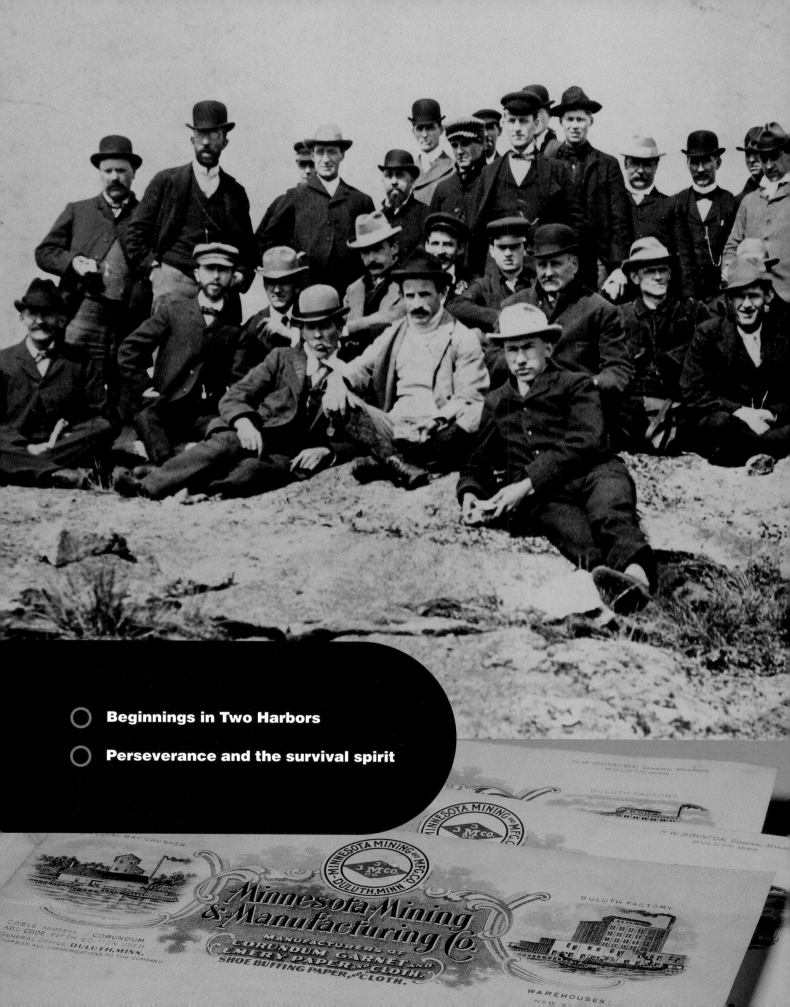

○ **Beginnings in Two Harbors**

○ **Perseverance and the survival spirit**

Early Struggles Plant the Seeds of Innovation

In today's business world, innovation is the mantra of success. For companies large and small, the big winners are those that match new, marketable ideas with customers before anyone else can. It takes flexibility and creativity and a willingness to risk. ● One hundred years ago, when 3M was founded as Minnesota Mining and Manufacturing, the formula for business success was the same. But for 3M, perseverance mattered even more. The multiple crises that rocked 3M a century ago could have easily destroyed a young company in the 21st century. Imagine, for example, that your "big idea" for a new product has properties that will leave your competition in the dust. You attract venture capital, invest in production facilities, and set your sales force loose to beat the market leaders. Then—as now—everything is riding on a marketable innovation with immense promise.

But instead of soaring revenues and customer orders, your big idea fails. Your product is flawed. Your major investors have given you all the funding they can. This is precisely what happened when five northern Minnesota entrepreneurs extracted a mineral from the shores of Lake Superior. The optimistic partners believed their "Crystal Bay" mineral was corundum, almost as tough as diamonds and an ideal substitute for garnet, the mineral abrasive found in grinding wheels used by furniture makers.

The founders of 3M were banking on success when the company was born in 1902. Each man contributed $1,000 in start-up funds in exchange for 1,000 shares. They started their venture in Two Harbors, a booming frontier village on the North Shore of Lake Superior, where the winds of entrepreneurship were as strong as Alberta Clippers blowing across the lake. Iron ore had been discovered in the region and prospectors hoped to get rich with new mineral claims, including the possibility of finding gold.

> **Incorporate First, Investigate Later**

Leaps of faith were common in those days, as one observer noted: "Like so many others who organized mining ventures in the early 1900s . . . 3M apparently incorporated first and investigated later." The company sold shares and made plans to start mining before they were even certain they had customers. Finally, Hermon Cable, a 3M co-founder and successful Two Harbors meat market owner, traveled to Chicago and Detroit to test samples of 3M's corundum with potential customers. Though Cable came home describing only "fairly satisfactory" results, he encouraged his four partners—who all seemed infected with Cable's enthusiasm—to move ahead.

It was almost two years after 3M's founding that the company sold its first batch of minerals, one ton of Crystal Bay corundum, in March 1904. Fortunately, based on the founders' own solid reputations, the local bank had no qualms about loaning the company operating capital until more sales revenues materialized.

Chapter opening photos

Prospective stockholders were offered a free boat trip from Two Harbors to the 3M Crystal Bay plant to inspect 3M's corundum; 3M company letterhead; Original 3M plant on North Shore of Lake Superior at Crystal Bay, Minnesota, 1903; Label on back of Crystal Bay corundum paper.

ARTICLES OF INCORPORATION
OF THE
MINNESOTA MINING AND MANUFACTURING COMPANY.

KNOW ALL MEN BY THESE PRESENTS, That we, the undersigned, do hereby associate ourselves together as a body corporate for the purposes hereinafter mentioned, under the provisions of title two (2), of Chapter thirty-four (34) of the General Statutes of the State of Minnesota of 1894, and the various acts amendatory thereof and supplemental thereto, and to that end, do hereby execute and adopt the following Articles of Incorporation.

ARTICLE I.

The name of this corporation shall be "MINNESOTA MINING AND MANUFACTURING COMPANY".

ARTICLE II.

The general nature of the business of this corporation shall be as follows: to engage in and carry on the busines of Mining, Quarrying, Crushing, Analysing Smelting, Shipping and Marketing abrasives and all kinds of Minerals and Metals and the Manufacturing of abrasives of all kinds and other mineral products; to acquire, buy, sell, lease, own, control, examine, explore, develop and operate Iron Mines, and all kinds of quarrying and mining property, and to market the product thereof; to build, own, control and operate and market
machine

But a long dry spell followed because 3M's product was actually anorthosite, a soft mineral that is inferior to garnet. 3M's partners voted to cut their salaries and then abolished them altogether. Meanwhile, impatient suppliers wanted their money, and 3M owed its own employees back pay. (Each of the partners contributed

> The first key issue the company faced was failing to make quality sandpaper. They could have given up and gone under. It's incredible that they persisted and looked beyond a short-term vision of success. **> Dick Lidstad** *retired vice president, Human Resources*

money to cover the payroll.) 3M had little success selling its stock to raise operating capital, and the company was racing head-long for disaster. Only two investors stepped forward—Edgar Ober, a St. Paul railroad man, and John Dwan, a Two Harbors lawyer and co-founder of 3M, who had a reputation for smart investments.

Ober came from modest means. After graduating from high school in St. Paul, he became a clerk at the Chicago, St. Paul, Minneapolis and Omaha Railroad. The hardworking Ober was promoted often, but his ambitions soared beyond his job. That's when Ober took a chance and bought 5,000 shares in 3M. He had high aspirations and faith in the venture. In 12 of the early, touch-and-go years of 3M, Ober served as

president and never drew a paycheck. To scrape along in those years, Cable also worked without pay and so did Dwan. Decades later, William McKnight, considered the "architect" of 3M growth, credited Dwan, Ober and Cable with "remarkable faith and tenacity." They also shared a strong work ethic and Midwestern roots, a background that worked in their favor during difficult times.

With no revenues in sight and the treasury bare, 3M's founders tried another approach in 1904. If grinding wheel manufacturers aren't buying our corundum to make their wheels, let's make the wheels ourselves, they reasoned. Deciding to become a manufacturer of

> You have an idea, you take this idea and you pull all the things that need to come together and it's called 'believing.' Innovation boils down to conceive it, believe it, achieve it. **> Leon Royer** *retired executive director, 3M Leadership Development Center, Human Resources, formerly a technical director*

finished goods, rather than merely a supplier of raw materials, set 3M on a new, stronger course, but it didn't seem so at the time. The partners had no knowledge of the grinding wheel business. They also didn't know that an ambitious New York inventor named Edward Acheson had discovered how to make an artificial abrasive combining carbon and silicon at high temperatures.

1 Anorthosite, mistaken for corundum, was mined at 3M's Crystal Bay property. **2** Articles of Incorporation, signed on June 13, 1902, by the five founders (Henry Bryan, Hermon Cable, Dr. J. Danley Budd, John Dwan and William McGonagle.) **3** John Dwan in his law office, where the company had its headquarters until 1916, when 3M moved to St. Paul.

Acheson's "carborundum" was taking off on the East Coast, especially with grinding wheel manufacturers.

Searching for other options to keep the company afloat, the founders jettisoned the grinding wheel idea a year later and chose to focus on manufacturing sandpaper, another business they knew nothing about. To get started, the company needed about $40,000 to pay its debts and finance a sandpaper plant. Who would be the financial supporter this time? Ober called his younger friend, Lucius Ordway,

> Ober had a clear vision that 3M could be built on manufacturing abrasives when the United States was becoming an industrial nation. If he hadn't been bold and courageous, 3M wouldn't exist today. > **Roger Appeldorn**
>
> *retired corporate scientist*

co-owner of Crane and Ordway, a plumbing supply firm in St. Paul and a man of means who liked to take risks. Ordway invested $25,000 on the assurance that he wouldn't need to be involved in the day-to-day affairs of 3M.

Ordway migrated to St. Paul, at age 21, after graduating from Brown University. He married into St. Paul society, promoted new business development in the city, sailed the waters of White Bear Lake as his yacht club's first commodore, and pursued his own company's

1 Letter from John Dwan to Edgar Ober, July 13, 1906, questioning the future of 3M. **2** Sheets of unsuccessful Crystal Bay corundum paper. **3** Early 3M sandpaper factory, in a converted flour mill in Duluth. Its location on the waterfront made it easily accessible to Lake Superior boats.

growth. By the time Ober appealed to his friend for an investment in 3M, Ordway was already worth nearly $1 million.

After Ordway had invested $25,000, the founders came back for more money. Within two years, Ordway had invested $200,000 in the fledgling enterprise. Even though sales had begun to pick up, 3M still needed more cash. Breaking his own rules about daily involvement, Ordway became 3M's president and personally approved every purchase and every check issued. In the back of his mind, Ordway considered getting out, but he couldn't think of anyone else who was a likely prospect to buy his majority share of 3M.

A survival spirit dominated the little company and, thankfully, a modicum of good sense. Even though there was talk of large copper deposits at Carlton Peak in northern Minnesota, Ordway argued that 3M could go broke using all its resources trying to find the precious metal. Ordway also refused to engage in price fixing when two other abrasives companies suggested to 3M in 1907 that life would be ever so much better if all three just "cooperated on prices."

> **Perseverance and a Spirit of Survival**

About that time, 3M's partners learned that their Crystal Bay corundum wasn't corundum at all, but a low-grade anorthosite that was useless for abrasive work. If the company was going to make sandpaper, it needed a source of garnet and only two deposits existed in the United States. Both were in the Adirondack Mountains

of New York and both mines were dominated by larger sandpaper manufacturers.

3M had no domestic source of raw materials, no ready cash and no product. This might have been a logical time to admit defeat. Instead, the company moved to Duluth in 1905 and found a source of Spanish garnet. It received its first shipment in 1907.

At just about the same time, 3M's first and only "angel," Ordway, introduced the concept of patient money—a term that is still used today at 3M to represent long-term investment in an idea, technology or

> If you look at 3M technologies and the strongest programs we have today, they've been long-term. It's not the money that's patient, it's the people supporting the new idea that are patient.
>
> **> Leon Royer**

product that shows promise, even when others argue otherwise. The angel in Ordway resurfaced again in 1910 when he acquired property to move 3M from Duluth to St. Paul. The first step was construction of a new sandpaper plant. It was a big gamble, given 3M's ragged history. In fact, McKnight said years later that without Ordway's investment of patient money, 3M would have disappeared before 1910.

The company seemed star-crossed. First, a worthless mineral, then virtually no sales, poor product quality

4 Workers taking a break during construction of 3M's original St. Paul building. 5 Harriet (Hattie) Swailes, 3M's first female employee, began as a "general office girl" in 1903. Later she transferred to St. Paul as secretary to McKnight and retired in 1923.

and formidable competition. All the founders had to keep them going was perseverance, a spirit of survival and optimism. What would happen next? It was the equivalent of the sky falling, only at ground level. 3M built its new plant, a two-story, 85-foot by 165-foot

The founders had unshakable faith in the future of 3M. Even though they almost went bankrupt, they kept pouring money in. You succeed if you have faith. **> Walter Meyers** *retired vice president, Marketing*

structure with a basement. It wasn't the best construction, but it was all the budget allowed. When raw materials arrived from Duluth and were stacked on the first floor, one Saturday, the weight tested the timbers—and the timbers lost. The floor of the new plant collapsed and every carton, bag and container landed in a heap in the basement.

With the plant finally restored, 3M faced quality problems. The company had sales of $212,898 in 1911, but disgruntled customers were sending its inferior sandpaper back. To make matters worse, 3M had no lab or technical expertise to figure out what was wrong with its sandpaper or how to fix it. 3M's naturally ambitious sales manager, John Pearce, grew dispirited and quit. For a solution, Ober turned to 3M's young office manager.

"Much to my surprise," McKnight recalled years later, "Mr. Ober appointed me sales manager to succeed Mr. Pearce and to fall heir to his troubles." McKnight knew nothing about sales or quality assurance, but he experienced a dimension of 3M's young culture that has become a key strength for 100 years. It was to provide promising people with new opportunities, support them and give them time to learn and thrive. That is precisely what happened. When McKnight proved he could take initiative, be creative and produce, Ober promoted him to general manager in 1914, ahead of two men who were older and more experienced.

3M recognized the importance of quality assurance and technology excellence sooner than most companies. The builders of 3M knew that if their company was to be a leader, they had to identify and solve problems.

> Ken Schoen *retired executive vice president,*

Information and Imaging Technologies Sector

1

1 Letter to 3M Secretary John Dwan from an early stock-holder, 1910.

Lou Weyand got a taste of 3M's work ethic and frugal temperament early in his career. Weyand joined the company in 1915 as an office clerk in the company's five-person national sales office, based in downtown Chicago. When a price changed or a special order came in, it was not unusual for Sales Manager Archibald Bush to work with Weyand and a shipping clerk until midnight, packing products, labeling and preparing them for shipping. Because he was away most of the week making sales calls, Bush worked Saturdays and often Sundays with Weyand to catch up on paper work. Weyand's wife frequently volunteered as a stenographer and the trio warmed themselves with a kerosene stove in the drafty 3M office.

When Weyand, who later retired as executive vice president and director, Sales, began selling four years later and covered six states, he said, "Mr. Bush finally condescended to provide a Dodge sedan which relieved me of a lot of foot travel, buses and trains." The bargain vehicle had only a rear bumper, but that didn't concern the frugal Bush. He told Weyand that he was responsible for watching carefully and not hitting anything. Weyand wasn't allowed a spare tire either, only tire patches. Traveling salesmen couldn't charge laundry costs to the company and, if there was a choice of restaurants for meals, they were expected to go to a coffee shop and sit on a stool.

Walter Meyers was a marketing student at Wayne State University in 1935 when he came up with a unique idea to promote a new product. 3M had introduced a blockbuster product, Scotch cellophane tape, five years earlier in 1930, the year after the U.S. stock market crashed. "I got to thinking about new ways to use the tape; one was putting up posters in grocery stores to advertise specials," Meyers recalled. "3M didn't know their tape turned dark brown and stained windows when it was exposed to sun. I wrote them a letter about this problem."

Even though the country was deep in the Depression and 3M wasn't hiring, Meyers' letter landed him a job unloading boxcars for $75 and $10 in stock a month. But Meyers' first assignment wasn't the loading dock. It was a trip to St. Paul to meet privately with Bush. If there was something the company could learn from an 18-year-old, Bush, who by then was general sales manager, wanted to know it. Meyers spent his entire career at 3M and eventually became vice president, Marketing.

When **Harry Heltzer** graduated from the University of Minnesota in 1933 with his metallurgical engineering degree, he remembered a class field trip to 3M's minerals processing department. "I was intrigued with how they crushed and sized minerals to make abrasives for sandpaper in a six-floor building nicknamed 'six floors of fun and frolic,'" Heltzer said. The Benz building was physically isolated from 3M headquarters and had a reputation for creativity and freedom to experiment.

Heltzer applied for work and became a $12-per-week factory worker unloading boxcars, as most newcomers did. About the time Heltzer moved to 3M's minerals department lab, a customer asked Sales Manager George Halpin why 3M couldn't use its mineral expertise to make reflective glass beads to improve highway markings. Young and inexperienced as he was, Heltzer got to use his education and had the chance to "fool around with the challenge."

"One of the things that has always been important at 3M is giving people a chance to branch out and spend some time on projects that excite them," said Heltzer. "I was intrigued with how to make glass beads. My first ones involved melting glass in a crucible about the size of a cup and pouring it out of the sixth floor of the Benz Building. When you melt glass and pour it in a thin stream, it breaks into particles that turn into bubbles. I'd run down the six floors and sweep up what I had." Those early experiments led to 3M's Scotchlite reflective products and the chance for a young man to try his ideas: "Mr. McKnight and the people around him recognized the value of gambling on people instead of things," he said. Forty years later, Heltzer became 3M chairman of the board and chief executive officer (CEO).

It was McKnight who went straight to customers' factories to find out why 3M's sandpaper was failing. And, it was McKnight who told Ober—with all due respect—3M would never succeed unless its general manager supervised both sales and manufacturing.

The one-two punch in 1914 and 1915 that hit 3M might have been the end of this start-up story, but once again, perseverance prevailed. Once the plant was restored, McKnight dealt with what he called "an epidemic of complaints" that spread like a nasty virus

'We want you to inspect everything,' Mr. McKnight told me. He outlined what he wanted me to do and I said, 'I don't know how long it's going to take.' He said, 'All your life if you like; we've got to get a good product.' > **Bill Vievering** *3M's first quality assurance employee and a Carlton Society member*

among customers and "what little reputation we had . . . was badly impaired." In the daily mail, every complaint was the same . . . pieces of bare, rumpled sandpaper. Quite simply, the crushed garnet fell off when the customers tried to use 3M's product.

After weeks of frantic study, a worker noticed some crushed garnet left from manufacturing that had been tossed in a water pail. The water's surface was oily. If the garnet had been contaminated with oil, it would resist glue and never stick to the sandpaper backing.

Retracing the route of the Spanish garnet shipment, 3M discovered that its sacks of garnet had crossed a stormy Atlantic Ocean with an olive oil shipment. When the ship pitched and rolled, a couple of casks broke and oil soaked into the garnet bound for St. Paul.

3M was left with 200 tons of oily garnet and a pack of angry customers. Fortunately, Orson Hull, 3M's resourceful and determined factory superintendent, finally found a solution after many experiments. He "cooked" the garnet and roasted the oil away. That incident led to 3M's first quality program. But, regaining the trust of customers would take much longer and that task fell to a young up-and-comer, Archibald Bush.

Like McKnight, Bush was raised on a Midwestern farm, paid his way through business school in Duluth, then joined 3M as a bookkeeper. But, the extroverted, ambitious and energetic Bush seemed far better suited to sales. It was Bush who is credited with building a strong sales culture at 3M in the company's early years. He later held leadership positions on 3M's Executive Committee.

The second punch in the one-two punch came on the heels of 3M's first real success. When the large and established Carborundum Company of Niagara Falls, New York, introduced a cloth coated with an artificial abrasive as a substitute for emery cloth used in the auto industry, scrappy little 3M responded in kind. "We very quickly made arrangements to obtain a competing artificial mineral produced by the Norton Company of Worcester, Massachusetts, and we made 'Three-M-ite

1 Archibald G. Bush, sales manager in the national sales office in Chicago, circa 1919, seated at a desk received in payment from a craftsman who owed 3M $16.84. 2 William L. McKnight as a young man. 3 McKnight pictured in 1939, inspecting the cornerstone of Building 21, which would serve as company headquarters until 1962. 4 McKnight in the 1950s. It was rare to find him working in his shirtsleeves.

Background: 3M aluminum oxide sandpaper

Even though he started his business career as an assistant bookkeeper, in 1907, and never graduated from Duluth Business University, William L. McKnight developed a personal business philosophy that was profoundly progressive. In fact, what McKnight espoused 75 years ago is echoed in today's best-selling business books.

McKnight broke into business at a time when a U.S. businessman was often a larger-than-life economic hero who ruled his enterprise with an autocratic hand. Workers should be seen and not heard. If a breakthrough idea surfaced, it would surely come from the top.

McKnight saw business and the workplace differently. He understood interdependence as well as the importance of personal freedom. "It is proper to emphasize how much we depend on each other," McKnight said on his 60th anniversary with 3M. In business, he said, "the first principle is the promotion of entrepreneurship and insistence upon freedom in the workplace to pursue innovative ideas."

McKnight knew risk was necessary to achieve success. "The best and hardest work is done," he said, "in the spirit of adventure and challenge . . . Mistakes will be made." McKnight put his faith in the good judgment of 3M employees. He warned against micromanagement and the chilling effect that accompanies intolerance of failure. "Management that is destructively critical when mistakes are made can kill initiative," he said. "It's essential that we have many people with initiative if we are to continue to grow."

McKnight knew that others could rise to leadership. "As our business grows," McKnight said in 1944, "it becomes increasingly necessary to delegate responsibility and to encourage men and women to exercise their initiative." For a man who liked to control most aspects of his life, McKnight demonstrated a rare ability to see beyond his own needs. Delegating responsibility and authority, he said, "requires considerable tolerance because good people . . . are going to want to do their jobs in their own way."

Born in a sod-covered house in South Dakota and raised working on his father's farm, where and how did McKnight develop

these progressive ideas? McKnight's Scottish parents were pioneering settlers on the Midwestern prairie. From Joseph and Cordelia McKnight, the boy learned about risk-taking, self-determination and personal ambition. Growing up in an era when farmers were plagued by drought and grasshoppers, he learned about interdependence. Watching his father struggle to sustain and build the family farm from season to season taught McKnight the rudiments of entrepreneurship. Cordelia McKnight's faith in the goodness of people gave her son an enduring idealism. Joseph McKnight's activism on behalf of struggling fellow farmers taught his son to stand for his ideals.

When William broke the news to his parents that he would not be a farmer, one parent said to the other: "Let him have his dreams." From that simple response, McKnight learned how the support of personal freedom can set creativity free.

DIVIDEND NO. 1.
Sheet 2

NAME	ADDRESS	Dec.18 1916	STOCK	DIV 6%

28. Catherall, Sidney E. 10 Phoenix Blk.Duluth
29 Cobb,E.R. 504 Lyceum Bldg.,Duluth 6 STOCK DIV 6%
30 Constantine,J.H. 114 W.1st St.,Duluth 25 1 50
31 Campbell,T.B. Mgr.Mariaggi Hotel,Winnipeg,Can 4 .24
32 Cotton,Jos.B. 4th Floor Wolvin Bldg.Duluth 72 4 32
33 Cable,Rhoada A. 903 Beech St St.Paul 40 2 40
34 Cable,John E. do 1600 96 90
35 Canfield,Tillie, 88 Harrison Ave.Detroit,Mich 6672 400 00
193 Canfield,Katie do 6386 383 16
36 Clark,Margaret, P.O.Box 112,Big Rapids,Mich 6 .36
37 Collins,Henry Oakland Tribune,Oakland,Cal. 6 .36
38 Dion,Theophile, 513 8st Ave E.Duluth 45 2 70
39 Decker,Mary, 914 E 5th St.,Duluth 45 2 70 returned
(cancelled)
5 Dwan,Dennis, Two Harbors,Minn 4 .24
Dorsey,Mrs.John, Detroit, Minn 107 6 42
cancelled
Dutton,Lilla R. Amer.Exchange Natl Bank,Duluth 353 21 18
cancelled
Dwan,John, Two Harbors, Minn 125 7 50
Dwan,John C. do 7 .42
dman,Axel 1425 E 4th St., Duluth 23723 1423 38
oar,Mose P. 213 East 2nd St.,Duluth 1025 61 50
tinger,Matthew, 308 18½ Ave W.,Duluth 141 8 46
elled
wards,Est.R.M. 206 W 2nd St. Duluth 10 .60
ns,J.E., Est. 1101 Minn.Ave Duluth 54 3 24
art,Joseph 2317 Woodland Ave Duluth 130 7 80 returned
a,Lillian A. St.Paul 240 14 40
May Agnes,% Northwestern Trust Co St Paul 200 12 00
acher,Wm.607 1st NatlBank,Bldg.Duluth 6 .36
nry, 27 2nd A e We.Duluth 315 18 90
132 7 92
100 6 00

1

cloth,' " McKnight recalled years later. But, it was no instant success. While Carborundum's product was very flexible, Three-M-ite cloth was stiff and brittle. Like roasting oil from garnet, solving this problem required creativity and a little luck.

Three-M-ite cloth became 3M's first profitable product, 12 long years after its founding in 1902. The start-up company in Minnesota was thrilled to challenge a New York behemoth—that is, until the letter arrived. The Carborundum Company charged 3M with patent infringement and demanded that they stop making Three-M-ite cloth. Goliath was on the offensive.

Bush, 3M's sales manager, suggested that the company hire Paul Carpenter, a tough Chicago lawyer who knew patent law cold and was noted for standing his ground in the face of formidable odds. 3M did not back down and Carpenter did his home-

Beginnings are slow. Beginnings are hard. Somewhere along 1920, it began to ease up.

> **Bill Vievering**

work. Ultimately, Carpenter argued that Carborundum's patent was invalid: his argument was so strong 3M prevailed. This was 3M's first experience with the power of patents, and the positive outcome saved the company from a terminal case of red ink. It also educated the

1 Record of early dividends paid out on December 18, 1916.
2 Early view of sandpaper production. Before machinery like this, sandpaper had to be coated by hand.

young company about the importance of patents, a philosophy that endures today.

Thanks to Three-M-ite cloth and a boost in business from World War I, 3M finally posted substantial profits and declared its first dividend of 6 cents per share in the last quarter of 1916. The dividend totaled $13,497 on 224,956 shares outstanding. When Edgar Ober, William McKnight, Samuel Ordway (son of Lucius)

and John Dwan gathered to share the good news, Ober was jubilant: "Gentlemen," he said, "this is the day we've been waiting for. Some of us wondered if it would ever come. We're out of debt and the future looks good. Business has more than doubled in the past two years; and, for the first time, we'll have enough left after expenses to pay a dividend . . . There are a lot of people who thought we'd never make it."

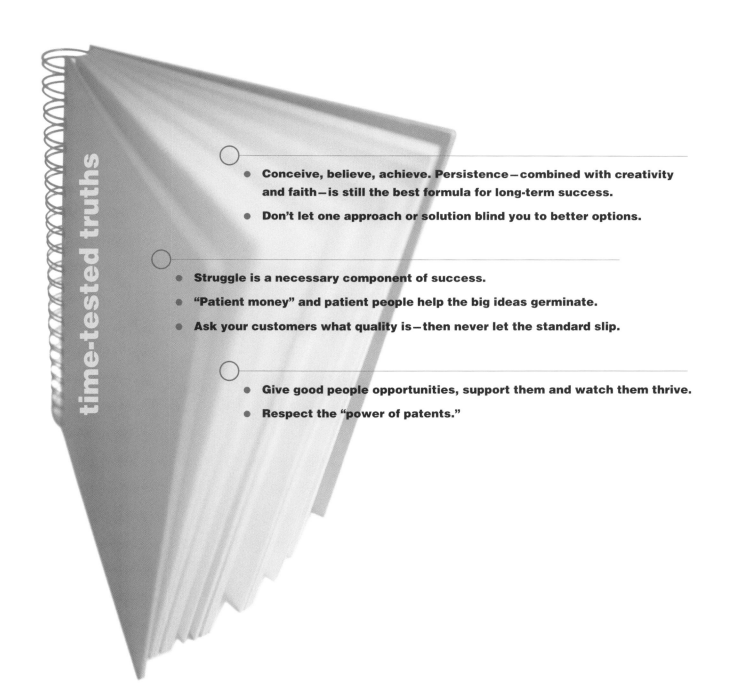

time-tested truths

- Conceive, believe, achieve. Persistence—combined with creativity and faith—is still the best formula for long-term success.
- Don't let one approach or solution blind you to better options.

- Struggle is a necessary component of success.
- "Patient money" and patient people help the big ideas germinate.
- Ask your customers what quality is—then never let the standard slip.

- Give good people opportunities, support them and watch them thrive.
- Respect the "power of patents."

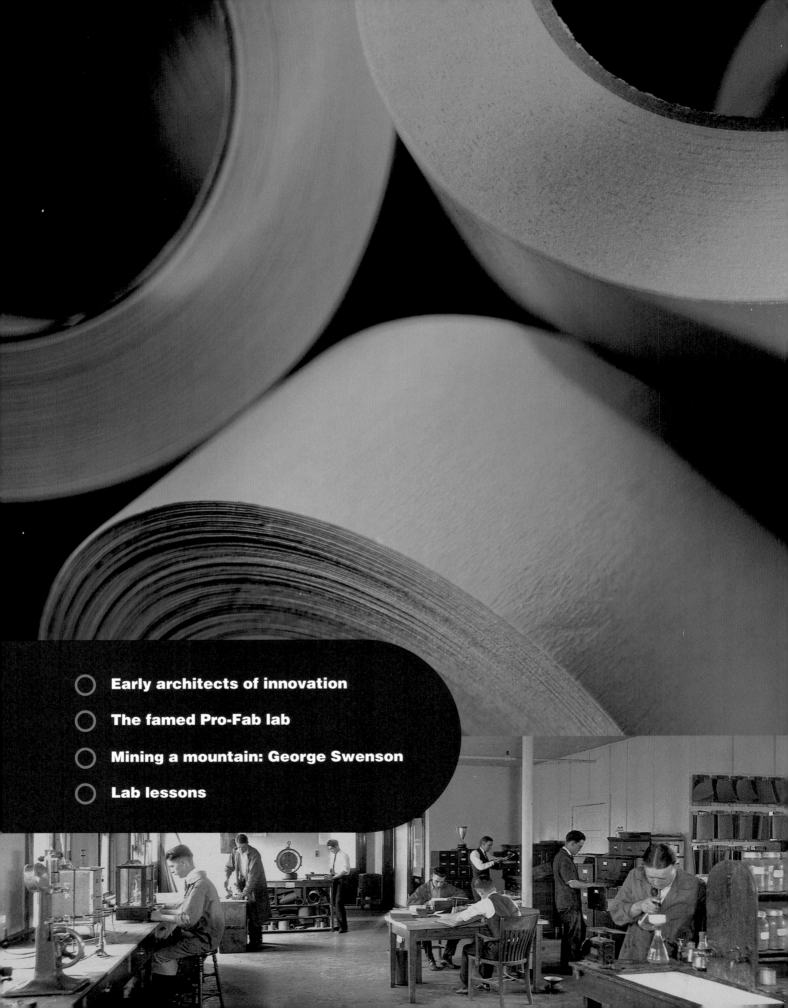

2

3M Innovation— A 'Tolerance for Tinkerers'

In the same year a baseball game was broadcast on U.S. radio for the first time and French scientists developed a vaccine to combat tuberculosis, 3M welcomed three men who turned the company into an innovation powerhouse that would attract admiration—and analysis—for 80 years to come. ● The year was 1921. The early architects of innovation were Richard Carlton, Dick Drew and Francis Okie. Looking back, observers might call this one of the most "harmonic convergences" in the annals of business.

With his company in the black and annual sales exceeding $1 million, President William McKnight knew it was time to hire a strong technical person to lead and coordinate 3M's research, manufacturing and engineering activities. Carlton was an affable, quick, 27-year-old engineering graduate from the University of Minnesota

> We've made a lot of mistakes. And we've been very lucky at times. Some of our products are things you might say we've just stumbled on. But, you can't stumble if you're not in motion.

> **Richard Carlton** quoted in "The 3M Way to Innovation: Balancing People and Profit," Kodansha International Ltd., 2000

with experience in drafting and electrical contracting. The only trouble was that McKnight could pay Carlton only $65 a month—less than one-third of what he was already making. No problem, the ambitious Carlton answered, "Your company can't get along without a technically trained man like me. I'll take $65." Carlton became the first member of the lab staff with a college degree and made the first steps toward turning 3M into a well-oiled innovation machine.

> ### Probing the Impossible
More than a few people in the industry had turned Okie down when he asked for samples of sandpaper grit. They thought Okie was a wild-eyed inventor. But when he

wrote to McKnight asking for samples of every sandpaper grit size 3M made, McKnight responded. Okie was a young printing ink manufacturer who had an idea far removed from his own business. 3M didn't sell bulk materials to anyone, but McKnight was curious about Okie's unusual request typed on sky blue stationery.

McKnight dispatched his East Coast sales manager, Robert Skillman, to check out Okie. Sitting at a worn oak desk (that Okie used to test his sandpaper), he told Skillman he hadn't planned to share his idea with anyone, but he had been unable to find a reliable supply of

> Okie created quite a stir among the workers, for he was the first live inventor they had ever met. Like William McKnight, he was quiet, soft-spoken and unaffected. But he said he hated 'to be confined to the specific.'

> **Mildred Houghton Comfort** author, "William L. McKnight, Industrialist"

raw materials. Furthermore, his financial backers had cold feet. Here was a young entrepreneur with a great idea and no way to bring it to market. Could 3M help? Okie agreed to sell his patented waterproof sandpaper, later called Wetordry, to 3M. He moved to St. Paul, joining 3M in 1921.

Okie made his first Wetordry experimental batches in a washtub until someone suggested he could make

Chapter opening photos Rolls of Scotch masking tape; The 3M tape lab where Scotch brand pressure-sensitive tapes were developed in the 1920s; A prolific writer, Francis Okie scratched notes on anything, even the back of 3M sandpaper; Samples of Wetordry Tri-M-Ite sandpaper.

1 Richard Carlton (top row, far right) and Francis Okie (holding trophy) were members of the 3M bowling team. **2** William McKnight and Okie traded telegrams in 1920 concerning 3M's request to experiment with Okie's sandpaper binding agent. **3** Dick Drew's letter in 1921 was in response to a 3M employment ad.

smaller ones in a bowl. He often forgot to record ingredient amounts. When he had a particularly good batch, Okie didn't know why. In later years, the absent-minded and research-focused Okie frequently forgot where he had parked his car in the 3M lot and an accommodating colleague took him home. On the next day, Okie often drove another car to work, then forgot where it was. Another colleague drove him home.

> ### The 'Irresistible Force'

At 22, Drew was an engineering school dropout who made his living playing the banjo for dance bands while studying mechanical engineering through correspondence school. There was a job open in 3M's tiny research lab. "I have not as yet been employed in commercial work and am eager to get started," he wrote Bill Vievering, 3M's first quality assurance expert. "I realize that my services would not be worth much until a certain amount of practical experience is gained, and I would be glad to start with any salary you see fit to give . . . I am accustomed to physical labor, if this be required, as I drove a tractor and did general farm work . . . "

Drew spent his first two years at 3M checking raw materials and running tests on sandpaper. Next, he was assigned to make "handspreads" of Okie's revolutionary Wetordry waterproof sandpaper and take them to a local auto-body paint shop for testing. (This product gave 3M an important entry into the automotive marketplace.) While waiting for the test results on the sandpaper, Drew

Dick Drew had an instinct that compelled him to push beyond reasonable limits and . . . in some cases . . . unreasonable limits. He was an irresistible force drawn toward any immovable object. > **Lew Lehr** retired 3M chairman of the board and chief executive officer (CEO)

couldn't help but notice—or hear about—the problems people had painting cars in the popular, two-tone style of the day. Either the paint came off when painters tried to remove the plaster tape they used, or the tape's adhesive—softened by lacquer solvent—remained on the car's surface. Profanity peppered the air.

Not knowing how he would do it, the irrepressible Drew promised he could produce a better, nondrying adhesive tape and solve their sticky problems—even though, after weeks of experimentation, McKnight ordered him to quit his work and get back to improving Okie's Wetordry sandpaper. Drew's "contraband" Scotch masking tape debuted two years later in 1925.

> ### The 'Dream Team'

The trio that joined 3M in 1921 shared characteristics that set the tone for 3M's innovative climate. Carlton was an optimist, go-getter, calculated risk-taker and a leader. Drew shared Carlton's optimism. He was also unconventional, innately curious, a rule-breaker and a leader who had his own distinctive style. Okie was the consummate inventor: open to new ideas, resisting limits, probing the impossible. He might have been a misfit in a more traditional organization, but at 3M, he was very successful.

Carlton set the tone for 3M's innovative future and echoed McKnight's operating philosophy when he blended research, manu-

facturing and sales objectives. Looking back, he was a visionary when he wrote in a manual he published in 1925:

● The time to get closest control of your product is during your manufacturing process. What you do after this is just history, except in isolated cases.

● There is no room for a thin-skinned man in this organization. Carelessness cannot exist. The future is in building even more exacting requirements so refinements on machinery can be designed to meet the demand.

● The technical phase has passed from the laboratory to the production department. A free exchange of data and ideas, we hope, will always be our policy and creed.

● The laboratory of the modern industrial plant must have something more than the men and equipment to do control work. It must be a two-fisted department generating and testing ideas. This work, dressed in its best Sunday clothes, is termed "research."

● No plant can rest on its laurels—either it develops and improves or loses ground.

● Every idea evolved should have a chance to prove its worth. This is true for two reasons: 1. If it is good, we want it;

1 Soft-spoken Francis Okie, pictured in 1963, was 3M's first authentic inventor. He was brilliant, but absent-minded— there often were eight to 10 hats on the hat tree in his office because he forgot to wear them home at night. **2** Richard Carlton was lauded for his ability to inspire creativity. **3** The first Central Research Lab was established in 1937 to spur new product development.

2. If it is not good, we will have purchased our insurance and peace of mind when we have proved it impractical. Research in business pays.

During the dark days of the Depression, when money was almost nonexistent, Carlton fought tooth and nail to keep the laboratories in existence and to keep the people from being hurt. I have never known a man more kind, more considerate, more companionable or more inspirational than him. **> Clarence Sampair**

retired president, International Division

Like McKnight, Carlton—who later succeeded McKnight as 3M's president—was a "management by walking around" leader who didn't stay at his desk. He could blend the talents of the nontechnical, the college-trained and the "idea" people who operated on the fringes of policy and practice.

For its first 35 years, 3M's definition of research was "product development" not "pure" or "fundamental" research as research scientists define it. To the leaders of 3M, research meant growth and, according to early company records,

every dollar invested in research and development (R&D) from 1926 to the early 1950s had a strong "multiplier effect." Each dollar invested returned $28 in gross sales. Even so, Carlton said, there were broader research horizons to explore. What about pure research that focused on products not even imagined yet?

Thanks to Carlton's sponsorship, 3M created its first Central Research Laboratory in 1937 with a twofold purpose: to supplement activities of 3M's division labs that worked on product refinements and to explore independent, long-range scientific problems beyond the ken of any division. The Carlton Society, which even today recognizes 3M technical employees for career achievements, is named after Richard Carlton.

Innovation has more to do with inventing the future than with redesigning the past.

> Alex Cirillo Jr. *division vice president, Commercial Graphics Division*

Strong, annual investment in research was a financial imperative for McKnight. He wanted his company to aim for a 10 percent increase in sales annually, a 25 percent profit target and 5 percent of sales plowed back into R&D every year. It was a sum above the average for U.S. companies at the time.

Looking back, 3M people agree that this early and consistent commitment to R&D was crucial. By the 1970s, the annual investment averaged 6 to 7 percent

Say What?

Almost 50 years after 3M's founding, Bob Adams, then senior vice president, Research and Development, and Les Krogh hosted two University of Illinois professors at 3M. One guest was John Bardeen, co-inventor of the transistor and 1956 Nobel Prize winner. After the visiting professors gave technical presentations at 3M, they piled into Krogh's van to head for a local golf course.

"We were driving down 35E in St. Paul and passed the Benz Building," Krogh, who later became senior vice president, Research and Development, recalled. "I pointed at it and said, quite proudly, 'That's where Central Research got its start.' "

The car was silent. From the seat beside Krogh came a hesitant question, "You don't use the building any more do you?" Bardeen asked.

Beauty is in the eyes of the beholder. "I was proud of the Benz Building heritage," said Krogh, "and all they saw was an old, run-down factory building. The fact is, we were still doing experiments through the 1990s."

Background: Post-it note

of sales. "It was one of the most important decisions ever made," said Ray Richelsen, retired executive vice president, Transportation, Graphics and Safety Markets. "Every business we're in today is based on having invented something new to the world and taking that invention to customers around the world. 3M has spent a lot of time, money and effort to create a culture of invention."

> **Among Cinders . . . Creativity**

The first Central Research Laboratory location was hardly conducive to creativity—it was located below an adhesive maker in Building #14, in space that Les Krogh, retired senior vice president, Research and Development, called "too bad to describe." Before long, however, Central Research moved to the Benz Building on Grove Street in St. Paul.

Annual investment in R&D in good years— and bad—is a cornerstone of the company. The consistency in the bad years is especially important. > **David Powell** *vice president, Marketing*

"I heard the building had been a candy factory and a whiskey warehouse," said Krogh, who started work there in 1948. "It was extremely well-built, but it had large factory windows. We were right next to a railroad switching yard with a steam locomotive that spouted cinders. Standard operating procedure

1 The Benz Building housed Central Research until the mid-1950s. **2** An early lab notebook used to record experiments.

every morning was to dust cinders off your desk before starting work. With no air conditioning, it was hot. One day, I remember a reading of 107 degrees Fahrenheit in the building. It was hard to conduct experiments."

Even 3M technical directors might be spotted visiting the lab in their sandals, shorts and short-sleeved shirts. In spite of the heat and grit, however, Krogh said, it was one of the most productive labs he'd ever seen in his long career. "A plaque at the entrance names the discoveries that led to major products," said Krogh, "including magnetic tape, printing products, modern pressure-sensitive adhesives, acrylate adhesives (providing the basis for medical tapes), Thermo-Fax copying,

3M has a tolerance for tinkerers and a pattern of experimentation that led to our broadly based, diversified company today. To borrow a line from 'Finian's Rainbow,' you might say we learned to 'follow the fellow who follows a dream.'

> **Gordon Engdahl** *retired vice president, Human Resources*

fluorochemicals that led to Scotchgard fabric protector, reflective sheeting and Scotch black vinyl electrical tape. Carlton set the tone for the lab. He was an idea man and he had a huge tolerance for experimentation."

Jim Hendricks, who spent 16 years in the Central Research Laboratory during its formative years and was a founding member of the 3M Technical Forum, remembered Carlton calling his lab staff the "shock troops," after the members of a university football team who played the role of the team's next opponent and bumped heads with the first string players. "Dick's idea was to have a group of us handle the dicey problems that 3M's product labs didn't have time for," Hendricks said.

Thomas Edison believed that a small group of people with varied backgrounds could be the most inventive. That's what I found when I joined Central Research. I could talk to an analytical chemist, a physicist, people working in biology and organic chemistry—people in all the sciences. They were all within 50 yards. > **Spencer Silver**

retired corporate scientist, Office Supplies Division

People in Central Research were on their honor when it came to working hours, said Krogh. If a guy decided to go fishing on a weekday, Carlton knew the time would be made up. If he decided to work independently on his own product idea, he had the freedom to do it—even if the boss said otherwise. From the early days of 3M, "bootlegging" was a time-honored practice. The leaders of 3M understood that no one should stand in the way of a creative person with passion because that person might invent the next product or manufacturing breakthrough.

2

First You Find a Flower Pot . . .

William McKnight's desire for diversification sometimes led to surprising results and a motherlode of innovative thinking. About the time the United States stock market crashed in 1929, McKnight learned that 3M's only Midwest competitor, Wausau Abrasives Company of Wausau, Wisconsin, was on the block. For $260,000, McKnight made his first acquisition for 3M. He picked up one roadster, three trucks, two plants—and one mountain. McKnight called his entire management and laboratory force together and asked, "What can you do to make a mountain of silica quartz profitable?"

George Swenson was one of the research chemists in the room. He remembered H. Colby Rowell, a specialty salesman for 3M, telling the group that a huge market existed if 3M could make colored minerals for the roofing industry. Consumers were tired

of their dull gray and brown roofs. But early versions of colored roofs faded much too soon.

Because he had some experience with resins and coatings, Swenson, at age 24, was told to figure out how to make the granules fade-proof. Here was the big

that practical considerations limited the amount of coating used on roofing materials to only a fraction of an ordinary coat of paint. Normally, paints last five years, at best, but roofs were expected to survive 20 years.

Swenson experimented by mixing powdered ceramic glazes with paint and firing that mixture at nearly 2,000 degrees Fahrenheit. He and his team created a little rotary pot furnace to test the approach. They mounted a flower pot on a spindle that rotated on a 45-degree angle. The heat came from an open gas flame. During the firing, the paint burned off and the glaze fused with the roofing material. Voila— it worked and 3M delivered its first 200 pounds of colored roofing granules to Bird & Son of Chicago in 1932. The company was so impressed that it asked for two carloads—80 tons— in six weeks. Because speed was important (even in those days), 3M acquired a small enamel smelting furnace, installed it in the 3M minerals building, filled the order and began manufacturing between 40 and 80 tons in multiple colors every week by operating all day, every day.

With major improvements in manufacturing that cut costs sig-

nificantly, thanks to the work of a young newcomer to the 3M minerals department, Cliff Jewett, 3M manufactured more and more tons for less cost. Even in its first year—producing 18,000 tons— 3M managed to run in the black. Its product was decidedly better than the competition's, in part, Swenson said, because 3M had strong cooperative relationships with the labs at the roofing companies. In about four years, however, calamity struck.

"It's not unusual in new products," Swenson recalled. "Our quartz granules were losing their adhesion and falling off the roofs." Like the olive oil incident in the earlier years, this product failure threatened to put 3M out of a booming business where it could charge premium prices, even during the Great Depression.

Swenson and his colleagues went to work as sleuths. "There was a real feeling of camaraderie on our team. Everybody was young and full of energy," said Swenson. "I didn't see people who were thinking first about 'What will this do for my career?'" With persistence and no small amount of creativity, they found the problem. Light— and damaging ultraviolet light—was passing through the roofing granules and causing the asphalt underneath to lose its adhesive properties. How would they solve the problem? Make the granules more opaque to let in less light? Would they have to find a new material altogether?

Meanwhile, consumers were asking for blue roofs—a color 3M didn't offer. Richard Carlton inspired the team when their spirits waned. "On many occasions, we'd try every approach to a problem without success, and we were feeling pretty down," Swenson said. "Five or 10 minutes with Mr. Carlton would often bring out some avenues we hadn't explored, and I'd leave his office ready to take up the fight again." When things looked their worst, luck intervened.

"All these problems descended upon us at once," Swenson said. Jack Brown, 3M geologist, went in search of other minerals with more opacity and luckily found a large deposit of greystone rock about five miles away from 3M's Wausau plant. "Without this extreme good fortune," Swenson said, "we probably would have discontinued the business." 3M wound up making all of its colored roofing granules using this base rock and quickly patented the manufacturing processes.

Because of its long-term success, the roofing granules business became the first separate division created at 3M with its own management team—a pattern that would be replicated many times as the company grew. And, after 39 years, Swenson ended his career as vice president of the division.

Drew was an early icon for bootlegging. Krogh and others agreed that Drew's response to McKnight led to what is known today as the 15 percent rule at 3M. Regardless of their assignment, 3M technical employees

Entrepreneurship, in my definition, is a spirit— a quality—that believes so strongly in an idea that it risks the security of the present for the reward of the future. > **Gordon Engdahl**

are encouraged to devote up to 15 percent of their working hours to independent projects. With the development of Scotch masking tape, McKnight and Carlton saw what Drew could do by saying, "Management, you're wrong. I'm right and I'm going to prove it." After that, McKnight and Carlton both supported the idea that technical people could disagree with management, experiment, and do some fooling around on their own.

"I was only with 3M a couple years," said Roger Appeldorn, retired corporate scientist, "when we were

I started working as a 'lab flunkie.' It dawned on me that, even without formal education, a guy could use his brains and further himself. You weren't paid to do the job: you were paid to think. > **Don Douglas** *retired vice president, Reflective Products Division*

❸

1 3M's Wausau Plant supplied Midwestern roofing manufacturers with quartz roofing granules. **2** A trend in brightly colored rooftops began with the introduction of 3M Colorquartz roofing granules. **3** The roofing granule business fit well with 3M's strategy to diversify.

Background: 3M algae block copper roofing granule system

in a staff meeting and someone asked, 'I have a new idea that could be useful to 3M, but it's not related to the business I'm working in right now. Am I allowed to work on it?' The vice president of Research and Development answered, 'The facilities we have here—the lab and all the equipment—are for you to use. If you want to work on those programs on your own time, you're welcome to do it.' "

The 15 percent rule is unique to 3M. Most of the inventions that 3M depends upon today came out of that kind of individual initiative . . . You don't make a difference by just following orders. **> Bill Coyne** *retired senior vice president,*

Research and Development

During his years as senior vice president, Research and Development, Krogh said the 15 percent rule was often greeted with skepticism by technical people from other large companies. "They couldn't understand how we could allow people 15 percent of their time to do what they wanted and still meet important deadlines. It was inconceivable that we would permit so much freedom," said Krogh. "Here was my answer. If 3Mers have to get something done, they'll do it. They'll take their 15 percent on Saturdays or Sundays, if need be. The 15 percent philosophy flies in the face of standard management ideas about control."

> **Incubating the 'Birth Rate'**

Innovation isn't complete until an idea explored in the laboratory is transformed into a product—and that product goes to market. 3M's most successful stories revolve around innovative products that solved problems and met customer needs. In the best cases, these products changed the basis of competition by introducing a never-before-seen idea to the marketplace. But, that wasn't happening fast enough to satisfy McKnight in 1940.

One Saturday morning, McKnight analyzed the "birth rate" of 3M products. He ticked them off: Wetordry waterproof sandpaper in 1921, Scotch masking tape in 1925, Scotch transparent tape in 1930, Colorquartz roofing granules in 1933 and rubber cement in 1934. Then there was a six-year dry spell. Although Scotchlite reflective sheeting was created in 1937, the rewards of that new product had not yet been recognized.

"While these dates are only approximate and are really predicated on when the product commenced to yield some profit, it indicates rather a long period of hunger . . . nothing appears to have been developed since the rubber cement birthday," McKnight wrote Carlton. He urged Carlton to push some of the ideas in development stage to marketable products generating revenue or "to move on to other fields."

In his memo to Carlton, McKnight said, "I do not think there is anything we can do about it immediately." In spite of his own comments, later that same day, McKnight took action. After thinking about the innovation dilemma and talking with

1

1 The equivalent of two daily coffee breaks plus lunch time gave inventors "15 percent time" for their own projects. 2 Dick Drew (right) set the company's standard for perseverance and encouraged his lab team to follow their instincts.

Carlton and others, McKnight created 3M's first New Products Department that Saturday afternoon. In a second memo dated October 12, 1940, McKnight described his plan.

"3M is spending a substantial and an increasing amount on research every year," McKnight said. "It's time to create a department to cooperate with all interested parties in studying the commercial value of each research project upon which money is being spent." The goal was to recommend to management whether or not work should continue on a project. McKnight gave Joe Duke, who later retired as executive vice president, Sales Administration, the responsibility of leading the effort. He told Duke to keep him informed on all new development work in research at 3M; learn about the large new markets with product needs; conduct market surveys to identify the potential size and profitability of a market; supervise product quality; design a sales and distribution network; and—most importantly— decide which research projects lived or died.

Duke was a 1940s genius. He helped introduce Wetordry sandpaper to the automotive industry;

Everything I Learned in a Lab, I Learned From . . .

Much of what Paul E. Hansen, who retired as technical director, Nonwoven Technical Center, learned about working successfully in a lab, he learned from Dick Drew. They are timeless lessons:

Anything worth doing is worth doing before it is perfected. Don't wait to try to do everything exactly on your first attempts in an experiment. If you knew how to "do it right the first time," you would, but in most first attempts, you don't.

Be a jack of all trades and a master of one. It is good to know how to do a lot of things but also good to be an authority in a specific area.

Put things in a nutshell. It is good to take a broader approach to things and look for a simple definition of the task or problem. Always update these objectives because the task can constantly evolve.

It is easier to ask forgiveness than permission. With a sincere attitude toward one's work, the chances of doing real damage or harm are small. Consequences from bad calls, in the long run, do not outweigh the time waiting to get everyone's blessing.

If you can do the task today, don't wait for tomorrow. A quick and marginally successful experiment will fuel thought that evening for your next attempt.

Keep the ball in the other person's court. With everyone doing their job responsibly and promptly, tasks stay current and fresh and move quickly to an end.

Don't keep blinders on all the time. It's good to have defined goals, but don't get so engrossed that you miss other opportunities that may spawn from your efforts.

Most people aren't stubborn enough. Too many people quit easily at the first sign of failure.

The reward for persistence is internal. The person who is persistent and eventually succeeds is usually only recognized for accomplishing the feat. Seldom does anyone appreciate all that went into making the success a reality.

Follow your instincts. Your instincts are actually your total experience in practice.

Background: Scotchlite Diamond Grade reflective sheeting

quickly became Eastern division sales manager; and was sales manager of 3M's entire Abrasives Division when McKnight tapped him to lead the New Products Department.

To succeed, McKnight said, Duke "should be a free-lancer in our organization" and interact with sales, manufacturing, engineering and research. Anticipating the obvious, McKnight said that when "differences of opinion" became serious enough, the 3M management group would have the final vote on a product's future. Eight years later, the New Products Department became a division and its most productive years continued through 1955. In about 13 years, the division produced new business that represented 12 percent of company sales and 25 percent of 3M's profits.

There was more than one way to identify and launch new products and 3M still was learning. McKnight created a second option in the early 1940s. He was a good judge of people and he noticed that young Drew—the inventor of Scotch masking tape and the even-more-popular Scotch cellophane tape—was stuck. Stalled. Unhappy. "Here was Dick Drew at age 35, a successful inventor. 3M was busy developing many more tapes," said Paul E. Hansen, retired technical director, Non-woven Technical Center, and a member of the Carlton Society. "However, Dick was not a happy fit in this thriving business where his maverick, free-wheeling style didn't fit the company's organized, technical approach to product development and line extensions." Seeing this, McKnight took Drew aside, encouraged

---

1 Among 3M products that had direct applications during WWII were Safety-Walk treads on ship decks, and 3M adhesives were used in everything from planes to artillery. **2** Intended for 3M men in the service, 'Tape-Up Girls'—pretty, young 3M employees—were featured on the back covers of the *Megaphone* during the war. **3** Lou Spiess, pictured in 1942, held one of the $5 money orders the 3M Club sent to 3M servicemen at Christmas.

3M Goes to War

World War II called for a special kind of innovation at 3M. When the war broke out, the company was making its Scotch transparent tape using natural rubber adhesives. But, the United States government cut off the supply for commercial applications in order to stockpile rubber for the war effort. "The big push to develop substitutes for rubber that could make a reasonable adhesive started," said John Pearson, retired vice president, Development, who created a new

device to test the adhesion of various resins. "Synthetic resins became the next frontier, and the big advance was acrylate that we discovered during the rubber crisis. It was a whole new platform, to use today's language."

Work in the lab in those years could occur at any hour. "Lab people would work at all hours of the day or night," said Pearson,

who was later named a Carlton Society member. "There was a limited amount of equipment available and, if you wanted to use it, it might mean coming in at midnight to get it."

Another research scientist, Don Douglas, experimented with melting old inner tubes to make adhesive for Scotch electrical tape. "One night I snapped a rubber band. It fell on a hot plate," he said. "I wiped the plate off with a paper towel and the rubber impregnated the towel. When I told my lab mates, they said, 'But we can't get any rubber,' and I said, 'If a rubber band works, I'll take inner tubes.' Too bad the smell was so bad when I melted a whole box car of inner tubes that the neighbors complained. That marked the end of my idea of using that substitute."

3M products had direct applications to the war effort. Safety-Walk general purpose tread, a 3M product used in industry to keep people from slipping on wet surfaces, was a natural for ship decks. Many 3M adhesives were used in manufacturing airplanes and ships as well as the equipment in them. Scotch masking tape was essential in painting ships, planes and tanks. Scotchlite reflective sheeting marked airports, runways and life rafts for downed airmen in the ocean. It also marked road signs during bombing blackouts.

"It was hard to keep Scotchlite reflective sheeting alive during the war," said Bert Cross, retired

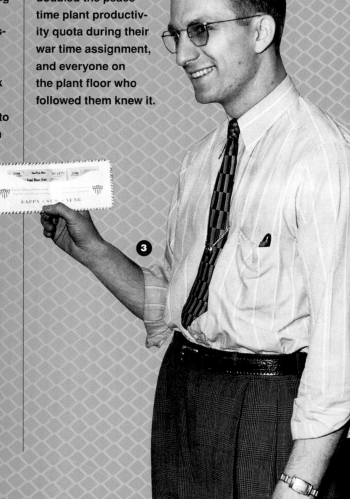

"TAPE-UP" GIRL FROM HOME

3·M MEGAPHONE

❷

3M chairman of the board and chief executive officer (CEO), with 18 patents to his name. "Our success hinged on creating reflectorized products for the Air Force, Army, Navy and Transportation Corps."

Lou Spiess was chair of the 3M Club during the war. He took up a collection for 3M's fighting men in 1942. The club managed to send each soldier about $5 with a special holiday message. The gifts reached most of the men, but remarkably, six letters were returned to 3M in 1997 after moving around the world for 55 years in search of their recipients.

By 1945, more than 2,000 3M employees were on military leave. While the 3M men were away fighting in the war, 3M women stepped in. Virginia Mulvaney was 17 in 1942 and she got a job working in sandpaper manufacturing. Mulvaney was part of a 19-person plant crew, dominated by women and led by a "matron" plant super-

visor. "She was the one who told us, 'Double your quotas! We'll win the war and bring the boys home,' " Mulvaney said. "The girls worked like heck. We were going to win that war. What camaraderie we had in a crisis. It felt like we were doing something with our hearts, souls and guts.

"Most of us lived in apartments within walking distance of 3M and we were bounced off the machines when the heroes came home. Nobody said we were heroes . . . and most of us married them."

In fact, the women were heroes. They doubled the peace time plant productivity quota during their war time assignment, and everyone on the plant floor who followed them knew it.

❸

him to hire a few co-workers and return to his greatest strength: inventing.

Drew started the Products Fabrication Laboratory, known as the Pro-Fab Lab, a group that—60 years later—has garnered admiration that far exceeds its own tenure as a lab. In many ways, the Pro-Fab Lab of the 1940s was a precursor to 3M's Technical Centers today.

> Dick Drew took a bunch of misfits—people who wouldn't fly in formation—and he put together a lab that created technologies that account for 20 percent of 3M's sales in 2000. **> Art Fry**
>
> *retired corporate scientist, Office Supplies Division*

Because the tape business was thriving in the 1940s, Drew's Pro-Fab Lab focused on creating better backings and coating processes. During its 20-year lifetime, the lab was known for product breakthroughs that led to Scotchlite reflective sheeting, Micropore surgical tape, foam tape, decorative ribbon, face masks and respirators. In addition, the lab experimented with adhesives that—almost four decades later—led to development of the blockbuster product, Post-it notes.

The environment of the Pro-Fab Lab and Drew's leadership is remembered most. Drew kept his lab group small, about 20 people. Like Drew, they were considered corporate "misfits"—the people who, by their own admission, didn't seem to fit anywhere else

in 3M. Drew saw something in them—something valuable and creative.

"I was lucky enough to get hired in 1954 into Drew's lab," said Hansen. "We were in an old dairy building on Seventh Street in downtown St. Paul, away from 3M headquarters. Dick created an environment where people were always encouraged. He had passion but also was easy going. He was a great mentor but probably not a strong manager. He created a greenhouse environment—a skunkworks—where we could do anything, try anything. When you're an oddball in a permissive environment, very often things turn out well."

> Four of us were the original inhabitants of the Pro-Fab Lab—Al Boese, Ralph Oase, Warren Hurd and me. I could purchase stuff and build things, and the engineering department agreed to a hands-off policy. There was complete freedom to build and do. **> John Pearson** *retired vice president, Development, and Carlton Society member*

"Dick never turned anyone away from his office, even though they came in with the strangest ideas," said Ray Hunder, who experimented with an edge-adhesive coated memo pad in the Pro-Fab Lab 40 years ago, a predecessor to the Post-it note. "He never discouraged people. He thought of himself as a bit of an underdog and he had compassion for others like him. He allowed

1 Hulda Meissner performed tests in the Pro-Fab lab, which was known for product breakthroughs.

his lab team to freely follow their instincts. Dick encouraged people to be themselves. He'd say, 'Hey, your idea's as good as anybody else's.' When people can be themselves, they use their gifts and talents to the fullest."

Drew advocated the power of serendipity, said Hunder. "He called it the gift of finding something valuable in something not even sought out."

Hunder said Drew's highest priority was new products. In fact, he never gave up trying to find a replacement for cellophane tape, his own creation. Drew liked people who were good with their hands, as well as their heads. He was leery of too many college degrees, although he hired people with extensive technical training. "What I really want is a creative person," Hunder recalled Drew saying. "You can always hire a Ph.D. to take care of the details." Drew was concerned that too

much education risked making people too rigid and reduced their ability to "think outside the box."

Some members of senior management made jokes about the Pro-Fab Lab, on occasion calling it the "funny farm." Although that lab was the target of humor, it attracted considerable resources and some of the most creative people in 3M's early years. Drew never seemed to have trouble funding projects, said Hunder. It helped to have a champion in McKnight.

More than 60 years after 3M created its first Central Research Lab and the legendary Pro-Fab Lab, innovation is still the hallmark. In 2000, 3M was issued 525 patents and filed for 860 more. It invested $1.1 billion in property, plants and equipment. To target even greater returns on 3M's investment in research and development, the company sharpened its focus on growth areas that had the greatest return for investors.

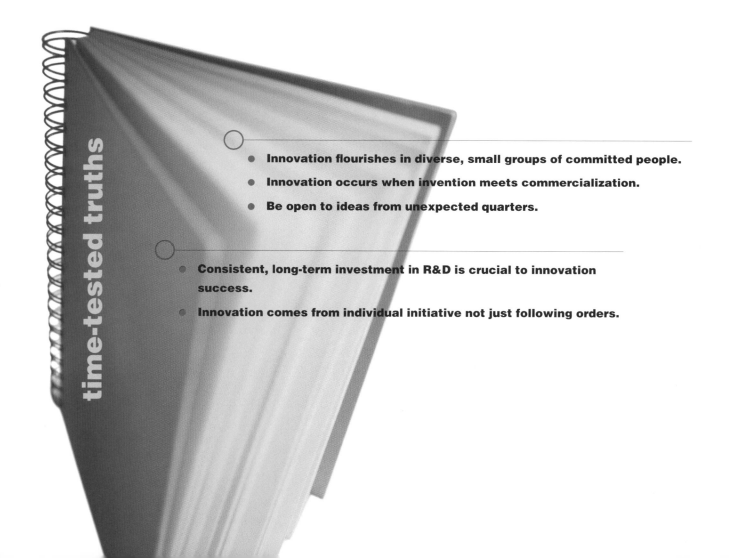

time-tested truths

- Innovation flourishes in diverse, small groups of committed people.
- Innovation occurs when invention meets commercialization.
- Be open to ideas from unexpected quarters.

- Consistent, long-term investment in R&D is crucial to innovation success.
- Innovation comes from individual initiative not just following orders.

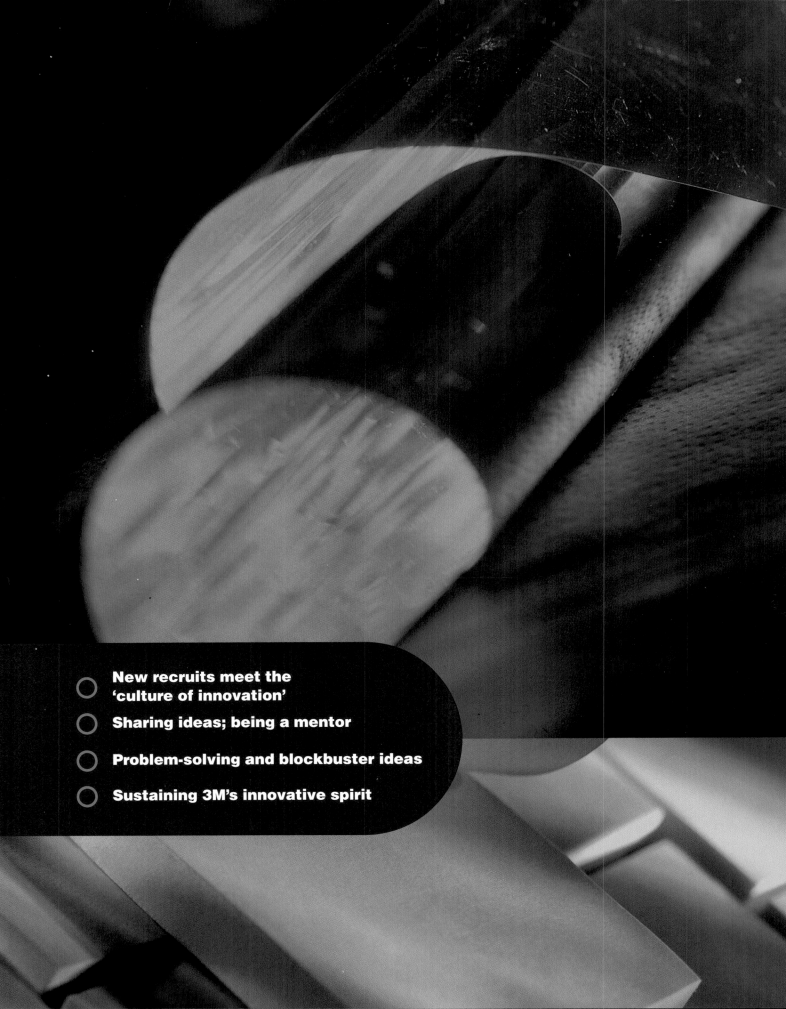

- New recruits meet the 'culture of innovation'
- Sharing ideas; being a mentor
- Problem-solving and blockbuster ideas
- Sustaining 3M's innovative spirit

3

3M Innovation — How It Flourished

What did a native of the Deep South know about the "culture of innovation" at a Yankee company in Minnesota? Joe Bailey was a 25-year-old ceramic engineering graduate of South Carolina's Clemson University when he joined 3M in 1962. Thirty-seven years later, Bailey would become vice president, Research and Development, responsible for Adhesives, Advanced Materials, Corporate Analytical and Science Research Technology Centers. ● Bailey worked for American Lava, a 3M subsidiary based in Chattanooga, Tennessee, and he made quarterly trips to 3M's Central Research lab in St. Paul during the 1960s. The environment was unmistakable. "I discovered that the technologies belonged to the company not the business units," Bailey said. Rather than protecting what they knew, 3M employees shared knowledge. "I saw openness and a spirit of immense cooperation that helped people get things done," he said. "I soon learned that the most successful people at 3M were good at getting out of their offices, meeting people, interacting and knowing where to find the expertise they needed."

The young engineer also learned the difference between invention and innovation. "Invention isn't innovation until you've delivered something to the marketplace," said Bailey. "The engine that drives innovation is technology, but understanding what people need and delivering the right product at the right price is equally important."

> Tell Your Story

Although he held an advanced degree in chemistry, Manley Johnston didn't want to put down roots in an isolated lab. He wanted to be close to the marketplace. "3M was diverse and entrepreneurial," said Johnston, who joined the company right out of college, in 1968. "I wanted to work on things that would be commercialized quickly. I was drawn to the business side of innovation. I learned that if you have a good story to tell in this company—and if you have the guts to tell it—people will listen and support you." After 29 years in 3M labs around the world, Johnston became technical director, Bonding

Systems Division. It produces products as diverse as repositionable systems for Post-it notes to high-performance tapes that replace rivets, bolts and screws on airplanes, cars and trucks. In late 2001, he was named staff vice president, International Technical Operations.

> An Electric Atmosphere

When he looks back on his 31 years at 3M, Moe Nozari, executive vice president, Consumer and Office Markets, said he will remember most and miss the innovators that he met—particularly those he encountered during his first week in Central Research, Building 201. There was Cliff Jewett, inventor of the pre-sensitized printing plate. "The last guy before Cliff who brought significant innovation to the printing industry was Guttenberg," Nozari said with a laugh. "There I was, at 29 years old, meeting him and shaking hands. Next, a guy across the hall walked into my lab and said, 'You know, I've just made this adhesive. Look how interesting it is. It sticks to paper, but I can lift it off and it doesn't tear the paper.' His name was Spence Silver, and he was showing me the adhesive that made Post-it notes. Spence and colleague, Bob Olivera, took that adhesive to the Commercial Tape Division and the rest, as they say, is history."

Nozari met Harry Heltzer, then chairman and CEO of 3M, and discovered that Heltzer had invented reflective sheeting. Next, Nozari was introduced to Ray Herzog, then president of 3M, who championed office copying products, an innovation that produced

Chapter opening photos
3M multilayer optical film, one of 3M's new, innovative products with multiple applications, was developed using funding from two Genesis Grants; 3M recently entered the touch-screen market, which simplifies computer usage, by making two acquisitions; 3M Pharmaceuticals continues investigating a newly developed, proprietary family of drugs that stimulates the immune response system to fight disease.

1 Sumita Mitra, a 3M corporate scientist, serves as a mentor to young scientists by introducing them to the 3M culture. **2** Cheryl Moore, also a 3M corporate scientist, benefited from the experience of an older mentor and now has become an informal mentor to three other scientists.

20 percent of the company's sales in the 1970s. "I had never seen this much diversity in research and applied science in one building. The atmosphere was electric. What we knew we shared, because technology at 3M doesn't have owners."

Early in his career, Nozari discovered a catalyst that could be used to create urethane, a component in many 3M products, including sponge brushes for surgeons, Tartan Track surfacing material for running and race-tracks, and Tartan Turf surfacing material designed for stadiums. "I went to my boss, George Allen, who later retired as senior vice president, Research and Development, and said, 'I've finished this. What do I do now.' His answer was, 'No, you're not finished. Now you go to every division in this company and show them what you've done and work with them to incorporate your invention into their product lines.' That was the best professional growth opportunity for me, because I learned about the company and the wide range of skills and responsibilities that 3M people have."

> **We Can Be Anything We Want To Be**
Paul Guehler was 27 when he joined 3M as a senior chemist in Central Research. "They told us to identify, develop and commercialize new products. Every new product had to have a 30 percent operating income with specific growth targets. There was an attitude of 'just do it, seize the opportunity.' It was a way of life. The administrative systems existed to support the work. There was a will to grow—and to succeed.'"

Scientists as Mentors

Sumita Mitra of 3M ESPE (formerly Dental Products Division) is a corporate scientist and a member of the Carlton Society. She joined 3M right out of college, in 1978. "The climate of sharing and openness is unusual here. I discovered that in talking to colleagues in other companies," she said. "As a young person, I took it for granted. Now I realize that it's something I have a responsibility to foster." Among many accomplishments, Mitra invented light-cure glass ionomer technology, which is considered one of the significant breakthroughs in dental materials. When she is asked—as she often is—how to make a mark at 3M in the technical area, Mitra's answer is pragmatic. "I tell my younger peers that they must meet two criteria: there must be a market need, whether articulated or unarticulated, and there must be a feasible technical pathway for getting there. That's when things come together." While there is no formal mentoring program, Mitra, who has approximately 30 patents to her name, is frequently asked to advise younger scientists and introduce them to the 3M culture.

Cheryl Moore, 3M corporate scientist, Specialty Materials Manufacturing Division, and Carlton Society member, started her career at 3M as a technician and took advantage of 3M's Tuition Refund Program, earning her chemistry degree in her off-hours. Her development and application of acrylate pressure-sensitive adhesive technology led to new products that generated nearly $1 billion in sales for 3M. "I had a chance to work with technical giants, and my mentor, Francis Brown, still comes into our lab," Moore said. "I'd be lost without people like Fran, because he has so many years of experience and knowledge that aren't recorded. Fran and other 3M 'veterans' are also willing to say, 'Give it a try; what have you got to lose?'" Like Brown, Moore has become an informal mentor to three scientists. "They want feedback and they're eager to learn about what happened in the past," said Moore. "Sometimes they want to know if they should take a risk and how to go about it. Mentoring our newest recruits is very important to 3M's future."

Thirty-five years later, in 2000, when Guehler succeeded Bill Coyne as senior vice president, Research and Development, his belief was unchanged. "We'll continue to emphasize new technologies, new products and—especially—our ability to use them to build new businesses," Guehler said. "I want to make sure that our technologies are converted into commercialized products." And, in the characteristic "can-do" spirit of a man who made his career at 3M, he added, "We can be anything we want to be."

> Walking the Innovation 'High Wire'

When asked to describe his company in one sentence, Coyne was succinct. In a 1996 book titled "Innovation: Breakthrough Thinking at 3M, DuPont, GE, Pfizer and Rubbermaid," Coyne said, "At 3M, we live by our wits. Innovation may be an important element of other corporate strategies; but for us, innovation is our strategy." For decades, Coyne said, 3M has been balancing on "the innovation high wire" and funding research and

When I joined 3M in 1962 as an organic chemist, some of us called 3M 'the big red sandbox.' Product innovation is our magic and our soul. Today, 3M is the best and biggest sandbox to play in. **> Leon Royer** *retired executive director, Leadership Development Center, formerly technical director, Commercial Office Supply Division*

development efforts annually with up to seven cents of every sales dollar.

Many have wondered how 3M could create and sustain a culture of innovation, especially as the company grew and reached global proportions. Some observers have said that size—and its inevitable, creeping bureaucracy—stifles creativity and innovation. Others heartily disagree by pointing out that 3M's magnitude and considerable resources—human, financial and technological—actually make the company better equipped to innovate more and faster.

People who know the company best point to four key ingredients that foster a culture of innovation at 3M: attracting and retaining imaginative and productive people; creating a challenging environment; designing an organization that doesn't get in people's way; and offering rewards that nourish both self-esteem and personal bank accounts.

> A Forum for Honesty and Thorny Problems

Innovation has thrived at 3M because people talk. They strike up lively conversations in hallways, cafeterias and labs. They talk across departments and divisions. They meet to share ideas in brainstorming sessions and forums. While more traditional organizations have kept researchers and engineers within their own areas or divisions, where their loyalties were strongest, 3M has instead fostered a strong sense of attachment to the company as a whole. The "granddaddy" of that concept was the Technical Forum, which had its start in 1951—

the same year that the company formed the International Division. While the latter merited a press conference, the Tech Forum's birth was quiet and just 17 people were at the inaugural meeting.

We share ideas at their earliest stages, before we have an idea of a product. We talk about our problems, our failures. That takes a lot of courage and trust. **> Art Fry** *retired corporate scientist, Office Supplies Division*

Tech Forum's first chair, James Hendricks, retired manager, Tape Research, a tall man with a professorial style, invited every technical person at 3M—400 in all—to join the forum. An organization in which participation was purely voluntary, its original goals were to foster idea sharing, discussion and inquiry among members of the 3M technical community, while educating technical employees. To accomplish that, the Tech Forum brought in Nobel Laureates and other luminaries to address the group. The Tech Forum sponsored problem-solving sessions at which businesses presented their most recent technical nightmares with the hope that their colleagues would help them find answers. For innovators who had newly issued patents in their name, the forum began the annual Inventor Recognition Program.

The forum also launched an annual event at which each 3M division put up a booth to show off its latest technologies. In 2001, it was combined with the Engineering Information Exchange and is now known as the Technical Information Exchange.

The Tech Forum sponsored specialty subgroups or "chapters." Each of these chapters focuses on a scientific discipline, such as polymer chemistry or coating processes. Scientists in each discipline gather to compare notes and share their technical expertise and prowess. "Think of the power of that concept," said Marlyce

The forum built morale and respect among colleagues. It got people talking—young with senior, basic scientist with applied technologist, experienced or famous with people new to the company. Pride in being a 3M technical person often began right there. **> Roger Evans** *retired research scientist*

Paulson, now retired, who coordinated Tech Forum activities from 1979 to 1992. "3M has lots of polymer chemists. They may be in tape; they may be in medical or several other divisions. The forum pulls them from across 3M to share what they know. It is a simple but amazingly effective way to bring like minds together."

Illustrating its forward-thinking nature, the Tech Forum sponsored a meeting to review the "computing machines" at the University of Minnesota in 1951. It

1 In 1951, all 3M technical people were encouraged to join the newly organized 3M Technical Forum, which promoted the sharing of ideas. Pictured is an early event where 3M scientists demonstrated their inventions and asked for advice.
2 Scientist Francis Okie, one of 3M's earliest inventors, credited with Wetordry sandpaper, was inducted into the Carlton Society and given the same bust of Richard Carlton that is presented to new members today.

was followed by a series of lectures on the industrial uses of computers. Two years later, believing that science education in the schools was crucial, the forum sponsored its first science fair for Minnesota high school students. By 1971, the Tech Forum had its first

> The forum has not been bound by any set of rules but has been allowed to develop naturally.
>
> > **James Hendricks** *retired manager, Tape Research, and first chair, 3M Technology Forum*

female chair. Julianne Prager, who retired as executive director, Corporate Technical Planning, was then a member of the Central Research technical staff. In an effort to encourage young women to pursue careers in science and technology, the Tech Forum started its Visiting Technical Women program in St. Paul area schools during the 1970s.

During that same decade, recognizing the significant global reach of 3M, the Tech Forum "cloned itself," establishing Tech Forums in Harlow, England, and St. Marys, Australia. More Tech Forum outreach continued in the 1980s: Teachers Working in Science and Technology (TWIST) introduced teachers to science in industry through summer internships, and STEP (Science Training Encouragement Program) combined education and work experience to give a boost to a diverse group of high school students interested in science and math. To enrich 3M's relationships with the schools, the forum began a 3M Visiting Wizards program in 1985 to the "oohs" and "ahs" of children. 3M volunteers visit elementary schools and perform eye-popping science demonstrations that rival magic tricks—another way to inspire the next generation of innovators.

By 2001, 3M's Tech Forum had grown to 9,500 members in eight U.S. locations and 19 countries.

> ### The Rule That Isn't

The 15 Percent Rule, inspired by 3M inventor Dick Drew decades earlier in 3M's life, lost none of its power as the company matured. In fact, the stories told and re-told inside 3M have "institutionalized" this so-called rule. It encourages technical people to devote 15 percent of their time to projects of their own choosing.

> The beauty of 3M's 15 percent rule is that it's not a rule at all: it's permission. Most big businesses are run like grade schools. 3M is college. > **Dale Dauten** *newspaper columnist, nationally syndicated Corporate Curmudgeon*

> ### A Wild Idea With No Home

Ted "Flipper" Buchholtz, retired research scientist, never saw himself as an inventor. He just liked to do things that no one else had done. He resisted reading instructions; he wanted to solve puzzles on his own.

1 Julianne Prager, retired executive director, Corporate Technical Planning, was the first woman to head the Tech Forum. **2** Ted Buchholtz (left), retired research scientist, and Don Bemlott, retired senior lab technician with the Pro-Fab Lab, laid out a 110-foot-long strip of Tartan Track surfacing material in 1959. They tested a portable runway for use at a track and field competition in the Los Angeles Colliseum.

When Buchholtz joined 3M in the early 1950s, he was a young native of Canada with street smarts but no high school diploma. After hearing about a "little gadget" that Buchholtz devised while working at a local car dealership, Drew "drafted" him for 3M's fabled and eccentric ProFab lab. "Dick didn't care about an individual's education," Buchholtz said. "He felt that even if you flunked kindergarten, if you stayed in motion, you'd get things done." Buchholtz had his own internal momentum.

On his own, Buchholtz began experimenting with ways to make urethane foam, adding colors and making designs with it to explore how that foam might be used. His first 3M patent, shared with colleague Doug Campbell, was the chair rail, which used the foam to protect walls from chairs bumping into them. Continuing to explore more ways to use that foam, Buchholtz put adhesive on both sides of it, calling it double-coated foam tape. This discovery was the precursor to 3M's successful Scotch mounting tape. Buchholtz faced his greatest challenge when two researchers asked the ProFab staff if they could solve a thorny problem. William McKnight, an avid owner of race and harness horses, had seen one of his horses injured on a defective running track. Could 3M come up with a better, safer surface, George Rabacheck and Harvey Anderson of Central Research asked? "I don't think they wanted to be involved in such a crazy idea that had so little chance of success," said Buchholtz. "It was a wild idea and wild men had to work on wild ideas. When Drew asked for a volunteer, I raised my hand."

The goal, Buchholtz said, was to invent a soft, resilient and durable material that was shock absorbent and had the look of grass—the kind that could be used for race tracks and athletic fields.

After much experimentation, the first test turf was made with clay pipe sealant, a kind of urethane, and was still too rigid. Unwilling to give up, Buchholtz pressed on and, at one point, he brought a rented horse to the ProFab lab to test the prototype. "We went outside on a 20-by-30-foot sheet of the synthetic track and we ran the horse back and forth," said Buchholtz. By 1961, the new track surface had its first real test at New York's Belmont Park where it fared well in rain, mud,

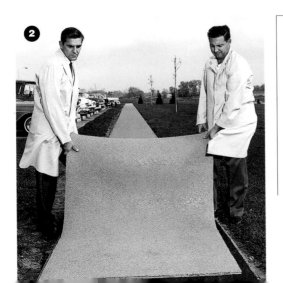

3 The Meadows near Pittsburgh, Pennsylvania, billed itself as the first racetrack to use Tartan Track synthetic surface, developed by 3M.
4 A model of a race track was used to display Tartan Track surfacing material at a Technical Forum meeting.

heat and cold. McKnight told Buchholtz he was the one to sell the new product to the 3M Board of Directors. "'Ted, it's your project; if you don't sell it, it's going to fail,' he told me," Buchholtz said. "I was scared." In spite of that, the young researcher, who had never seen the inside of a corporate board room before, was convincing enough to get $50,000 approved to pursue product commercialization.

Tartan Track and Tartan Turf synthetic surfaces were the first in the world. Sports Illustrated magazine hailed the breakthrough in 1963 and virtually all the major horse racing tracks used Tartan Track surfacing material. Tartan Turf surfacing material was used at a majority of high school, college and professional sports arenas and stadiums. Tartan Track surfacing material was used for the track and field events at the Olympic games held in Mexico City in 1968. Even with the introduction of competing Astro Turf, 3M held its market lead. But, when the company's patents began to expire in the 1970s, the days for Tartan Turf surfaces were numbered. "The market was saturated with our product," Buchholtz said, "and there was little or no replacement business. The surfacing material wasn't like so many 3M products; it wasn't disposable. People didn't use it up and buy more." Tartan surfacing materials were innovative, but their market life was short. "It was a big let-down," said Buchholtz, "but then you grab yourself by your bootstraps and start a new project. And you get excited all over again. I was excited a lot in my career at 3M."

> **'Give Me a Problem to Solve'**

Roman Schoenherr, retired corporate engineer, was a novice engineer in 1965 when he had his first brush with innovation at the Decatur, Alabama, plant where polyester film backing was produced for Scotch magnetic tape. "The plant was producing film 18 inches wide at about 600 pounds per hour and they needed to increase output to 2,400 pounds an hour. Without changing the fundamental process, the production lines would have to have been four times larger, a very costly proposition," Schoenherr said. He searched for an innovative manufacturing solution and found it using computer simulations to test different ways to produce the film. "My job was to understand what was happening so we could design the proper size equipment to do the job."

Retired Corporate Engineer Bob Vytlacil thought he had invented a better idea for slitting 3M tape products during manufacturing in 1980. "It started with a young engineer writing a letter," Vytlacil said. "He knew what he wanted to accomplish, but he didn't know what the mechanism would look like." A few months later, Vytlacil was cleaning his garage and ran across an old fishing reel. "I played with it for a few minutes, then I tossed it out," he said. "That night, I was staring at the ceiling and the idea hit me between the eyes. That's it!

"I didn't have any money to pursue the idea, but Frank Vikingstad, then manager, Engineering, Science and Technology lab, who later retired as staff vice president, Engineering, did. He told me I could use his little lab machine shop and he gave me a couple bucks to

1 The University of Minnesota's Memorial Football Stadium was one of many to use Tartan Turf surfacing material. **2** Len Volin used Tinkertoys to fashion his first prototype of a machine to improve adhesive tape manufacturing. Volin received the Engineering Achievement Award for the project. He estimates that each of the seven machines installed at various 3M plants around the globe saves the company $1 million each year.

make the crudest prototype you ever saw," Vytlacil said. "Next, I got permission to canvass the divisions at 3M that I thought could use this new device, and I ended up raising $10,000 for my project. I called it CAMITE because those were the initials of the divisions (Commercial Products, Abrasives, Medical, Industrial Minerals, Tape and Electrical Products) that chipped in money. I built a better prototype with a hand crank, like the old fishing reel but larger, and I put together a little slide show."

By this time, Vytlacil's work was becoming more visible inside 3M and, despite being told by his boss to turn his energies to other, more promising assignments or "lose my job," he persevered in classic 3M style. It was about 1980 when Vytlacil got his big break at a gathering of specialist engineers. "I invited every vice president I could think of to come and see my prototype and try it out personally," Vytlacil said. "People really liked it." Later, at an engineering research meeting at which Vytlacil was testing the waters in hopes of raising $250,000 to see his project through, Joe Ramey, then group vice president, Commercial Markets Group, now retired, spoke up. "Joe said, 'If this thing can do a lot of good, then somebody should pick it up . . . and I will.'"

John Pearson, retired vice president, Development, and a Carlton Society member, served as a mentor to many young 3M engineers. He said Vytlacil had admirable staying power. "The development of that tape slitter didn't go like clockwork," he said. "It was a very difficult project."

Ultimately, Vytlacil's manufacturing innovation was heralded as one of the most significant in the company's manufacturing history.

> ### There's No Place Like Home
Like Vytlacil, Len Volin, associate corporate engineer, Bonding Systems Division, was searching for a more efficient way to make 3M adhesive tape. "Traditionally, we started with tape backing, then we applied adhesive and wound the finished tape on a big roll called a 'jumbo,'" Volin said. "The jumbo was stored and later slit into individual rolls of tape. We thought

we could save a lot of time and money if we slit the tape as it was made."

Volin fashioned his first prototype using his child's Tinkertoys. "That just illustrated the idea, but it didn't confirm that the concept could work," said Volin. "We didn't have a lot of lab space available in our engineering department, but I had what I needed at home. I was building a house and that's where I also built the first functioning prototype. My 'lab' was a couple of saw-horses in the hallway leading to the garage in my unfinished house. When I needed a vacuum source, I used my home shop vac." Two years passed from the initial idea to construction of the first production machine in 1988. Volin's invention—created with his 15 percent time—had multiple patents.
Today, there are seven of these machines

used around the globe, and Volin estimates that each machine saves the company about $1 million annually.

For their innovative efforts, all three men, Schoenherr, Vytlacil and Volin, received the prestigious Engineering Achievement Award, the engineering equivalent of membership in 3M's Carlton Society.

> The Beginning of a Blockbuster Idea

Spencer Silver, retired corporate scientist, Office Supplies Division, was a senior scientist studying adhesives in the Central Research lab in 1968 when he discovered an adhesive that didn't act like any others. Instead of forming a film, this adhesive turned into clear spheres that, according to Silver, "kind of sparkled in the light." Silver spent the next few years shopping his new adhesive around 3M to find a product use for it, but the

My discovery was a solution waiting for a problem to solve. > **Spencer Silver** *retired*

corporate scientist, Office Supplies Division

reception wasn't stellar. In other companies, this might have been discouraging enough to scrap the idea, but Silver didn't give up.

Five years after Silver's initial discovery, Art Fry was warming his vocal chords while sitting in the choir loft at his church. Frustration rose with

At 3M we're a bunch of ideas. We never throw an idea away because you never know when someone else may need it. > **Art Fry**

his scales as Fry turned to a hymn and his scrap paper bookmark fell to the floor. "My mind began to wander during the sermon," Fry confessed. "I thought about Spence's adhesive. If I could coat it on paper, that would be just the ticket for a better bookmark." Fry went to work the next day, ordered a sample of the adhesive and began coating it on paper. He only coated the edge of the paper so the part protruding from his hymnal wouldn't be sticky. "When I used these 'bookmarks' to write messages to my boss, I came across the heart of the idea. It wasn't a bookmark at all, but a note," said Fry. "Spence's adhesive was most useful for making

1 Art Fry used an adhesive developed earlier by Spencer Silver to create one of 3M's most famous products, Post-it notes. The idea came to him as he sang in a church choir. **2** Today, there are more than 400 Post-it products sold in more than 100 countries around the world.

paper adhere to paper and a whole lot of other surfaces. Yet, it wasn't so sticky that it would damage those surfaces when it was pulled off. This was the insight. It was a whole new concept in pressure-sensitive adhesives. It was like moving from the outer ring of the target to the bull's eye."

We conducted a direct-mail program to the secretaries of CEOs of Fortune 100 companies, and we got letters back from the likes of Lee Iacoca, Chrysler's chairman and CEO, and the CEO of Phillip Morris telling us how much they loved our product [Post-it notes] and asking how they could get more! **> Jack Wilkins** *retired marketing director, Commercial Office Supplies Division*

Fry encountered serious technical problems very early and his boss, Bob Molenda, encouraged him to takes things one step at a time. First, there was the problem of getting the adhesive to stay in place on the note instead of transferring to other surfaces. And, although 3M was known for its coating expertise, the company didn't have coating equipment that could be precise on an imprecise backing such as paper. It was difficult to maintain a consistent range of adhesion. "All of these things bothered our production people," Fry said, "but I was delighted by the problems. If there is anything that 3M loves, it's to create a product that is easy for the customer to use but hard for competitors to make." Fry used his 15 percent time to find manufacturing and technical solutions over about 18 months, and Molenda helped Fry find the time and money to dedicate to his pet project.

It would be years before the Post-it notes adhesive was perfected, prototypes created and the manufacturing process developed. All the while, Fry busily handed out product samples and Geoff Nicholson, then Fry's technical director, made sure that secretaries of 3M senior executives got them. Before long, their bosses were borrowing the little yellow pads. Everyone who tried them wanted more.

In 1977, with a host of product literature in tow, 3M conducted market tests in four major cities. But, consumers were lukewarm at best. Ramey was a new division vice president when Post-it notes tested so poorly. Seeing how many 3Mers truly believed in the product, Ramey decided to figure out why the notes weren't faring well. He and Nicholson traveled to a test market and met with people, only to discover that advertising and brochures weren't good enough. What consumers really wanted was the product itself. Sampling, however, was an

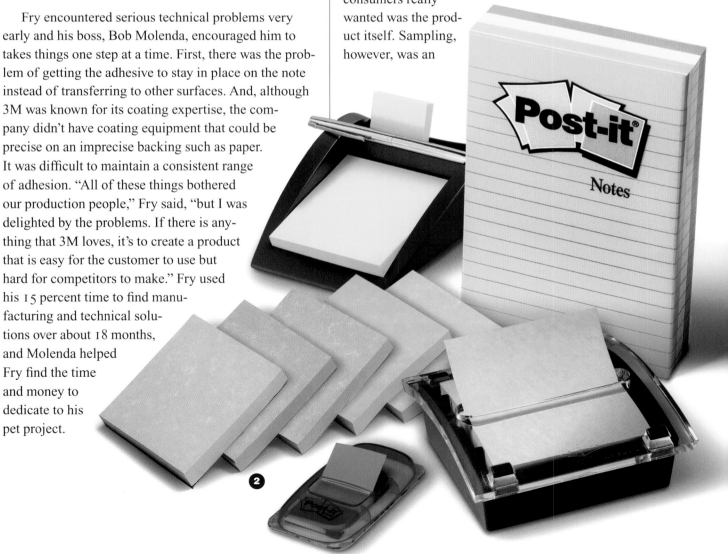

expensive proposition—especially for a product with a questionable future. Ramey bypassed the traditional approval channels and went straight to Chairman of the Board and CEO Lew Lehr to fund the Post-it note sampling.

In 1978, 3Mers descended on Boise, Idaho, with samples for what would later be called the "Boise Blitz." The town was a perfect venue—not too big, not too small and remote enough to truly be able to measure results accurately. Sample upon sample were handed out, and 3M discovered that more than 90 percent of the people who tried them would buy them. With success in Boise, 3M was convinced that the market potential for the yellow note was enormous and, in 1980, Post-it notes were introduced nationally.

For their efforts, the Post-it note team was awarded the Golden Step Award, the highly coveted internal award recognizing teams that develop significant profitable products generating major new sales for 3M. By meeting this criteria twice, the team won the award two years in a row, 1981 and 1982.

> **Innovation: How Do We Sustain It?**
Even with public kudos from business observers, as 3M entered the 1980s, Lehr wanted to ensure that his company's growth curve could be sustained in a global economy where the innovation rate was accelerating and competition had multiplied. Perhaps on the heels of the blockbuster Post-it note, some 3Mers wondered how the company could produce more revolutionary prod-

ucts that quickly increased sales. Lehr championed aggressive "stretch goals" for the company at the start of the new decade and employees delivered. Five years earlier, in 1977, 3M had inaugurated Challenge '81, a program aimed at achieving 25 percent of all sales from products less than five years on the market. By the 1990s, that stretch goal was raised to 30 percent and the total years reduced to less than four.

Lehr also created a 16-member Innovation Task Force led by Gary Pint, now retired group vice president, Electrical Products Group, to take a candid look inside the company. "We wanted people in 3M to understand that management, starting with Lehr, was sure that the environment for innovation at 3M hasn't deteriorated," Pint said. "Or if it had, that the commitment and means were available to get it back to where it was. We've been successful because of innovators in the past and we wanted to continue to make sure that innovators, the people who have that flair for making things happen, feel like they're working in a supportive environment."

The task force goal was to not only stimulate innovation in technical areas of 3M but at all levels and in every kind of job at 3M. And, to gain a clearer picture of 3M's climate of innovation, the group hired Gifford Pinchot III, a management consultant and author who had coined a new term in his successful business book, "Intrapreneuring: Why You Don't Have to Leave the Corporation to Become an Entrepreneur." Pinchot conducted a four-month "innovation audit" for 3M aimed at better understanding the delicate "climate."

1 Cathy Arsenault, product development specialist, Software, Electronics and Mechanical Systems Lab, uses computer aided design and analysis to help improve the Pharmaceutical Division's metered dose inhalers.

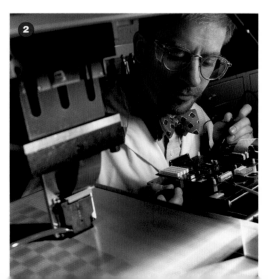

During their inquiry, Pint's task force made some discoveries that ratified long-held ideas within 3M. For example, innovative people are motivated when they have freedom, support and encouragement. 3M intrapreneurs also have a way of making middle managers and supervisors uncomfortable.

"Innovation," Pint affirmed, "is generally an untidy process." A majority of new ideas fail, but people shouldn't fear for their jobs when that happens. "We estimate that 60 percent of our formal, new product programs never make it," Lehr said. "When this happens, the important thing is not to punish the people involved."

> **'Give Us the Attention and Support We Need'**
One key outcome of the task force study was the confirmation that innovation thrives on personal recognition matched with financial and moral support. Coincidentally, a brand new project to support innovation surfaced in 1984. The Genesis Program was spearheaded by Joe Abere, a highly respected corporate scientist, with full support from 3M's technical leaders, Bob Adams and Les Krogh. The idea had been percolating for some time, but Abere said it fit beautifully with 3M's renewed focus on innovation. "Genesis is all about optimizing the innovative spirit at 3M," Abere said. The parameters are simple. The grant encourages technical entrepreneurship by funding research projects that have not yet qualified for 3M budget support through regular channels. In the first year, proposals came in a flood not a trickle, even though people had less than two months to develop proposals and win lab management support for it. "Two days before the deadline, we had 14 entries and I thought that was good," said Prager. "Two days later we had 60 with still more coming in."

Genesis struck a chord. "We're telling people who work here that all the positive changes in 3M's future weren't going to come from management," said Prager. "We told them that they are the innovators." Other grant and recognition programs to spark creativity would later be added to time-honored programs such as the Carlton Society and the Engineering Achievement Award of Excellence. Alpha Grants for innovation in administrative, marketing and other nontechnical areas were made available in 1986. The Technical Circle of Excellence and Innovation honors technical people for exercising innovation and creativity to produce a significant impact on 3M's products, processes or programs. These efforts ultimately lead to

2 Scott Iverson, senior design engineer, in the same lab, works on the design of a new piece of equipment which will help evaluate inkjet inks. **3** The Engineering Achievement Award of Excellence, established in 1973, is awarded for engineering innovation, proficiency and contributions to 3M's growth. **4** Diane North, senior process development engineer, Polymer Processing Laboratory, Engineering Systems and Technology, investigates new techniques for measuring the thickness of film. **5** The Technical Circle of Excellence and Innovation Award.

measurable business or technical success and allow 3M to change the basis of competition. To largely recognize manufacturing breakthroughs, 3M created the Corporate Quality Achievement and the Process Technology awards.

> Charge of the Light Brigade

One of the recipients of Genesis funding was a team that developed a whole new technology platform based on multilayer film. It was not only strong and durable, it also possessed never-before-seen optical properties. It

3M doesn't have the structural boundaries of other companies. It's perfectly OK to call someone anywhere in the company and offer help or ask for help. We're a good example. Jim was looking for applications; I was looking for a way to know if this was a useable technology; and Mike wanted to solve the problem.

> Andy Ouderkirk *corporate scientist, Film and Light Management Technology Center*

was a film that could create a mirror that was 99 percent reflective, could be combined in up to 1,000 layers with a total thickness of 100 nanometers, and—to the surprise of many experts—it broke the 200-year-old Brewster's Law of Physics, which defines the characteristics of reflection based on the angle between transmitted and reflected light.

Research into multilayer film began in the 1970s when the Central Research Process Technology Lab (CRPTL) explored how a multilayer film could be used as a relatively inexpensive backing on tapes. But, as scientists began combining those layers, said John Stephan, technical director, Traffic Control Materials Division, "the whole was greater than the sum of the parts." While multilayer film was first used for tape backings, 3M scientists later found it useful in products that required puncture and tear resistance, such as substrates for signs and in safety films for window glass.

The next breakthrough occurred in the 1990s when 3M researchers Andy Ouderkirk and Jim Jonza attended the annual Technical Forum science fair highlighting new technologies. Ouderkirk, then a researcher in CRPTL, had been experimenting with "flash-lamp" treatments of films to prepare them for adhesion by applying a sudden burst of energy to a film surface, melting it to a depth of .1 micron. Ouderkirk noticed a difference in light refraction between the melted surface and the rest of the film. He told Jonza, a researcher in Safety and Security Systems Division, that even more variations could be created by combining several film layers that had different refractive properties. "And, if you could put together layer after layer of film," Ouderkirk speculated, "you could make a very interesting reflective polarizer." To Ouderkirk's delight, Jonza answered quickly, "We can do that."

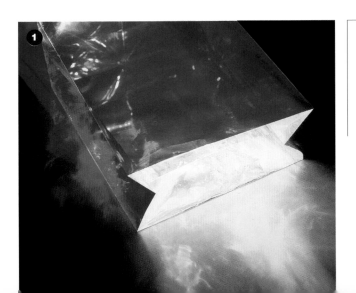

1-2 Material made from multilayered optical film is amazingly reflective and versatile. **3** Andy Ouderkirk, corporate scientist, 3M Film and Light Management Technology Center, works with three different multilayered optical films, each of which reflects light differently.

The two men went to work. Jonza had a special co-polymer made and demonstrated the feasibility of the first reflective polarizer. Ouderkirk demonstrated the brightness enhancement this film provided to a liquid crystal display. Mike Weber, a senior specialist in specialty materials, Film and Light Management Technical Center, provided optical calculations. The trio received two Genesis Grants to fund additional research and began pilot production. Several groups within 3M helped sponsor development of the technology, including the Optical Systems Division.

"Our multilayer film mirrors are significantly more reflective and versatile than competing products," Stephan said, "and we can do so many other things with this technology. Right now, we're looking for the best applications—where we should focus our investment—and we're in the steepest part of the learning curve."

When Ouderkirk explains how the potential applications embody "new-to-the-world physics," with a nod to expanding Brewster's Law of Physics, it's clear that he's not playing around.

"Take this standard glitter ball," Ouderkirk, now a corporate scientist in the Film and Light Management Technical Center, said, "and turn it slightly away from the light. The reflectivity washes out. Now take the mul-

tilayer ball and turn it any way you want. It never loses its reflectivity. No one has been able to do that before with a film." That property has value in more serious applications such as computer displays, window reflectors, light piping products and the reflective liners in light fixtures and signs. There are other applications for the auto industry, marine supplies, commercial graphics, security products and next-generation projectors and displays.

The multilayer film project has been a passion, particularly for Ouderkirk, Jonza and Weber, whose time and energy have been consumed by the technology. Now, a significant number of patents protect 3M's multilayer film, and its commercialization is expected to generate $1 billion in annual revenues for the company.

> **It's Imperative . . .**

It was the early 1990s when Chairman of the Board and CEO Allen Jacobson asked Ron Mitsch, then group vice president, Traffic and Personal Safety Products Group, to take six months off from his position at that time and examine how to take innovation to the next level at 3M. From that work came a set of "R&D Imperatives" that heavily influenced new product development in the 1990s. "We have a great track record; we

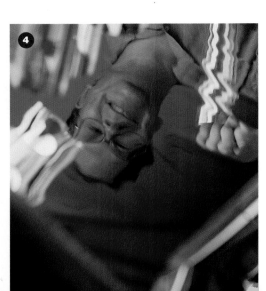

4 Ouderkirk was a leader in the development team that broke what was once considered a basic law of physics by creating the 3M high efficiency mirror. It uses 3M film technology to create a surface that is 99 percent reflective at all angles.

3M Engineers—Getting Their Hands Dirty

Taking a page out of the Technical Forum history, Gerry Mueller, director, Engineering, in the early 1970s, encouraged the company's engineers to organize and share their ideas and brainpower. These are the people who—over decades in the life of 3M—have designed manufacturing equipment and processes that ultimately produce the products that 3M sells. "There were engineering specialists in each 3M division—some of them following the same technology—but we never met and exchanged ideas until Gerry got us together," said Bob Vytlacil, retired corporate engineer. Soon afterward, the group broke into minichapters, each with a specific focus. "We recognized that we had shared expertise and common experience, so the minichapters began actively consulting within 3M," Vytlacil said.

Vytlacil believed that these consultants couldn't be effective without getting their hands dirty. "You can't just give advice and not be responsible for the results," he said. "Someone in the Consumer Products Division called and said, 'We'd like you to go to our Prairie du Chien, Wisconsin, plant. The plant is yours for three days. We're not going to tell you what to do. The employees can answer all your questions. After three days, we're going to meet here in a conference room and we want you to tell us the two biggest things that need to be fixed." The specialist engineers came back with answers and saved the division, in Vytlacil's words, "a lot of money and our advice was free."

During the 1970s, 3M was making major investments in its manufacturing facilities and the advice of the newly formed "minichapters" was invaluable. "We used them as expert consultants to critique what was being planned," said John Pearson, retired vice president, Development, "and they performed a tremendous service."

For the specialist engineers, the minichapters were a shot in the arm, personally and professionally, said Roman Schoenherr, retired corporate engineer. "I saw people suddenly rise up and get involved," he said. "They became engaged with the whole corporation, rather than sitting back in their corners just doing their jobs."

As time passed, the engineering group added education and mentoring to its program and, in recent years, more consulting with 3M divisions. "Some of our minichapters schedule regular consulting sessions as often as twice weekly," said Len Volin, associate corporate engineer, Bonding Systems. "Our automation minichapter has done this so that when somebody has a question, they don't have to wait too long for the answer." In recent years, the minichapters have begun exploring how they can supply consultations across oceans, making use of fast communications now available via the Internet.

Dean Shafer, retired manager, Engineering, worked with 3M's automation minichapter for 10 years, serving as the group's sponsor, to help clear roadblocks, secure funding or offer organizational guidance. Shafer specialized in assembly and automation within 3M from 1982 until his retirement. "We had about 24 people who were dedicated to automated assembly technology and we served any 3M division worldwide that assembled a product," Shafer said.

Shafer said that 3M's engineering minichapters are ideal mechanisms for promoting information sharing and education. "We had two one-hour sessions every Friday morning involving our engineers with expertise in automation," Shafer said. "Because of their broad experience, they could handle just about any question. It was informal. We saw people from the labs and product development areas of the company come to our sessions. The minichapter likes having a chance to offer suggestions early in product development, rather than down the line when the product is more fully formed and we discover that manufacturing is difficult or too costly or both."

have a great culture and the way we operate is fine," Mitsch said in his team's recommendations. "But, at the same time, we believe we can move to a new level of performance by taking the best practices in the company and spreading them company-wide."

The first imperative was to implement the national Baldrige Quality Award criteria that called for meeting customer expectations combined with a need for "time compression"—moving products faster from concept through development and to the market. 3M called that new quality process Q90s.

The second imperative was Pacing Programs. Each of the company's sectors was asked to select product development programs that could really make a difference in achieving profitable, global growth. Because as many as 200 programs were selected by individual sectors, the programs had limited success.

However, the concept was a good one. To channel limited research dollars into the most important product development efforts, the Pacing Plus Program was developed in 1994. That program asked businesses to select a small number of programs for consideration, but the company's top executives made the final decision on which products won support. The selected programs received additional corporate resources so they could be brought to market more quickly.

Initially, the list included 25 product development programs, according to Coyne, although it eventually grew to include nearly 60. "The product development programs that had been selected received additional corporate resources," Coyne said, "and by the end of two years, 20 percent of the company's R&D expenditures were directed at those product development programs.

"Narrowing the number down was significantly more effective in speeding product development," Coyne explained. "Because the numbers were smaller, it was also easier for international companies to address the programs effectively, so that these new products could be brought to market on a global basis." Among

Pacing Plus focused on 'leapfrog technologies,' revolutionary ideas that changed the basis of competition and introduced whole new technology platforms. > **John Pearson** *retired vice president, Development*

the successful programs were those in optics (brightness enhancement film and dual brightness enhancement film), microelectronics, pharmaceuticals (immune response modifiers) and fluorochemical fluids.

Other imperatives called for an increase in 3M's R&D investments yearly, a technical plan for growth in every division, a global R&D strategy and the creation of technology centers and more international labs.

1 One of the successful projects selected for Pacing Plus Program status is the CFC-free metered dose inhaler for asthma patients.

Background: Vikuiti light management film

'We're the Audit Team . . . and We're Here to Help You'

Technical audits have been a valuable form of feedback at 3M. They've been around since about 1960 when Chuck Walton, senior vice president, Research and Development (R&D), at that time, decided he needed to know more about what was working—or not working—in the company's labs. Realizing that personal visits to each lab were too time-consuming for one man, Walton asked his colleague Les Krogh, now retired senior vice president, Research and Development, to invent a peer review process. Julianne Prager continued the tradition in 1980 when she became executive director, Corporate Technical Planning, as did Dave Sorensen who followed her.

"The idea has been to provide internal appraisals of major R&D programs in the company's many labs," Prager said. "The audit team, composed of about 10 to 15 business and technical people including technical directors and senior scientists from other laboratories, conducts the 'exam' and does the analysis. They look at program strengths, weaknesses and probabilities of success—both technical and business." The team makes recommendations, but they're not binding. "Even so, people in management take them seriously," Prager said.

"From the start, the goal was to be positive," said Prager. "The audit team focused on what was good about a project and areas that needed improvement. Some people have used them to get support for more resources. If the audit team said, 'This is a terrific project, but terribly underfunded,' management would usually pay attention.' "

Conversely, when a project didn't "score" well with the audit team, it was often a motivator, said Prager. "I've seen it happen. We've said, 'We'd love it if you can prove that our rating is wrong.' And, the response has often been, 'I'm going to go out and make this project work, if it's the last thing I do.'

"3M has done a good job of combining the best of both—the small, flexible and unorthodox attributes of a small company, combined with the large technology, manufacturing and financial base of a large company," Prager said. "As 3M grew and the divisional structure continued to prove its worth, tech audits have helped institutionalize that 'small company' ethic of sharing."

> **Technology for 'Winners'**

3M's 14 technology centers actually evolved from "sector labs" that were created initially to serve the company's large business "sectors" that were identified in a company-wide reorganization during the early 1980s. As time passed, those labs evolved into today's technical centers that focus on specific technology platforms and serve the entire company. "Their charge is simple," said Bailey. "They develop new technologies that they transfer into divisions to create products that will be the next winners. People in those centers are judged based on their ability to invent and share their knowledge. The question I usually ask is 'Who's using what you developed?' A tech center will get ahead when it's recognized for making contributions." Similarly, said Bailey, successful 3M divisions are those that seek ideas from tech centers and staff their product teams with tech center scientists.

The centers are diverse, focusing on adhesives, nonwovens, manufacturing engineering, microreplication, ceramics, fiber optics and "advanced materials" such as technology for use on new generations of computer chips. "I know of no other company that has taken this technology center approach," said Bailey. "In most companies, R&D is located in a major business unit. Our next step will be to set up satellite tech centers for some of our large labs overseas."

The evolution of 3M's labs outside the United States followed its business growth. Nicholson, retired staff vice president, Corporate Technical Planning and

International Technical Operations, said, "As 3M developed businesses around the world, the companies needed technical support and service to customers." Back in the 1960s and 1970s, labs were usually part of 3M manufacturing and their key role was to check the quality of local raw materials. By 1978, 3M had created full service labs in Japan, Germany, Italy and the United Kingdom, and by the 1980s, technical service labs were established in every company that 3M operated outside the United States.

"Technical people at 3M work very hard at being a community around the world," said Nicholson. "They feel a strong need to share both their knowledge and their problems. There's a lot of synergism. This is one of the key ingredients for innovation." Nicholson, who traveled the world working with 3M labs and customers, has a strong message. "3M has a 'candy store' full of technologies," he said. "Take a look and help yourself. My job was to stimulate people to imagine how these technologies could be used in their countries. They're likely to come up with new applications and products that could be of value to all of us. I love music, so I like to think of our technologies as notes on a piano, and every day, people are inventing new tunes with them."

By the millennium, 3M had world-class expertise in about 30 technologies and excellent grounding in about 100 more. By operating in dozens of markets and believing in the importance of sharing these technologies, 3M has a competitive advantage that few other companies enjoy.

time-tested truths

- The most successful innovators network, interact and share their knowledge—and problems.

- Get your hands dirty in the innovation process; it's meant to be messy.

- It's not up to 3M's customers to ask for products they need; it's up to the company to anticipate the needs customers don't even know they have and develop product solutions.

- Listen, when your heart says, "Don't stop."

- Use the tools at your disposal to support and give protection to embryonic ideas with great promise.

- Be a mentor; you'll never regret it.

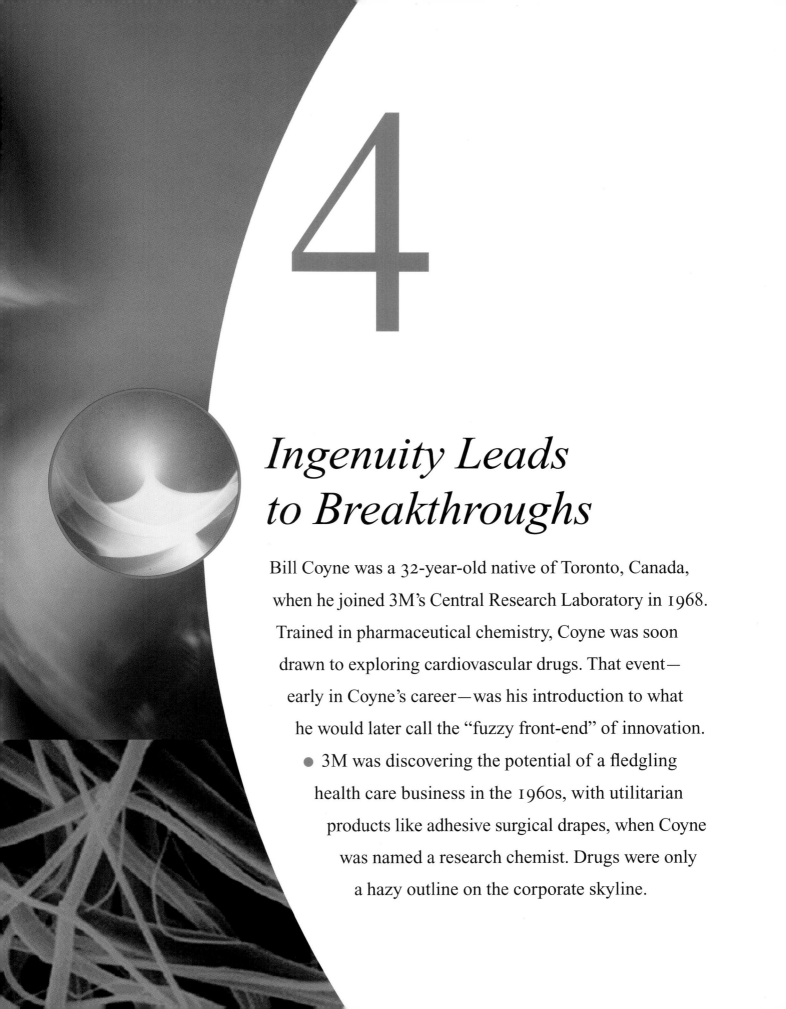

4

Ingenuity Leads to Breakthroughs

Bill Coyne was a 32-year-old native of Toronto, Canada, when he joined 3M's Central Research Laboratory in 1968. Trained in pharmaceutical chemistry, Coyne was soon drawn to exploring cardiovascular drugs. That event— early in Coyne's career—was his introduction to what he would later call the "fuzzy front-end" of innovation.

● 3M was discovering the potential of a fledgling health care business in the 1960s, with utilitarian products like adhesive surgical drapes, when Coyne was named a research chemist. Drugs were only a hazy outline on the corporate skyline.

"My boss told me that 3M was interested in pharmaceuticals and he said, 'Why don't you start working on it,'" Coyne remembered. "What I liked was that he didn't tell me what to do. He just said, 'Have at it.'" Ultimately, Coyne's early fuzzy front-end exploration led to 3M's introduction of a major heart anti-arrhythmic drug called Tambocor (flecainide acetate), 14 years later in 1982.

For 100 years, 3M employees—in virtually every job assignment—have been told, "Have at it." Many of the company's most significant product breakthroughs have emerged because 3M employees were open and patient enough to let the fuzzy front-end sharpen.

"There are always random events—good and bad—that affect an innovation," Coyne said. "The mix of randomness and chaos is always part of the pattern."

Horace Walpole coined the word 'serendipity.' It came from a tale about three princes from Serendip, Sri Lanka. They were always discovering things they weren't in search of. The key is: You must recognize it as a discovery.

> **Spencer Silver** *retired corporate scientist, Office Supplies Division*

①

On the eve of his retirement in 2000 as senior vice president, Research and Development, Coyne addressed the American Association for the Advancement of Science annual meeting in Washington, D.C. He was asked to dissect the nature of innovation at 3M. "In our experience," Coyne said, "the most important innovations respond to an unarticulated need—not as a response to an identified customer need. In other words, the fuzzy front-end is inherently fuzzy—and should be. This is true for every voyage of discovery. We go out looking for the Spice Islands. Sometimes, we find a new world—and then it takes us years to figure out how big it is and what to do with it."

> **Al's Lonely Voyage**

Al Boese's voyage of discovery began in 1938 when his boss in 3M's tape lab, Dick Drew, suggested that he might not be cut out for technical work. Perhaps, Drew counseled, Boese should take time off to find a different job. Boese hung around the lab anyway. One day, Drew off handedly mentioned that 3M specifications called for an inexpensive, noncorrosive backing that was fibrous, but not woven, for its popular electrical tape. The only noncorrosive backing anyone knew of was synthetic acetate cloth, clearly not covered by a 3M patent.

Chapter opening photos Close-up of Scotchgard fabric protector; Multilayer film more accurately senses daylight in electronic devices, such as cell phones, computers or pagers, and improves battery life; Close-up of Thinsulate insulation fibers; 3M mirror film reflects all parts of the color spectrum.

1 The National Medal of Technology was awarded to 3M in 1995, recognizing the company's nine decades of innovation. **2** Lab technicians assessed abrasives quality in the early 1900s. **3** Al Boese, pictured in 1947, with the nonwoven materials he invented. **4** Mistlon plastic ribbons were developed to be wilt-proof, waterproof and flame-resistant.

②

Rather than hunt for a new job, Boese found the best library on fibers at the University of Minnesota's Home Economics Department, and he spent the summer there. Boese—who started his career at 3M as a mail boy without a high school diploma—had begun exploring the fuzzy front-end of nonwoven science. When he retired 45 years later as a corporate scientist and Carlton Society member, his willingness to tackle this uncharted territory had led to a dizzying array of never-before-seen nonwoven products including ribbon; cleaning pads; surgical tapes, drapes and masks; fasteners; floppy disk liners; absorbent material to combat oil slicks; "metered" paint rollers for home improvements; and sound deadeners in cars.

All alone, Boese spent 1938 studying fibers, writing reports for Drew, conducting modest experiments and, in his words, "building half a dozen little machines with utter ineptness"—hoping to discover how to bind a mass of fibers together without weaving them. "One day I was walking by the rubber colander in the tape lab," Boese said. "I stuck a little tuft of acetate fiber in the colander. It heated the surface of the fibers and bonded them together. That was the opening to make nonwovens. Heat and pressure."

Knowing nothing about textile equipment, Boese took a colleague's advice and visited North Star Woolen Mills where he learned what a carding machine was. "I discovered that what I was trying to develop had been invented 10 years before," Boese said. "I got a little 12-inch machine, carded out the fibers to form a web, and applied heat and pressure to bond them. The next thing was to keep making it and find markets for it." Boese and the cohorts he attracted to his project named their group the Carfab Lab (for carded nonwoven fabrication) because they were an off-shoot of the eccentric, but highly productive, Pro-Fab Lab.

> **'You Have to Take Chances . . . '**

Boese's new process didn't produce a better backing for electrical tape, but gazing at a department store window one day in the mid-1940s, he had an idea. Maybe, if the new nonwoven material was dyed and sprinkled with color flecks, it could be used in decorative displays. Or, why not slit the material into strips and make ribbon for decorating gifts? Boese's early attempts at ribbon were modest, at best. The product, Mistlon ribbon (originally developed as a lint free lens cleaning tissue), was structurally weak for wrapping packages and it wasn't very attractive.

"It was obvious to everybody that we had a product failure," Boese said.

3M management gave him three years to improve the ribbon and still there was no solution. The ribbon brought in about $800,000 in revenues, Boese recalled, but the losses totaled about $200,000. "That was," he said, "enough money to have Mr. McKnight sit in on the meeting." Boese drew a deep breath and said his team could produce a saleable ribbon in three months. Management gave him the time.

"I went over to Beske's 10-cent store and got a 10-cent comb," he said. "I knew enough about handling yarn to know that they pulled it through combs as it went into the looms. We needed bobbins to wind the yarn so we bought 40 from Singer Sewing Machine Company for $4. We got a cone of acetate yarn from American Viscose, wound the fiber on bobbins and pulled it through the comb. We built a little set of hot drums and put the ribbon on the bottom and laid the yarn shoulder to shoulder on top. It worked like a dream. We had sheen, we had strength." In less than a year, 3M sold 250,000 yards of the ribbon. "I found out one thing," Boese said. "You have to take chances. You have to fight. Nonwovens never would have been successful if I hadn't pushed a little."

That is precisely what Boese remembered when Archibald Bush, head of 3M sales, chastised him for making a deal with a local St. Paul department store to sell his new, improved ribbon at 25 cents a roll. "Bush said in no uncertain terms, 'No kid in the lab is going to set prices for 'the Mining.'"

The new product, 3M Sasheen decorative ribbon, was a hit when it was introduced in 1950, along with a companion product, Lacelon ribbon. "3M developed the gift wrapping business with ribbon and then the paper companies came in with paper patterns in the early 1950s," Boese said. "We not only created a product, but a new market. Pursuing the nonwoven business was like being thrown up on shore when your ship gets wrecked. You don't know what you're going to do and you wind up doing what you never expected."

> ### Nonwoven 'Progeny'

From ribbon, 3M "married" nonwovens to abrasives in the 1950s to produce Scotch-Brite scrubbing and polishing pads, floor maintenance supplies and industrial polishing materials. A decade later, new dampening sleeves from 3M's nonwoven materials made offset printing much more economical. Nonwoven, disposable surgical face masks and Micropore surgical tape opened the door to other nonwoven medical products.

Still another nonwoven breakthrough product, called 3M oil sorbents, helped reduce the damage of oil spills. By the 1970s, government-approved industrial respirators made with nonwovens helped reduce certain workplace inhalation dangers to safe levels. Nonwoven technology led to the development of Buf-Puf cleansing sponges and Thinsulate thermal insulation, the product

1 In 1946, laboratory personnel worked on early development of nonwoven fabrics. **2** Industrial respirators, made with nonwovens, help reduce workplace inhalation. **3** Products incorporating nonwoven technology sold today include: 3M oil sorbents, Filtrete furnace filters and the Scotch-Brite wave-shaped scrub sponge.

that revolutionized cold weather apparel. By the 1990s, Filtrete furnace filters for home heating and air conditioning represented another application of this versatile technology. In most cases, 3M was first to the market.

There were some disappointments along the way, too. 3M never successfully developed nonwovens for book covers, draperies and window displays. A novel product called Skimmit was heralded as the easy way to skim oil off liquids like soups, but consumers never thought so. Early attempts at creating comfortable shoulder

> One of the imponderables of 3M is the multiplicity of interactions—it's not explainable and it's not orderly. > **Morgan Tamsky**
>
> *technical director, Adhesives Technology Center*

pads for clothing fizzled. Another nonwoven prototype seemed destined for failure, until Pat Carey, a project team member, had a bright idea. Walking through a local store, Carey noticed a display of Halloween masks. He

rushed back to the lab. "Here," Carey said, handing the curved prototype to his co-workers. "Try breathing through it." That bizarre demonstration led to applying nonwoven technology to the development of maintenance-free respirators and surgical masks.

Nonwovens had become a part of so many 3M products that a Nonwoven Technology Center was created in 1983 to offer technical knowledge and expertise across the company. By this time, about 10 percent of 3M's business, or nearly $1 billion in sales from about 20 divisions, represented some form of nonwoven application in products ranging from diapers to diskettes. By the late 1990s, that percentage had grown to approximately 15 percent overall and sales of about $2 billion.

> ### Gambling on the Unknown

In 1944, William McKnight approved the acquisition of the rights to a process for creating fluorochemical compounds from Professor Joseph Simons of Penn State University. No one knew how to use the compound.

Finding uses for this new technology was not easy. About a decade earlier, 3M had begun exploring silicone, thinking that the new material would help make 3M's tape products even better. However, three major companies, including General Electric, had a head start on silicone experimentation and, by the time World War II broke out, these competitors had already filed patents for silicone applications. The patents were "frozen" during the war, but as the fighting wound down, they were approved. Believing that the competition had beaten them, 3M asked the scientists at Penn State University what else they had in their inventory of new ideas.

Fluorochemicals held promise, although marketable products were elusive. At first, 3M's lab people could only make low-boiling and inert fluorocarbon liquids. Even so, the concept was so new—and the materials produced so unusual—that the technology aroused great excitement. But, this was a costly venture. Only a few good ideas surfaced and none led to practical applications. Equally disturbing, these "products" were called by insiders, "the most expensive organic chemicals known to man," costing about $40 a pound.

By 1952, as many as 100 people were focused on the promise of fluorochemicals—the largest research project ever undertaken, up to that time, by 3M. McKnight wondered if the gamble would ever pay off, so he asked his vice president of research and engineering, Dick Carlton, to

talk with 50 people on the project—one at a time. His question was simple: Should 3M continue to pursue fluorochemicals? Imbedded in that question was another: Will fluorochemicals make us money? When 48 said "yes," the project had new life.

Patsy Sherman joined 3M as a lab technician in 1952 armed with degrees in math and chemistry. She had dabbled in science as a young girl with her doting father—that is, until a failed experiment coated the kitchen ceiling and her mother called a halt to their embryonic "research." As Sherman became acquainted with Central Research, she saw tests being done on a new kind of rubber made with fluorochemicals, alongside natural rubber and other synthetic versions. The fluorochemical rubber could stand up to any solvent it faced in a test tube and Sherman was fascinated. "It wasn't bothered by any solvents," she said. "It was truly unique and I liked that. I asked for the assignment." Sherman was given a temporary task to find out if fluorochemical rubber could withstand exposure to a new jet fuel that Wright Patterson Air Force Base was testing. It did, but it failed in the bitter cold of the stratosphere.

> **'Tennis Shoes Don't Fly'**

With her lab job disappearing before her eyes and with an inquiring mind open to the fuzzy front-end of experimentation, Sherman dabbled more with fluorochemicals in 1953. She cooked up a brew of rubber particles suspended in water that looked like milky latex and handed

1 The Chemical Products Group, organized in 1955, was charged with coordinating specialized chemical research and production.

the sample to a younger colleague, Joan Mullin, after asking her to run a test. But, the glass bottle slipped from Mullin's hands, crashed to the floor and sprayed the milky brew on the assistant's new tennis shoes. No amount of water, soap or other solvents weakened the stubborn mixture. "Joan was bemoaning the loss of her new shoes to her boss, George Rathmann," Sherman said. "He said, 'Well, tennis shoes don't fly, so it's of no use to Wright Patterson, but maybe we should put some of this stuff on fabric and see what happens.' "

Sherman and Rathmann applied the sample to fabric, dried it and held it under a faucet. "Water splashed on the fabric," Sherman said, "and it took off 90 degrees the other way. So did solvent. That's when we thought, 'There's something here.' "

Patsy was a gifted experimentalist. She was capable of doing very painstaking experiments.

> **Sam Smith** *retired research scientist*

Sherman collaborated with her boss and mentor, Sam Smith, on the project, and Scotchgard fabric and upholstery protector was introduced in 1956. "It took three years to introduce Scotchgard protector to the textile industry and we had absolutely disastrous results," said Sherman. "Our first product worked only on wool, and it took many more years and many more discoveries to make a product with all the right properties and the right cost to make it affordable for textiles."

"Our product had to be compatible with all the equipment used by textile mills," said Smith. "That meant learning a great deal about the industry and relying on our marketing people to canvass the field. Our first product could tolerate dry cleaning, but not laundering. We knew we had to find a way to treat nylon and cotton, make it stand up in washing, and make the treatment cheaper than our original version."

Along the way, two well-respected experts in fluorochemicals told Sherman and Smith that it would be "thermo-dynamically impossible" to combine a stain repellent and a soil release component in the same product. The fluoro-chemical treatment for fabric made it water repellent, so how could it permit the removal of oily, ground-in soil in laundering? "That challenge," said Sherman, "was like waving a red flag in front of two bulls."

In her 15 percent time, Sherman went to the 3M library looking for a solution and found a new type of graft copolymer produced by a colleague, John

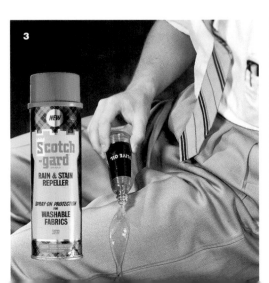

2 Patsy Sherman, who joined 3M as a chemical researcher, played an important role in the development of Scotchgard fabric protectors. Years later, she was the first woman named to the Carlton Society.
3 An early demonstration of Scotchgard stain repellent.

Erickson. "I asked him how he created it," Sherman said, "and he shipped a sample over to me." Sherman went to work experimenting and Smith challenged her to keep trying. "I was working on a new process and asked Sam if he could tell me why my idea wouldn't work," Sherman said. The next morning, Smith said he had an answer, but he was too late. "I said, 'Sam, I ran the process last night and I got a 100 percent perfect yield. It works great.'"

If you take the aggregate character of the company, I believe it's one in which we think we can do anything. That's what I look for in someone who runs a business. I want people who know they can run through walls. > Harold Wiens

executive vice president, Industrial Markets

In all, the fuzzy front-end experimentation that started with creating a viable fabric protector took about seven years. When Scotchgard carpet and upholstery protector was introduced to consumers in 1967, sales jumped from about $200,000 annually (largely to Australian wool producers) to $3 million in the first year.

"3M invested two decades in fluorine research and it took years to realize our first profits," said Smith. "This is a virtue of our company—having the patience to stand behind a good idea. That's where leapfrog technologies and a lot of new business comes from."

Since its introduction in 1956, Scotchgard products have been reformulated many times, always with an eye on improving the product. When 3M discovered environmental issues related to Scotchgard protectors in the late 1990s, the company developed a substitute formulation at considerable cost. By 2000, the popular Scotchgard line had grown to 100 commercially applied and six consumer applied protectors and cleaners.

More than 50 years have passed since McKnight put money on the fuzzy front-end of fluorochemical technology. "As recently as 1992, we were making new fluorine molecules and putting them in a catalogue and sending the catalogue around to people and saying, 'Can you use this?'" said Craig Burton, research manager, Fluorochemical Process and Technology Center.

3M's fluorochemical technology has managed to avoid maturity. It continues to generate new materials and new products at an impressive rate. > 3M Technology Platforms, 1996

"Now we can design molecules for specific applications. We work with the divisions to see what applications they have and then build a molecule we think will work." Ferro-electric liquid crystals are a good example of this approach. They were created in the mid-1990s for flat panel and desktop displays and other electronic devices, to give the screens higher resolution.

Fluorochemicals, and later, hydrofluoroethers (HFEs), have replaced ozone damaging chlorofluorocarbons (CFCs) used in cleaning circuit boards and other electronic components. They are used to cool supercomputers and are key ingredients in extra durable rubber and plastic seals, O-rings and gaskets for hostile environments. Versatile fluoropolymers are used in chemical processing, pollution control equipment and oil exploration. They even protect food from contamination.

Beyond their value as distinct products, small amounts of fluorochemicals allow 3M to manufacture extra thin films, and they help make 3M's tapes peel off their rolls more easily. "We receive about 23 patents a year based on fluorochemical technology and our high was 31 in 2000," said Burton, now laboratory manager, Fluoromaterials Research Group in the Advanced Materials Technology Center. "We're a long way from reaching the limits of this technology."

❸

> **Through a Lens Dimly**

Roger Appeldorn, a young physicist, was working in the Thermo-Fax (Copying Products) Laboratory in the late 1950s when he encountered the early fuzzy front-end of "incremental optics" later known as microreplication.

Appeldorn's mentor and boss, Emil Grieshaber, challenged him to find a use for the transparencies used in copying colored images. "3M was marketing a Thermo-Fax copier that reproduced colored images on white paper," said Appeldorn, but it was a two-step process and the intermediate step involved a transparency with no other use. We tried to project an image from the transparency on a screen using an old Bessler Vu-Graph machine, but the image was dim and brown."

Appeldorn said he then found a process that created a better image that led to 3M's first marketable transparency film. "One of our early, large customers was the Strategic Air Command base in Omaha," Appeldorn said. "They used about 20,000 sheets of film each month in their war room."

Up to that time, 3M had been selling an overhead projector, manufactured by an outside supplier. Appeldorn said 3M then decided to make its own projector to complement the new transparency film. The "improved" equipment turned out to be too costly, bulky, heavy, hot and noisy to be a big seller. Later adaptations improved the projector, but, said Appeldorn, "We were pushing for a lower cost, even lighter version. When we polled people, they said they wanted one as small as a briefcase; it had to unfold and light up automatically."

❹

1 Novec specialty fluids perform as well as chlorofluorocarbons, but do not deplete the earth's ozone layer. **2** 3M's specialty fluids clean printed circuit boards during manufacturing. **3** Fresnel lenses in overhead projectors are made with structured-surface plastic, which replaces expensive, hand-cut glass lenses. **4** Roger Appeldorn was an early leader in the development of microreplication technology.

Appeldorn and his team of five colleagues met these criteria, but the prototype was so expensive that the project was killed. When Appeldorn's team appealed to Bert Auger, manager of special projects, Auger gave them 30 days to produce a product that cost less. They did. It was 1961.

On January 15, 1962, Appeldorn's team demonstrated the first overhead projector with a new fresnel lens made with a structured-surface plastic that was superior to other plastic lenses and far less expensive than a cut glass lens. "We showed it to Ray Herzog,

> We didn't sit down and say, 'Microreplication is the next thing to do; let's go do it.' It doesn't work that way. It evolved. It reached a critical mass and it suddenly proliferated. **> Roger Appeldorn**
>
> *retired corporate scientist and Carlton Society member*

later named chairman of the board and CEO, and Auger," said Appeldorn. "We said the projector could be manufactured at a fraction of the cost of previous models. They told us to be ready to go into production in August and sales went through the roof the first year." Schools wanted them. Businesses needed them; so did government agencies. The product became the basis for the Visual Products Division within a few years.

> ### 'We Started Having Fun . . . '

That's when the fuzzy front-end reappeared for Appeldorn. "We started having fun with the idea," he said. "I'm a physicist. I was considering the science. My colleagues and I looked at the very fine pattern on the plastic fresnel lens and wondered, what else could we do with structured surfaces?" These could be surfaces with hundreds or even millions of structures per square inch repeated continuously and invisible to the naked eye.

"We soon renamed what we were experimenting with," said Appeldorn. "We called them 'structured surfaces.' 3M management was particularly enamored with the potential for replicating these surfaces, so we started to call it 'microreplication' in the early 1970s." At first, Appeldorn and his boss, Ron Mitsch, who later retired as vice chairman and executive vice president, resisted the "microreplication" term—not because it wasn't accurate, but because it might signal too much to the competition. That's why the Optics Technology Center—where microreplication was the motherlode of technology— kept its name until 1997, when it was officially renamed the Microreplication Technology Center.

The next application, after that initial breakthrough in the 1960s, was a 3M fresnel lens imbedded in a traffic signal light that gave U.S. drivers in the left lane a visible cue to turn. 3M also began producing lenses for LED watches and microfilm reader-printers. By the early 1970s, there were enough opportunities—particularly in the automotive industry—to warrant a new business initiative called the Industrial Optics Project. One of

1 A 3M overhead projector in a North St. Paul high school classroom in 1960.
2 Scotchlite Diamond Grade sheeting, widely used for traffic signs today, required a decade of development before its introduction in 1989.
3 Scotchlite Diamond Grade fluorescent sheeting makes directional signs more visible day or night.

the more advanced applications came with the 1974 acquisition of Polacoat, a company with the technological know-how to make liquid crystal displays (LCDs). "Our idea was to make LCDs that would combine with our overhead projectors to display electronic images," Appeldorn said. The idea was ahead of its time. Management didn't like it.

By the mid-1970s, Appeldorn was torn between putting his energy into making better fresnel lenses for the rapidly expanding overhead projector market, while also trying to respond to others in 3M who saw the value of structured surfaces—in abrasives, in magnetic recording, in traffic control materials, in new frontiers on the fuzzy front-end. Appeldorn went to Mitsch and suggested that Industrial Optics should stand alone as a business. Moreover, an Optics Technology Center could be created to nurture, expand and develop all the possibilities that structured surface science offered. About 20 percent of all products sold by 3M were rooted in optics technology when Appeldorn became the first director of the center in 1983.

> **A Highway Gem**
More promise for microreplication emerged when 3M tooled its manufacturing to make the first run of Scotchlite Diamond Grade reflective sheeting, a product that would revolutionize highway signs and vehicle markings many years later. "I was working in Traffic Control Materials when we put in the first small Diamond Grade maker in Menomonie, Wisconsin,

in 1975," said Charles Kiester, retired senior vice president, Engineering, Quality and Manufacturing Services. "Diamond Grade sheeting was the mother of all microreplication." It would be another 14 years before the product was formally introduced in 1989.

"The lab started working on Diamond Grade sheeting more than a decade before that introduction," said Robert Finocchiaro, former technical director, 3M Microreplication Technology Center, now technical director, Engineered Adhesives Division. "It was a challenging project because it involved creating several thousand identical retroreflective prisms in a square inch using plastic that could stand a wide range of conditions—weather and otherwise. 3M was the only company with this new application."

Since the late 1980s, there have been numerous iterations combining durable and flexible fluorescent materials and retroreflective surfaces—everything from daytime traffic signs that are fluorescent to flexible, fluorescent signs used on cones in the work zone and on canvas sidings on trucks in Europe.

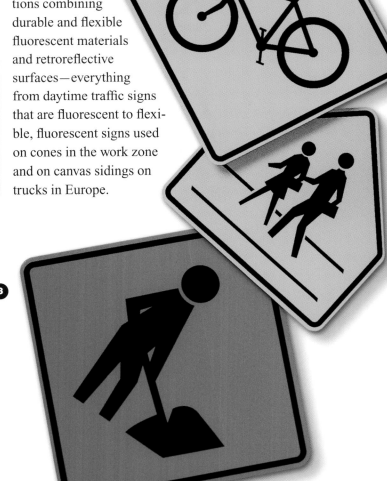

2

3

Scotchlite Diamond Grade sheeting has helped reduce traffic accidents, and the U.S. National Highway Traffic Safety Administration now requires all new trailers and truck tractors to use what's called "conspicuity markings." Other countries are instituting the same requirements.

> **Film Futures**

In the same year Scotchlite Diamond Grade sheeting was introduced, 3M also launched internal reflecting film, another new use of micro-replication. Later renamed 3M optical lighting film, the product had its start with research conducted by Lorne Whitehead at the University of British Columbia in Vancouver, Canada, a decade earlier. Whitehead had experimented with lining up prisms running the length of an acrylic sheet, then shaping that sheet into a square tube and transporting light, via the prisms, from one end to the other. He called it "total internal reflection."

Building on that concept, Appeldorn and Sandy Cobb focused on how microreplication could be used to produce micro-prismatic structures on a large scale. The team received a 3M Genesis Grant, designed to fund technical

pursuits that don't qualify for other financial support, and the work accelerated. The result was a reflective film. It looked ordinary on casual inspection, but a closer look revealed one smooth side and one structured side with tiny prismatic grooves. Rolled into a tube, the film was capable of "piping" light evenly throughout its length. It offered intriguing possibilities for street lights, traffic signals, manufacturing facilities, hospital operating rooms, airplane cabins, railroad cars and truck beds. "That film led to creating our Vikuiti brightness enhancement film (BEF) for laptop computers and cell phones," said Finocchiaro. "BEF is basically optical lighting film with a finer pitch. We were able to get into the market as fast as we did, in the early 1990s, because the technology had already been developed. The manufacturing processes were in place. 3M could offer a unique approach to solving an unarticulated customer need—namely, enhancing the brightness of backlit flat panel displays and extending the life of batteries. We were able to deliver 50 to 100 percent more light to a display using our film."

Appeldorn described much of this work as "still embryonic," even in the late

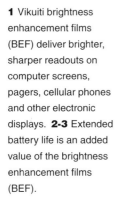

1 Vikuiti brightness enhancement films (BEF) deliver brighter, sharper readouts on computer screens, pagers, cellular phones and other electronic displays. **2-3** Extended battery life is an added value of the brightness enhancement films (BEF).

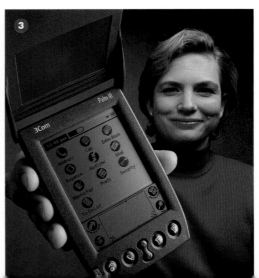

The pressure was on. After selling 3M optical lighting film to companies around the world for more than a decade, 3M decided to produce the end-product, a light pipe. The kind of light pipe that illuminates 900 miles of highway tunnels in Italy. A light pipe for sports arenas that eliminates blinding light on footballs or basketballs with a high arc or annoying reflection from the floor. A light pipe for greenhouses, museums, assembly halls, large manufacturing facilities, distribution centers, railway stations, indoor swimming pools and unique architectural designs.

Ken Kneipp, technical manager, 3M Consumer Safety and Light Management Department, is credited with the idea of not just selling the optical film, but the end product that uses the film, as well. "We decided to introduce our new product in 1996 at the Hannover, Germany, light show—a huge event that showcases new industrial and consumer lighting," said DuWayne Radke, project manufacturing manager, who joined the light piping team after spending 22 years in engineering. "We had about six weeks to design and fabricate our prototypes, then ship them to Germany. Ken, Steve Pojar, technical specialist, and I worked on them virtually nonstop until we were done. We said, 'O.K., we have a few weeks to do this,' so we just sat down and figured it out. We got a local extrusion house to build us a die and do some extruding. We figured out how we were going to assemble the piping. We built

some jigs in our home workshops. We invented as we went. We were committed and, whatever it took, we did it."

"3M had the first really big change in lighting technology at that Hannover show," said Pojar, who had joined the company in 1986 with a B.A. in physics. Show visitors wanted to place orders and even buy the prototypes. Several were lighting designers and one was particularly keen on the prototypes.

Two months later, 3M was gearing up to manufacture the first order and, by September, about a mile of piping was shipped to Hill Air Force Base in Salt Lake City, Utah.

Anyone observing the market reception to 3M light piping would have assumed the business was about to take off like a rocket. But, it didn't. As it turns out, the company supplying 3M with a superior, microwave-powered light source about the size of a golf ball had to remove its product from the market. 3M was left with light pipes and no light.

The scramble began to find an alternative light source and

one materialized with almost equally good lighting properties. By 1999, the light piping team was sure it could make their product in any size or shape, almost any length, for virtually any application, but they'd been set back about a year. With no real business yet, the focus was deciding which market segments held the greatest potential for 3M. "We weren't going to make 100 feet of light piping for someone," said Radke. "We wanted to sell hundreds of thousands of meters and feet of this product." This was the commercialization stage where the target buyers were identified, the manufacturing processes were refined and the price/value equation was defined. By the end of 1999, 3M was scheduled to ship and install about 1,000 3M light piping units for customers, ranging from as small as 10 inches in diameter to as long as 65 feet.

Pojar and Radke said they put their "heart, soul and emotions" into the 3M light piping program and there are still many unknowns. They agree that support from management is crucial in seeing an embryonic business to reality. "You need a committed team, funding and a general direction," said Radke. "We were working in a brand new area where we didn't have the details worked out. We had no idea what light piping was going to look like. We just starting working and necessity was our guide to invention. We needed the freedom . . . and we had it."

Necessity is the Guide to Invention

1980s, and he told a journalist, with obvious satisfaction, "Our learning curve, which began 25 years ago, is now trending sharply upward."

It was clear to Appeldorn that, if microreplication was to be a commercial success, 3M had to make products through a continuous process, "by the yard, not the inch" in Appeldorn's words. Process research efforts started in earnest because microreplication required a sophisticated, complicated set of steps including extrusion, casting, coating and molding.

> A Revolutionary Product and Process

When microreplication "met" coated abrasives in the 1980s, the result was new-to-the-world products. But, it would be 10 years before 3M Trizact abrasives debuted in 1995. The fuzzy front-end of "structured abrasives" required 15 percent time; boot-legging; collaboration among nine labs at 3M; and an ardent sponsor, In Sun Hong, then technical director, Abrasive Systems Laboratory.

Innovation tells us where to go; we don't tell innovation where to go.

> **L.D. DeSimone** *retired chairman of the board and chief executive officer (CEO)*

Mike Mucci was a technical service senior specialist in the Abrasive Systems Division during the mid-1980s. He was looking for ways to make aircraft more fuel efficient by sanding grooves into airplane wings. Meanwhile, Jon Pieper, process engineer, Abrasive Systems, was exploring how light curing could eliminate the use of solvents and heating by oven in the production of coated abrasives. Both Mucci and Pieper knew scientists in the Central Research Process Technology Laboratory (CRPTL) who were examining how to link microreplication to abrasives.

When this informal, though intensive, effort won a Genesis Grant, there were newly dedicated dollars

available for personnel and equipment. A retired manufacturing line from Traffic Control Materials Division—called the "blue monster"—became a testing ground and accelerated the process and product development work. Micro-replication experts from the Optics Technology Center became key advisors. Even Scott Culler, scientist, Dental Products Division, who knew nothing about sandpaper—but a lot about light curing—joined the team.

As it turned out, a major, early hurdle was figuring out how to coat and cure a mixture of mineral and resin (a "slurry") onto a backing, such as cloth, to form precise microscopic pyramids. Light curing became a key factor in making it work. "In 1991, we were lucky if we could make one sample a week before things started going wrong," said Stan Collins, who led the project's technical team. "For a management review at the end of the year, we were making product at 10 feet a minute and we were proud of that."

Once the project team was able to create 10-foot belts of the prototype, there were weeks and months of testing. Day after day, Mucci used the prototypes to sand golf club heads and plumbing fixtures. He became known as the single, most notorious, source of noise in his building.

With an effective prototype, the focus turned to boosting speed and quality in manufacturing so that 3M Trizact abrasives could be produced for a commercial market. Dave Quast, division engineer, Abrasive Systems, then technical director, Abrasive Systems Lab, designed all the equipment upgrades for the blue

1

monster, so the team could run small test batches. Hong was a relentless advocate and, through his efforts, Trizact abrasives became a Corporate Pacing Plus Program. That designation guaranteed them three years of funding to accelerate product development and commercialization.

The real breakthrough came in September 1992, when Culler field tested the new product for a manufacturer of titanium jet turbine blades. "That was the litmus test," Culler said. "We had a customer saying, 'You guys have something really unique here.' From that point on, it was 'Turn the crank and let's get scaled up and get this out as fast as we can.'"

> Today Golf Clubs, Tomorrow Semiconductors

In 1995, when 3M Trizact abrasive belts were formally introduced, 3M changed the basis of competition in the abrasives industry and there were significant sales by 2000. Hong called the structured abrasive discovery "a process revolution and a product revolution."

"When we first started," he said, "we didn't see the full scope of the product. There are still many applications that have not yet been thought of and many other market areas where we can change the basis of competition."

One of the most exciting prospects is semiconductor wafer polishing, called "planarization," a high-tech application that became a Pacing Plus Program in 1996. Put simply, planarization is sophisticated sanding that cuts the time required to make wafers used in semi-conductors and reduces the margin of error in the process. This product and application are in an industry expected to reach $1 billion by 2005. 3M hopes that it will generate $100 million in new sales by 2006. "This product is highly dependent on process," said Chuck Kummeth, business director, Chemical Mechanical Planarization Programs. "That's why we're partnering with the world's leaders, Rodel and Applied Material. It's an extremely challenging technology, but as electronic devices get smaller, there is even more growth potential."

> Partners in Microreplication

With new technologies in electronics emerging—on average—in two years or less, 3M decided to exploit its microreplication technology platform in the 1990s

As the semiconductor industry shifts to making semiconductor wafers that can process more and more information, they're looking to 3M to make the transition less costly. With our specialized abrasives, we can help a customer cut the number of process steps by as much as half.

> Harold Wiens

by finding worldwide manufacturing partners. In this way, new applications could reach the marketplace sooner. Finocchiaro traveled to Sumitomo 3M in Japan

1 Close-up of structured surface using micro-replication technology. **2** Structured abrasives, employing microreplication technology, offer superior performance for finishing metal products from golf clubs to medical implants. **3** Smoothing the surface of semiconductor wafers is faster using structured abrasives.

and called on companies including Hitachi, Sony, Fujitsu, Seiko-Epson and Canon. The objective was to introduce 3M's micro-replication expertise and find partnerships that would be mutual and strong. "I reviewed our capabilities," said Finocchiaro. "I said we're able to produce some of the most precise microstructures available and we can manufacture them into products in large volumes and on a large scale."

These exploratory discussions led to confidential agreements with manufacturers of plasma display panels in Japan and Korea.

Technologies have a shelf life. Micro-replication has a life of perhaps 15 years. We need to get as much out of the platform in the time that we can. Then, we'll migrate to something else. > **Robert Finocchiaro**

technical director, Engineered Adhesives Division

While relatively new to consumers, plasma displays are common in business, for example, serving as airline arrival and departure displays. The displays can be as large as 5 feet (on a diagonal measurement) and yet they are only about 3 inches thick. A hot gas, or plasma, is ignited in these panels to give off light, much like fluorescent gas illuminates a fluorescent lamp.

3M's stake in plasma display panel manufacturing is the rear panel of glass, called a "barrier rib," that has vertical channels less than 360 microns apart, five times smaller than the width of a human hair. Plasma, in the form of phosphors giving off color, is trapped in these narrow channels, then ignited to produce colored light that produces an image.

"The most expensive part of manufacturing the plasma display panel was producing that barrier rib," said Finocchiaro. "The glass was sandblasted under high pressure; it was a slow, messy and expensive process, taking about 30 minutes for each barrier rib. But, we have expertise in making structured surfaces. Not only could we make the structures, we also developed a manufacturing process to do it." Rather than make the barrier rib panels and sell them to manufacturers, 3M chose to license its process technology to manufacturers, saving them time and money and ensuring high-quality production. "Our Japanese customer, Fujitsu, has told us—of all the options they know of today—our solution has the potential to be the lowest cost in producing the barrier rib,"

Like a conspiracy in an Oliver Stone film, microreplication is suddenly everywhere in 3M.

> **Fortune magazine, February 5, 1996**

1 A model of a strand of DNA. **2** Senior research biologist Anila Prabhu, in the Biomaterials Technology Center, studied a gel used to analyze DNA. Micro-replication allows researchers to conduct thousands of tests on one protein at one time.

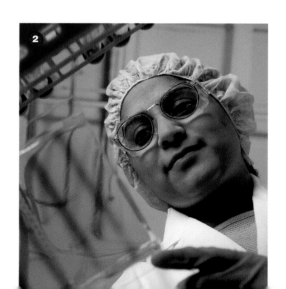

The barrier rib project is what we call 'white space' at 3M. Acceleration programs, like this one, address very large opportunities and markets. But there are other opportunities that we shouldn't ignore. 'White space' projects bring diversity to 3M's technology portfolio and that's what will keep us profitable.

> **Raymond C. Chiu** *product development specialist, 3M Microreplication Technology Center*

said Finocchiaro. This new application could cut the cost of in-home entertainment centers with plasma display panels from $10,000 to $2,000 in a matter of a few years.

Yet another white space for microreplication involves biomedical uses. "This would be a brand new application for our technology," said Finocchiaro. "In the human genome program, for example, researchers are decoding the genetic makeup of humans. To accomplish that, they must analyze hundreds of millions—if not billions—of protein samples. By using microreplication, we can create thousands of tiny channels on plastic so that researchers can conduct thousands of tests on one protein at the same time. This approach brings about huge improvements in efficiency while simultaneously enabling miniaturization of the process. I expect this will bring tremendous value in the marketplace."

By 2000, 3M products using microreplication technology generated more than $1 billion in revenue after peaking at about $200 million annually only a decade before. By 2002, 3M estimated that microreplication would be an integral part of one-fourth to one-third of all its products.

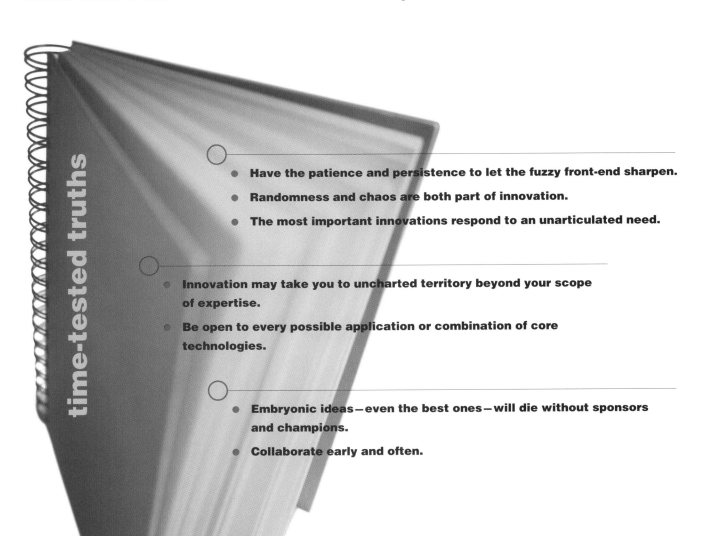

time-tested truths

- Have the patience and persistence to let the fuzzy front-end sharpen.
- Randomness and chaos are both part of innovation.
- The most important innovations respond to an unarticulated need.

- Innovation may take you to uncharted territory beyond your scope of expertise.
- Be open to every possible application or combination of core technologies.

- Embryonic ideas—even the best ones—will die without sponsors and champions.
- Collaborate early and often.

○ **Top leaders had support**

○ **3M legends**

○ **What it takes**

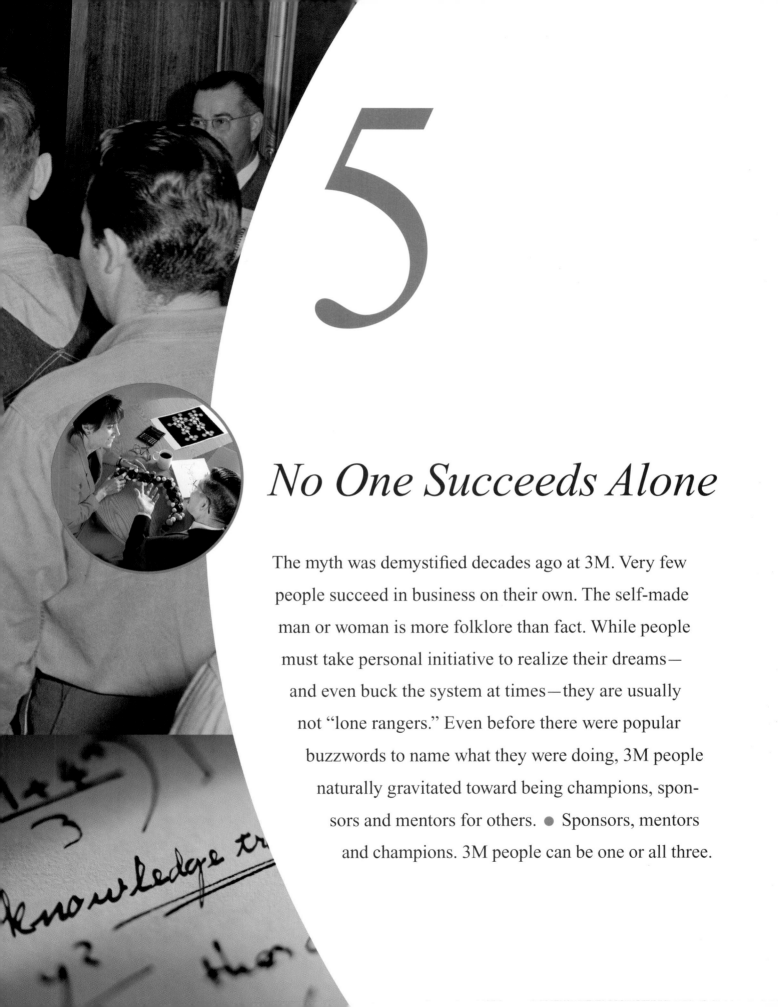

5

No One Succeeds Alone

The myth was demystified decades ago at 3M. Very few people succeed in business on their own. The self-made man or woman is more folklore than fact. While people must take personal initiative to realize their dreams— and even buck the system at times—they are usually not "lone rangers." Even before there were popular buzzwords to name what they were doing, 3M people naturally gravitated toward being champions, sponsors and mentors for others. ● Sponsors, mentors and champions. 3M people can be one or all three.

Kay Grenz became vice president, Human Resources, but 31 years before she was a novice HR coordinator in her first job at 3M. "I moved into manufacturing engineering and met Don Guthrie, now retired vice president, Engineering and Manufacturing," Grenz said. "I didn't walk into his office one day and say, 'Don, will you be my mentor?' Instead, when I had an issue to solve, we'd discuss the situation, talk about

It started with Lucius Ordway. 3M needed a sponsor who said, 'I believe in your company, I'm going to put money into it and I'm going to stay for the long haul.' **> Leon Royer**

retired executive director, Leadership Development Center, Human Resources

❶

what steps could be taken, examine how the approach fit 3M's decision-making process, and then we'd identify a solution. He took a personal interest in helping me understand the culture of the company and its strengths. It was an early version of knowledge transfer."

Guthrie was clear about how he wanted to coach Grenz but, she said, "I didn't know it was mentoring at the time and, if you asked him, I don't think he would have either—even though he'd been doing it for 30 years.

"Don's counsel was extraordinarily objective and yet personalized," Grenz said. "He could help a person find the answers, instead of giving them the answers."

Steve Buckingham, intellectual property counsel, explained his role as a mentor. "My goal is to teach people about the culture of 3M and the unwritten rules we live by here."

Dick Drew was the classic mentor. He always encouraged his people to pursue ideas . . . He said, 'If it's a dumb idea, you'll find out. You'll smack right into that brick wall, then you'll stagger back and see another opportunity that you wouldn't have seen otherwise.' **> Art Fry**

retired corporate scientist, Office Supplies Division

Chapter opening photos (From left) A.G. Bush, William McKnight and Richard Carlton were congratulated in 1949 as they took their new posts as chairman of the Executive Committee, chairman of the board, and president, respectively; Successful mentoring at 3M is informal and flourishes with personal contact and good rapport; The transfer of knowledge—encompassing both technical expertise and an understanding of 3M's culture—lies at the heart of the mentoring relationship.

❷

> **'Go South, Young Man'**

L.D. DeSimone became an engineer at 3M Canada, in his native country. But, when an opportunity surfaced to leave London, Ontario, and tackle a new assignment, DeSimone, who retired as 3M chairman and CEO, was reluctant. "I wasn't keen on going anywhere. I was happy

I was 20 years old in 1957... when Don Guthrie came in and talked with me. Having a person who was that interested in a young man's work was a real confidence builder. I think it's impossible to go from joining 3M to having a great career without some mentoring. It's part of the learning experience. > **L.D. DeSimone**

retired chairman of the board and chief executive officer

with what I was doing," he said. "But Jim Mingle, who hired me, said 'You know, Desi, you ought to go.' If he hadn't given me this advice, I'd still be in Canada."

DeSimone would not have become managing director of 3M Brazil without the mentoring and sponsorship of M.J. Monteiro (Em to his colleagues), who became executive vice president, International Operations. "He helped me make the transition from being an engineer with a technical orientation to becoming a business person," said DeSimone. "As I worked for him, Em taught me the business and financial considerations of man-

agement. The other thing he gave me was trust. I had a lot of freedom."

When 3M needed a new Scotch-Brite manufacturing plant in Brazil, DeSimone found a champion in John Whitcomb, group vice president, Abrasives, Adhesives, Building Services and Chemicals. 3M Brazil's business was growing at an astronomical rate in the early 1970s and DeSimone needed more production capacity. From experience, however, 3M had learned not to concentrate all of its manufacturing at one site, so Chairman Harry Heltzer and President Ray Herzog told DeSimone to find a new location on which to build a manufacturing plant for Scotch-Brite products. "We had a very skinny staff," DeSimone said, "and building a whole new location would have been tough." In the meantime, however,

Mentoring is an established part of the fabric of 3M and one of the key reasons why the culture has been sustained for so long. > **Kay Grenz**

vice president, Human Resources

DeSimone managed to get the OK to build the Scotch-Brite plant next to the existing facility. "We started building in a hurry," he said, "because we needed the plant so badly." Soon afterward, however, Monteiro wired DeSimone telling him to stop all work and come to St. Paul. 3M's international head of manufacturing didn't support the plan. "We had a hell of an argument,"

1 In the 1940s, the Cost Accounting Department, housed in Building 21 on the east side of St. Paul, instituted an early mentoring program: new employees learned how things were done from an "old timer." **2** Don Guthrie, pictured in 1959, mentored many 3M employees. **3** 3M scientists encouraged students' interest in science on a Twin Cities WMIN-TV television program in 1955.

Listeners, Teachers and Guides

"Don Guthrie, vice president, Engineering and Manufacturing; Bob Adams, head of Research and Development; and Lew Lehr, chairman of the board and chief executive officer, were all mentors, sponsors and champions in their careers," said Kay Grenz, vice president, Human Resources. What do these roles mean?

Mentoring is probably the best understood. It is a one-on-one relationship and often informal. People typically "self select" each other and they are usually in the same profession or field. The mentor is a good listener, teacher and guide. Relationships may be short and episodic or last for years through multiple careers. Mentors typically say that they gain as much—if not more—from the relationship as they give. Successful people in business can always cite at least one mentor and often more who helped them.

Spencer Silver, corporate scientist and creator of the Post-it note repositionable adhesive, said George Van Dykes Tiers left an indelible impression on him. "George was one of 3M's first corporate scientists and his mind soaked up knowledge like

a sponge. He showed me that you could do basic chemistry research in an industrial environment. Even in his 70s, he still lives, eats and sleeps research. His laboratory is a museum. George 'adopts' people and helps them immensely. He's as close to the real dictionary mentor as I can imagine."

An individual sponsor is someone who may have a formal responsibility to assure that an employee's career is on the right track. For example, if a 3M employee goes overseas, he or she is assigned a "re-entry sponsor." When employees return to St. Paul or 3M Austin Center in Texas, on home leave from an international assignment, they meet with their sponsors. "It's a formal relationship and people take it seriously," said Grenz, a re-entry sponsor herself. The sponsor wants to make sure that the person in the overseas assignment is making the most of that opportunity and, after the individual returns, the sponsor helps steer the person to the best opportunities stateside. The program was created in the early 1980s when international employees said they felt disconnected from 3M's United States operations.

Similarly, as 3M's technical infrastructure grew, the company's corporate scientists looked for ways to serve as sponsors or mentors to often younger colleagues on other continents. In 1996, a pilot program started with Sumitomo 3M in Japan involving four corporate scientists, from corporate headquarters in St. Paul, who spent several weeks there. "In Japan, they accept mentorship as a natural function; it's a fundamental part of their culture," said Steve Heilmann, one of the four mentors. "Our goal was to establish closer ties with the scientists and engineers in Japan. We wanted them to feel comfortable contacting us if they had technical problems or questions about their careers. Later visits to Japan involved staff and division scientists who served as mentors. Authentic mentoring," Heilmann said, "requires a lot of personal contact and rapport that builds over years."

It is not surprising that people in leadership roles are expected to serve in supporting roles. "One of the criteria used in assessing a technical career is whether that person engaged in mentoring," said Heilmann, whose own memorable mentor was lab mate Wayne Larson. "I saw how successful he was in getting his research out into the commercial arena," said Heilmann. "That takes so much skill—not just technical talent, but people skills." Now retired, Larson is a consultant to 3M and he has worked with Lockwood Carlson, another 3M corporate scientist, who organized a mentoring program involving retired 3M corporate scientists and current staff.

"A sponsor is someone who gives you advice as you go through life," said Les Krogh, retired senior vice president, Research and Development. "It's someone who talks to you about your future, who's there when you have a question. Sponsors say to others, 'Take a good look at this person.' I've sponsored a lot of people in my life; it's an important part of being a manager."

Project sponsors "adopt" and promote projects and not necessarily specific people. The people may change, but the project is the focus. Projects that sponsors choose to nurture and support are usually in their own business or organizational area.

Champions may come from unrelated business areas. They have strong credibility within 3M and they are persuasive "lobbyists" for company investments in new ideas or products. "Al Huber, retired executive vice president, Commercial and Consumer Sector, was the marketing champion in the company, even though he had sector responsibility and served as managing director, 3M Germany," said Grenz. "Ernie Moffet, retired group vice president, Consumer Group, was the consumer champion when 3M still thought of itself as strictly an industrial company. High rank is not mandatory for a champion, but the ability to listen, persuade and influence is."

3

1 Spencer Silver, the corporate scientist credited with inventing the microsphere adhesive used in Post-it notes. **2** Kay Grenz, mentored as a new 3M employee, was named vice president, Human Resources in 1998. **3** 3M's sales initiative and summer internship programs give students tips on building a successful sales career at 3M.

DeSimone recalled. "The talks went on for almost three days. Finally, the decision went to Whitcomb. We repeated the arguments in front of Mr. Whitcomb and he listened to our wrangling for 30 minutes. I was very aggressive and so was the other guy."

Finally Whitcomb put an end to the battle and DeSimone has never forgotten the outcome. "Whitcomb said, 'These guys in Brazil have the best business of all our businesses outside of the United States. Why don't you leave them alone and let them do what they want to do?'" End of discussion.

> **Sponsors with Vision and Pluck**
"Tom Reid was one of my first sponsors and mentors at 3M," said Les Krogh, retired senior vice president, Research and Development. "I worked for him in the summer of 1949. He talked to me about fluorochemicals and how they could carry 3M into agricultural chemicals and pharmaceuticals. I learned about vision from Tom." Mathew Miller, manager, 3M Abrasives Lab in 1954, told his colleagues to look seriously at that young guy, Krogh. "Matt taught me how to run a lab in one of the toughest situations—a division that was

William McKnight established fundamental operating principles for 3M including belief in people, trust in people and a willingness to let people try new things. > **Lew Lehr** retired chairman of the board and chief executive officer

losing market share," said Krogh. "The first thing he did was start Central Research Lab projects that examined the properties of adhesives. He hired me to work in a three-man research group to explore future abrasive backings. Because of those efforts, our lab knew so much about the function of abrasive structures that when our competition brought out a new product, we could analyze and duplicate it in two weeks flat."

Cecil March and Guthrie were champions who looked at the "bigger picture," said Krogh, who holds a Ph.D. in organic chemistry. "They

encouraged me to be the first technical director at 3M to leave a division lab and return to Central Research. The divisions were growing and they rarely hired Ph.D.s. Central Research did hire Ph.D.s and, soon, many became technical directors. Eventually, Central Research became a hiring pool for the divisions."

> **The Mentor and Motivator**
Jim Klein, retired, who held a variety of financial assignments during his 44-year 3M career, remembers the powerful role William McKnight played as a sponsor and mentor. "Tim Raymond, retired research scientist, had been working on a porous rubber sheeting for hospital beds," said Klein, who sat in on many management reviews of new products. "Tim called it Porcel rubber sheeting and he worked on it for years. Every six months, the product team reported to the Management Committee on their progress, expenses and projected costs. Tim knew, from the tone of one meeting, that the project was going to be killed."

Raymond had a huge emotional investment in the project and, as the meeting progressed, Klein remembered him saying, "You know, I've worked seven years of my life on this. You're not listening to me. You're going to kill this project." Tears ran down Raymond's cheeks. It was then, Klein said, that McKnight stepped in, "Wait a minute, Tim. What I want to tell you is we

have a project involving resin bond disks that is more important and we need you for that one. It's worth millions of dollars to 3M. Porcel sheeting is a good product, but we can't afford to have you focused on it right now."

Klein said Raymond went from fighting tears to "walking five feet off the ground because McKnight said, 'I've got a project for you; you're the best man in the company for this job.' "

> The Titan of Tape and TQM

Hugh Tierney, retired vice president, Reinforced Plastics Division, championed 3M's tape technology in the early years, Lew Lehr, retired chairman and CEO, said. "He forced the company to move from cellophane tape to acetate tape because cellophane crinkles and turns yellow. Acetate was a brand new concept in the marketplace. He pushed to develop a tape dispenser that was easy to use, load and unload. Even though he'd never been a salesman or marketer, he had a sense of what customers needed. All the new tape developments that emerged when he was head of technical operations were personally pushed by Tierney."

In 1950, when Lehr's embryonic medical products business spent more on advertising than it generated in sales, Lehr thought his project was doomed. "If you're an executive vice president, the logical thing to say is, 'It's dying. Kill it.' But we worked for Tierney and he said, 'Yeah, we'll stop, but let's make six months' inventory of our surgical drapes before we turn the equipment off. Then, you'll have to go out and sell the inventory.

We'll see if this is as good as you say it is.' " Six months later, 3M had two customers, the United States Air Force and the University of Minnesota. "We told them we were going out of business and they said, 'No, you're not,' " Lehr recalled. "That's how the medical business got reinstated at 3M. It was Tierney, a 3M champion, who had the faith to keep the program going. You could say he 'sat on the eggs and helped them hatch.' "

A champion has to have faith and the support of people at the top who have confidence in him. A champion also has to attract and retain a cadre of very capable, committed and loyal people, because no one accomplishes anything at 3M alone. **> Lew Lehr**

John Pearson, retired vice president, Development, and Carlton Society member, also credits Tierney with focusing on manufacturing process improvement decades before "total quality management" (TQM) became the mantra of American business. "Hugh was head of the Tape Division in the late 1940s. He recognized that as competition grew, we had to get our manufacturing economics in line by understanding the processes we used to make our products," said Pearson, who led the tape development engineering group at the time. "He took a risk and supported that work, even though it didn't generate any new products and was an expense item on his budget."

1 Acetate fibre tape, from the early 1950s. **2** Hugh Tierney (right), pictured in 1949, was a champion for 3M's fledgling medical products business and for manufacturing improvements long before total quality management was fashionable.

> The Persistence of Champions

Lehr said Jim Thwaits was the original champion of Post-it notes when he led 3M's Tape Group while Art Fry, retired corporate scientist, Office Supplies Division, pursued a lonely cause: trying to sell people on the value of a pad of yellow memo paper with impermanent adhesive. "Thwaits was the one who kept pushing and saying, 'This might be a product,'" Lehr said. Lehr's executive assistant, Shirley Tholander, was also a champion of Post-it notes. At the request of 3M marketers, she sent a letter to her executive secretary peers at Fortune 100 companies and enclosed a product sample. "All of a sudden, those little yellow things were coming from the CEO's offices in 100 companies," said Lehr. "The next question was, 'Where can I get more?'"

After Post-it notes failed in a five-city test, Joe Ramey, who retired as group vice president, Commercial Markets Group, and Geoff Nicholson, who retired as staff vice president, Corporate Technical Planning and International Technical Operations, were two champions who packed a pickup and trailer with samples and drove to one of those cities, Richmond, Virginia, to give the product one last try. "They traveled from one end of town to the other," said Jerry Chernivec, intellectual property counsel, who wrote the first Post-it note patent and has defended the product from competitive infringement around the world. "They gave Post-it notes to every potential customer and said, 'We'll be back in three weeks to see what you think.' When people actually had a chance to try them, Post-it notes were a hit."

The Boise, Idaho, blitz a few months later confirmed the fact that once consumers tried this product, they wanted more.

Clarence Sampair, Maynard Patterson, M.J. Monteiro and Thwaits, all long retired from leadership positions in International Operations, were the "international champions" who made 3M a global enterprise, as early as the 1950s, when other American companies were focused largely on domestic growth. "Establishing and expanding 3M's international operations was remarkable," said Lehr. "They had indomitable spirit. They were able to wear dirty shirts out of suitcases they'd been carrying around for three weeks. With little experience to guide them, Sampair and Patterson had uncanny, accurate instincts for international business." They, in turn, were mentors to Thwaits who followed them.

> The Champion of Shared Knowledge

Bob Bringer, retired staff vice president, Environmental Technology and Services, and former chair of 3M's Technical Council, said Bob Adams was the champion of technology sharing within 3M. "Bob, who retired as vice president, Research and Development, formed 3M's Technical Council," said Bringer. "He saw it as an open forum for technical leaders from all the laboratories in the company to share information about new technologies. This was the first time that peers got a chance to meet together for three or four days. Creating the council solidified the idea that technology belongs to the company."

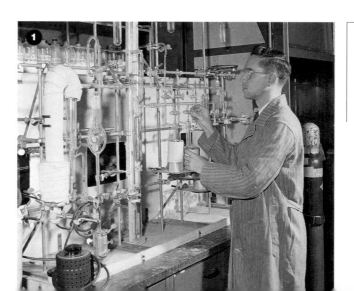

1 Bob Adams, pictured in 1949, created 3M's Technical Council for technical leaders from all the company's laboratories.

As the champion of knowledge transfer, Adams also advocated a strong market orientation, said Bringer. "He started at 3M as a salesman with a Ph.D. in chemical engineering. He encouraged all of us to think more about markets rather than just about technology."

Mentors, sponsors and champions often have long lasting impact. Roger Appeldorn, retired corporate scientist, remembers Emil Grieshaber, technical director, Visual Products Division, the nattily dressed individualist who arrived at work wearing a bow tie and a flower in his lapel. Appeldorn was taking additional courses at the University of Minnesota in 1956 when he went to work for Grieshaber in the Thermo-Fax laboratory. "3M didn't have an education policy at the time, so Emil covered for me when I attended day classes," said Appeldorn. "He was a taskmaster; he expected people to work hard. We all had projects that were important to the division, but he also encouraged us to think about new things—ideas that were completely apart from our normal lab assignments. He'd often walk in and ask 'What's new?'—and he'd expect an answer."

On most Friday afternoons, Grieshaber gathered his team for what he called, "show and tell." "He'd buy coffee and doughnuts and we'd all sit around and discuss the personal lab projects we were working on," Appeldorn said. "One idea sparked another. I can remember 30 people from other divisions attending, including some from Visual Products Division, the group working on overhead transparencies and later the overhead projector." Those early, casual meetings planted the seeds for 3M's microreplication technology platform. Even today, more than 40 years later, Appeldorn said Grieshaber's impact was pivotal. "He was my first major mentor. He influenced me more than anyone else in technical work and technical management."

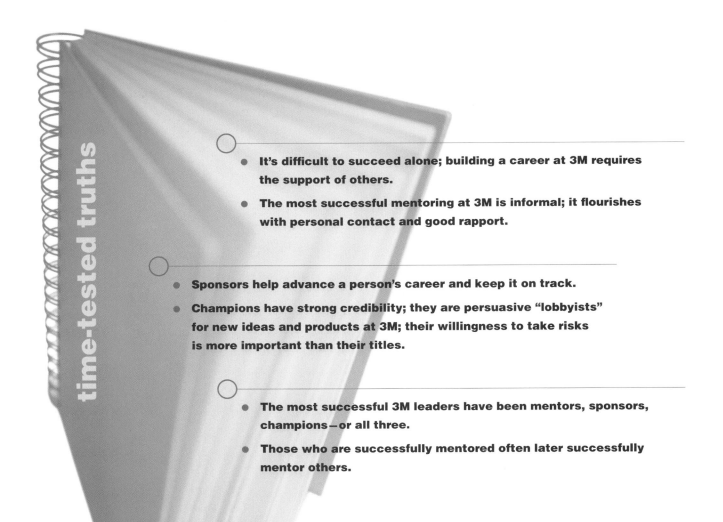

time-tested truths

- It's difficult to succeed alone; building a career at 3M requires the support of others.
- The most successful mentoring at 3M is informal; it flourishes with personal contact and good rapport.

- Sponsors help advance a person's career and keep it on track.
- Champions have strong credibility; they are persuasive "lobbyists" for new ideas and products at 3M; their willingness to take risks is more important than their titles.

- The most successful 3M leaders have been mentors, sponsors, champions—or all three.
- Those who are successfully mentored often later successfully mentor others.

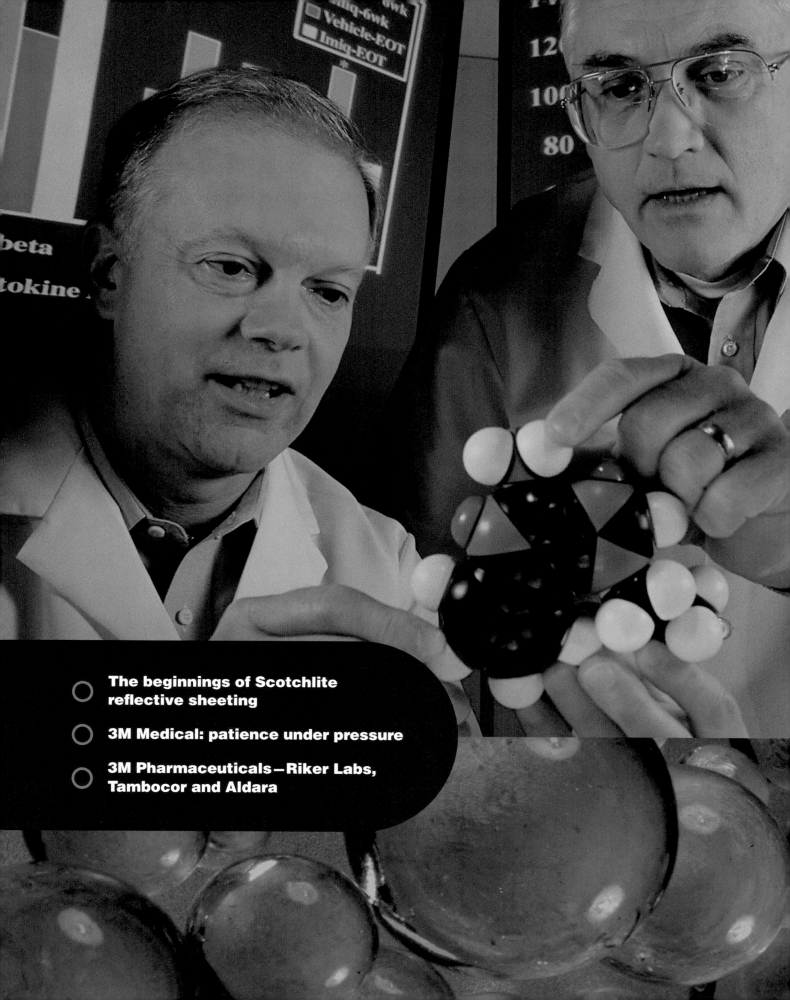

- The beginnings of Scotchlite reflective sheeting
- 3M Medical: patience under pressure
- 3M Pharmaceuticals—Riker Labs, Tambocor and Aldara

6

No Risk, No Reward—
'Patient Money'

Twelve years after its founding, 3M finally made money on
its sandpaper. Eight long, dry years plagued the company
before 3M Scotchlite reflective technology produced a
minimal profit. When 3M entered the health care business
in 1948 with surgical drapes, it was an inexperienced
newcomer with anemic product revenues taking on giant
Johnson & Johnson. In pharmaceuticals, 3M invested
in 25 years of research before Tambocor, a drug to
treat heart arrhythmia, was introduced. It took 20
years before Minitran, a transdermal nitroglycerin

drug delivery system, and 15 years before Aldara, an immune response modifier, made it to market.

For a century, 3M has demonstrated a bias toward growth through diversification. On many occasions, these new directions have involved considerable risk and long-term investment known as "patient money." This investment has often led to leapfrog technologies with far reaching applications. "We have to

Scotchlite sheeting didn't show much profit for nearly 10 years. The same was true for fluorochemicals and duplicating products. It takes 'patient money' to make some ideas succeed. > **Philip Palmquist** retired technical director, Reflective Products Division, and Carlton Society member

bring in new technologies that will enable 3M to win in the future, along with focusing on what we already do best," said Ron Baukol, retired executive vice president, International Operations, who started his career at 3M in 1966 as a new product development engineer in Medical Products. "I learned early on that the key to good product development is to 'iterate' as fast as you can. Make one model, give it a try, then try another. The more iterations you can make, the better, rather than trying to perfect one; it's probably flawed anyway."

3M has a tradition of applying patient money and patient support to ideas that ultimately can change the basis of competition. Baukol calls them the "holy grail" of 3M. "You just know that some things are going to be worth working on and that requires technological patience," said Baukol. "You don't put too much money into the investigation, but you keep one to five people working on it for 20 years, if you have to. You do it because you know that, once you crack the code, it's going to be big." Creating a reflective road striping material that is durable and replaces paint is an example of a "holy grail" product. Developing a dental

In the early stages of a new product or technology, it shouldn't be overly managed. If we start asking for business plans too early and insist on tight financial evaluations, we'll kill an idea or surely slow it down. > **Harry Hammerly** retired executive vice president, International Operations, formerly vice president, Finance

filling material that adheres directly to the natural tooth structure is another. An adhesive bandage that sticks to wet skin is still another. And, in pharmaceuticals, a major breakthrough would be a "smart medicine" or drug delivery system that sends medications straight to

Chapter opening photos Many years of anti-viral research led to Aldara, 3M's first immune response modifier drug; Close-up of reflective glass beads used in Scotchlite products; Scotch microporous surgical tape, introduced in the 1950s; 3M is a world leader in reflective sheeting.

1 Team leaders pictured from the 1975 Golden Step Awards. **2** The award program, which began in 1972, recognizes teams of people who develop successful breakthrough products. **3** The Scotchlite project team in 1943 included, from left: Donald Douglas, Edward Davis, Bert Cross, Robert Ackerberg, Paul Magoon, Philip Palmquist and Harry Heltzer. **4** From the beginning, researchers realized that glass beads were a key component to any future reflective sheeting or pavement marking product.

the place in the human body that needs them. "That's why 3M's metered-dose inhaler is such a strong product, because it delivers drugs for asthma directly to the lungs," said Baukol.

The challenge, of course, is to discern these holy grail product ideas from what Baukol calls the "evergreens"—products that demand years of attention and

The willingness to bet on embryonic businesses—and fund them—is the key to 3M's future. Fortunately for 3M Health Care, there was considerable patient money around 30 years ago. **> Jerry Robertson** *retired executive vice president, Life Sciences Sector*

investment but never blossom. "You have to have patience with some ideas, but not with everything you're working on," he said.

Golden Step Awards were created in 1972 at 3M to recognize teams of people who develop breakthrough, profitable products and demonstrate persistence, or stubbornness, to see their efforts through. "I remember our former chairman of the board, Harry Heltzer, once saying, 'The difference between persistence and stubbornness is, fundamentally,

whether you're successful or not. If you're successful, you're called persistent; if you aren't, you're stubborn. But, while you're doing it, nobody can tell the difference.'" Baukol said. "We have to have a lot of patience with our stubborn people."

> **Stubborn at First, Successful at Last**
A young research chemist named Phil Palmquist and rookie engineer Heltzer were probably considered stubborn when they wouldn't give up on the "Glass Beads Project," a product development team started in 1937. Assigned to develop durable roadway striping, the team coated a plastic adhesive tape with small glass beads, but it wasn't as reflective as it needed to be.

One year later, after 3M's senior management had told the team to stop work, Heltzer and Palmquist persevered. Working after hours, Palmquist managed to create a product 100 times brighter than white paint and 30 times better than earlier reflective prototypes. But, the stripes weren't tough enough to stand up to frost and heavy traffic; they peeled away from the road surface and waved in the breeze. Passing motorists dubbed the

product "3M's friendly tape." Undaunted, the team scrambled to improve the stripes before winter arrived by using asphalt to stick them to the pavement. Eight volunteers from several 3M departments helped lay a three-quarter-mile-long stripe on busy Highway 61 near the company's plant on the east side of St. Paul.

We had a machine to dispense the asphalt, but we had no way to keep it hot enough to go though the dispenser. Harry Heltzer volunteered to bring buckets of hot asphalt from the plant. That's when he got into trouble. On his third trip, a St. Paul policeman stopped him for speeding.

> **A Scotchlite project volunteer**

While the experimental reflective stripe survived the weather, it wasn't bright enough for highway engineers to accept the product's higher cost. It looked like the company's patience was running out. But, thanks to the suggestion of their internal "champion," Richard Carlton, then vice president, Research and Development, the embryonic reflective product was modified from a horizontal road strip to a reflective sheet for road signs.

Working out the technical kinks in the new product and selling it to highway engineers was a long, uphill battle. Cold was the worst enemy. One manufacturer put Scotchlite sheeting on the side-arm stop signal of school buses, but when the temperature dropped, so did the sheeting. Reflective "Go For Safety" emblems were distributed far and wide to car owners, but they became brittle in the cold and fell off the cars. Rain significantly cut the visibility of the reflective signs and dirt quickly lodged between the glass beads, making them look unsightly in daytime. Working with other technical people, Palmquist, who eventually retired as technical director, Reflective Products Division, improved the sheeting with a smooth topcoat that protected the glass beads from dirt and weather. In addition, the new Scotchlite engineer-grade, flattop sheeting made it possible to apply words and other design elements with weather-resistant inks. That breakthrough meant that Scotchlite sheeting could also be used in graphics and advertising.

> **Necessity: A Powerful Motivator**

World War II could have killed the reflective line altogether because 3M's supply of two essential raw materials, natural rubber and resin, was cut off during the war. That meant the lab had to start over and develop an entirely new process if it wanted to stay in business. As it turned out, necessity was a powerful motivator and, along with developing the new process, the product team increased the reflective power of the sheeting and perfected more sheeting colors. The U.S. government became such a big customer during the war that the Reflective Department was elevated to division status in 1943.

1 A 1940s advertisement recommended using Scotchlite reflective material on billboards like this one for Sweetheart bread. **2** Scotchlite reflective sheeting made taxi cabs in England more visible at night. **3** A 1948 advertisement for Scotchlite reflective fabrics.

The division didn't actually earn its own way until 1947. Bert Cross, the company's new products manager (and later CEO), became the next champion of reflective products when he envisioned multiple markets and applications. By fiscal year 1953, the division grossed about $10 million.

3M was a driving force in advocating a universal, international traffic sign system in the 1960s. When that agreement was successful, we went on to be—by far—the leading supplier of signing materials around the world. **> Donn Osmon** *retired group vice president, Traffic and Personal Safety Products Group*

By the late 1970s, the halting start of reflective sheeting four decades earlier had spawned one of 3M's largest product groups, including four units related to reflective technology—Traffic Control Materials Division, Safety Systems Division, Decorative Products Division and the Traffic Control Devices Department. Looking back, Heltzer said, "I don't think we fully appreciated that Scotchlite products represented such a high level of technology until after the basic patent ran out. In the early days, others were able to make swatches of reflective material that looked pretty good,

but nobody could produce it yard after yard and have the optical properties, the durability and the handling properties of Scotchlite products."

Over the decades, the original reflective technology has become more and more sophisticated and its uses have multiplied. According to a two-year study funded by the National Highway Traffic Safety administration in the 1990s, Scotchlite Diamond Grade sheeting on truck tractors and trailers has helped reduce accidents by 18 percent. Diamond Grade reflective sheeting also makes construction zones and pedestrian crossings safer. Scotchlite reflective fabric retains its reflectivity after repeated industrial washing. Reflective fabrics and yarns for shoes and clothing answer a safety

3M has a tradition of pursuing uninhibited research for uninhabited markets. The origin and development of our reflective products is a perfect demonstration of that. **> Hal Kosanke** *retired director, Civic Affairs*

need for a massive market. "The only thing on the road that isn't legally required to have lights or reflectors is a human being," said Donn Osmon, retired group vice president, Traffic and Personal Safety Products Group.

"When 3M moved into the highway safety business with Scotchlite sheeting, that was a high growth area," said Art de St. Aubin, retired executive director, Automotive Industry Center. "Our strong, early involvement made us one of the world leaders in safety products."

Workers building the Chunnel, linking England and France, in the early 1990s, wore clothing with Scotchlite brand high-visibility material while they labored 150 feet beneath the channel seabed. Thousands of signs covered with Scotchlite reflective sheeting guided workers through the huge, underground construction maze.

3M's reflective technology also became part of an anti-counterfeit system to ferret out fake records, audio and videotapes. Reflective technology even won 3M and Palmquist an Oscar when Scotchlite sheeting was used in a new reflex projection system for composite photography that greatly enhanced film quality in popular movies, including

"2001: A Space Odyssey" and "Barbarella." American film artists called it "a major advancement in the motion picture industry."

> **3M Medical: Patience Under Pressure**

Emergency medical care during World War II led physicians to think about making surgical conditions more sterile in peacetime. In the 1940s, the best a surgical team could do was sterilize a cloth towel and position it around the operation site, attaching it with pinchers to the patient's skin. But, the material got wet and the danger of bacteria migrating into the open wound was high.

"Three physicians from the Euclid Clinic in Cleveland (Ohio) came to 3M after the war with an idea," said Lew Lehr, retired chairman of the board and CEO. "Their idea was to make a plastic sheet with adhesive on it that could stick to the skin right up to the wound edge and prevent contamination. They

knew about Scotch brand tapes from 3M; that's why they came to us."

The physicians sought a licensing agreement with 3M to produce the surgical sheets, but Vice President of Research and Development Richard Carlton suggested collaboration instead. After all, he reasoned, 3M had experience with developing new products and the physicians didn't. Carlton assigned the project to 3M's tape lab where Lehr and Burt Auger, who later retired as staff vice president, Program Development, went to work. "It was a Rube Goldberg project; we were making

> We began marketing and we had about six sales people. After six months, we'd spent more on advertising and marketing than we sold . . . That wasn't the way 3M did things. > **Lew Lehr**
>
> *retired chairman of the board and CEO*

it up as we went along," said Lehr. The prototype combined polyvinyl chloride (plastic) with a very soft synthetic adhesive (an acrylic) and a treated paper liner to protect the adhesive. Starch or talcum powder kept the drape from sticking to itself. The package was folded, double wrapped in parchment paper, placed inside a foil bag and steam sterilized. The new surgical drape was introduced in 1948 to the American College of Surgeons in Cleveland.

Lou Weyand, who later retired as executive vice president and director, Sales, told Lehr, Auger and their boss, Hugh Tierney, who later retired as vice president, Reinforced Plastics Division, to halt production. "But, Hugh said, 'You guys say you have something. Before we stop, why don't you make enough so you'll have a six-month inventory to sell off and then go out and sell it,'" Lehr recalled.

> People were telling Lew Lehr, 'What the hell are you doing getting into health care?' He kept plugging away and he created a hugely successful business. > **Bill McLellan** *retired staff vice president, Corporate Services, Austin, Texas, and former division vice president, Orthopedic Products Division*

It was during this time that Lehr and Auger also converted 3M's masking tape into an "autoclave tape" that could be used to bundle hospital supplies for sterilization rather than using conventional string. The product was an easy conversion and it started generating modest revenues, but not enough. Management was insistent. Shut the business down.

1 3M reflective materials are used on pedestrian crosswalks to enhance visibility. **2** Throughout the world, countries rely on 3M reflective license plates. **3** Phil Palmquist won an Oscar in 1969 for developing a front projection screen using Scotchlite retroreflective technology. **4** Surgical drapes gave birth to an entire line of 3M health care products.

"We offered to buy the business from 3M," Lehr said. "People in management probably said, 'Those young punks want to buy it; they must know more about the venture than we do. Let's let them go ahead for a while.' We were serious, but we didn't have any money to buy it."

As fortune would have it, a branch of the U.S. Air Force and the University of Minnesota surgical department both decided to buy large quantities of 3M's new surgical drape. "At the end of six months, we told them we were going out of the business," Lehr recalled, "and our new customers said, 'No, you can't!'" Lehr and Tierney appealed to management and won a reprieve.

> A High-Risk Proposition

3M funded a pilot plant to supply its new medical customers and, by 1957, Lehr had convinced management to fund more research. Medical products was a tough arena for 3M and others. "No industrial company had successfully entered health care," Lehr said. "The two or three others that tried, failed." Success required significantly more investment in research; long, painstaking and expensive clinical studies before going to market; and selling physicians on new products. In addition, there was the threat of serious liability should a product fail. It was a new, risky world for 3M. Only ambitious people and patient money had a chance of success. "We were ignorant about dealing with the U.S. Food and Drug Administration (FDA)," said Lehr. "Our first drug application was refused because we had failed to specify a dosage for

We took our top tape salesmen and tried to have them sell surgical drapes to hospitals. They didn't know the chief surgeon from the intern or the purchasing agent from anybody else. It was very slow getting started. **> Frank Copeland** *retired research scientist, Medical Products Division*

our surgical tape. Our consultant had to fly out and tell the fellow at the FDA that tapes aren't put on by the spoonful or in capsule form."

By 1957, 3M had a lab staff of five people trying to develop new products. The team began using the company's new synthetic adhesive technology to develop tapes that could be applied to human skin because 3M's new adhesives were much less irritating than the common zinc oxide adhesive tapes used at the time. From this work came the introduction of Scotch plastic surgical tape, in the late 1950s, and a "breathable" tape, Scotch microporous surgical tape, later renamed

1 The early 3M surgical tapes carried the Scotch brand name.
2 Micropore surgical tape was advertised in medical journals in the 1960s as the first tape product to protect wounds while promising painless removal.

Micropore surgical tape in 1960. The two products became the leaders in reducing skin irritation.

"Johnson & Johnson was already selling an adhesive surgical tape, so we had to have something completely different," said Frank Copeland, retired 3M research scientist, a key developer of Micropore surgical tape. "Lew Lehr suggested that we look at nonwoven technology, which was in its infancy at 3M."

If you think about it, 3M's tape-type medical products fit the company's philosophy of 'make it by the mile and sell it by the inch,' which has served 3M well. **> Frank Copeland**

Soon after the introduction of Micropore tape, an inventive doctor snipped the tape into pieces and used it in place of stitches to close a wound. The opportunity was obvious. 3M cut the tape in ⅛-inch to ½-inch widths, sterilized it, packaged it and introduced Steri-Strip wound closures to the marketplace in 1962. After a few product improvements, the product became the best answer to closing a wound simply and painlessly.

About this time, Lehr and Frank Scully, a research scientist, paid a visit to William

McKnight, who was retired from day-to-day 3M operations and living in Florida. "We laid out a 10-year program of product development, sales and marketing," Lehr said. "We projected sales and profits 10 years out. McKnight was very enthusiastic and wondered out loud

When Lew Lehr was manager of the $5 million health care business, he was offered a higher ranking job in another 3M business. He turned it down because he wanted to build health care.

> Harry Hammerly

why we hadn't done this years before. When we looked into the records, we discovered that a researcher had proposed marketing a masking tape for medical use in the mid-1930s, but it went nowhere. McKnight was eager to take on Johnson & Johnson."

McKnight; Chuck Walton, senior vice president, Research and Development; and Clarence "Sam" Sampair, the architect of 3M International, all became champions of 3M's fledgling business. This is probably why Medical Products was named a division in 1962 even though it fell short of 3M's stringent revenue requirements. After 10 years, the actual numbers for the Medical

2

comes
off with
a smile

Products Division exceeded even Lehr's projections. "Our cumulative sales were 102 percent of our forecast, and our cumulative profit was 162 percent—even though only about 25 percent of the products we projected were actually developed," Lehr said.

Lehr assigned a young chemist, Jerry Robertson, who later retired as executive vice president, Life Sciences Sector, to manage a new Surgical Products Department. "We were small, probably $12 million in sales," Robertson said, "but we grew it over about eight years with a compound annual rate that I don't think has been equaled. We had to change the way surgeons practiced medicine, one surgeon at a time. We had to

It takes the right group of people to get involved and really push a new idea. The more these stories are told, the more they will give people confidence that they can do it, too. > **Lew Lehr**

teach them about the advantages of tape to close wounds, the benefits of a molded mask over a flat mask and why plastic surgical drapes worked so well. These were 'concept sells' and we had our own sales force of knowledgeable, driven people."

With more support and patient money still flowing, a string of new medical products began to emerge from the 1960s to the 1980s: a molded

mask, later called the Aseptex surgical mask (1961); Reston foam pads (1963), created to reduce bed sores; Transpore surgical tape (1969), a nonirritating, transparent, easy-to-use tape that caught on quickly around the world; Durapore surgical tape (1972), made of strong cloth; soft, stretchy Microfoam surgical tape

You have the freedom at 3M to maneuver things to your benefit if you want to take advantage of it. Some things won't work, so you fail once in a while, but that's a lot better than the cost of a missed opportunity. > **Les Krogh** *retired senior vice president, Research and Development*

(1976); Tegaderm transparent dressing (1981); and DuraPrep substantive iodine prep (1988). In the 1990s, 3M introduced two advanced stethoscopes capable of detecting low- and high-frequency sounds; the 3M universal electrosurgical pad; a higher adhesion Micropore tape called Micropore II; and, for consumers, Nexcare Active strips, comfort strips and waterproof bandages, as well as the popular Nexcare Tattoo bandages for the younger crowd.

By 1989, 3M's health care business had grown so much that the Life Sciences Sector was divided into two strategic business groups, hospital products and pharmaceutical and dental products. Annual global sales were nearly $2 billion. By 2000, those revenues

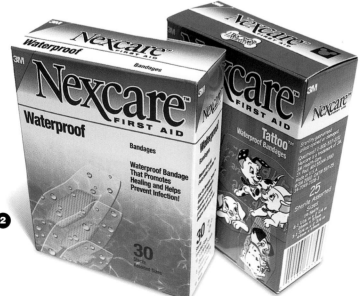

exploded to $3.1 billion, representing nearly 20 percent of the company's total business worldwide. Health Care Markets became one of 3M's strategic market centers in 2000.

Pharmaceutical research is not for the weak of heart. The stakes are high: years of development and testing and millions of dollars of investment . . . then it still has to succeed in the marketplace. Given all that, wouldn't it be easier and more rewarding to invest in lottery tickets?

> **3M Technology Platforms, 1996**

> **3M Pharmaceuticals: 'All We Had Were Wishes'**
Investing in fluorine chemistry back in the 1940s may have been much like buying a lottery ticket because 3M had no specific product in mind. But, even as early as 1951, 3M's annual report mentioned using fluorochemicals to make drugs. It wasn't until 1963, however, that 3M created a Biochemical Research Group Laboratory inside Central Research. Robertson was hired as the company's first experienced biochemist. Don Kvan, the first pharmacologist, and Bob Nelson, the first veterinarian/toxicologist, made up the rest of the team. They started investigating drugs for the heart, central nervous system and high blood pressure. They even dabbled in agricultural herbicides.

Patience was necessary from the start. "I remember the first technical audit the Biochemical Research Lab had in about 1963," Tom Reid, then the lab's manager, said. "Our audit was combined with the Medical Products Division because we had so little to talk about. They had all these projects and all we had were wishes. It was a pretty embarrassing review and some of the auditors weren't impressed." Even so, Lehr took an active interest in the team's work because he knew it was a logical extension for medical products. So did McKnight and Cross, McKnight's successor as chairman of the board and CEO in 1966.

About six years earlier, McKnight had struck up a merger conversation with his Florida neighbor, the chairman of Warner-Lambert Company. Though that idea fell through, it set the stage for 3M considering growth in pharmaceuticals through a strategic acquisition. "We knew we either would have to build the business ourselves or acquire it," Lehr said. "It was becoming more and more obvious that this would require a different mentality than selling sandpaper. Along with a different mentality, we needed a sales force familiar with the market."

Cross knew Justin Dart, chairman, Dart Industries, the parent company of Riker Laboratories, a Los Angeles-based pharmaceutical company. Riker had made its mark in 1950 by introducing Veriloid, a breakthrough drug for high blood pressure. But, Dart was reluctant to sell. "3M doesn't have enough money to buy Riker," Dart challenged Cross. "Try us," was Cross'

1 Superior acoustics make Littmann stethoscopes popular with health care professionals. 2 Nexcare waterproof and Tattoo bandages are recent additions to the 3M Health Care product line. 3 Central Research was home to the Biochemical Research Group Laboratory in 1968.

reply. Within two months, the two companies had a deal and Riker—with its 2,500 employees worldwide—officially became a subsidiary of 3M on January 1, 1970. Many observers later said that Riker was 3M's most successful acquisition because it grew—by a factor of 10—after becoming part of 3M. "It moved from a little understood, peripheral activity of 3M to a business area recognized as a major contributor," said W. George Meredith, who became executive vice president, Life Sciences Sector, and retired as executive vice president, Corporate Services and Supply Chain Management.

Along with a strong portfolio of products and a solid reputation with the Food and Drug Administration, Riker had a 700-person global sales and marketing staff. It also brought, according to Robertson, a "loose confederacy

3M realized that it couldn't grow everything from within. The Riker acquisition gave us a new direction. > **Arlo Levi** *retired vice president and corporate secretary*

of fiefdoms" that ran Riker's international business, not unlike 3M's own highly independent managing directors in its evolving global businesses. Robertson later said that Riker's savvy, successful international managers sustained 3M's pharmaceutical business while it struggled to gain a toehold in the U.S. market. The two com-

panies worked through the agonizing intricacies of integration, while learning from each other.

"I was predicting that 3M would move toward the pharmaceutical model as Riker moved toward 3M," said Baukol, who was named general manager of Riker in 1982. "I said we couldn't go it alone—that Riker was not going to succeed as a stand-alone pharmaceutical company, maybe not even survive. The competitive

3M's acquisition of Riker signaled the real start of our drug discovery era. > **Richard Miller** *corporate scientist, Pharmaceuticals Division*

advantage we had was 3M, its image, infrastructure, technology, reputation and people."

On January 1, 1991, Riker Laboratories ceased to be a subsidiary and was fully merged into the company as 3M Pharmaceuticals Division. The integration was difficult, said Robertson, who was the first 3M person to lead Riker worldwide. "Nearly everyone at 3M thinks their business is different from the rest of the company, but pharmaceuticals truly is different," he said. "Management took a long time to get used to it." Even so, Robertson said in retrospect, 3M handled the assimilation better than most nonmedical companies.

> **Tambocor: A Long-Term Investment**
The invention of Tambocor (flecainide acetate), a drug designed to control irregular heart beats, was Riker's

1 3M's acquisition of Riker Laboratories in 1970 expanded the company's health care business. **2** Riker brought a strong portfolio of pharmaceutical products and a solid reputation with the U.S. Food and Drug Administration. **3** Elden Banitt was one of the creators of Tambocor.

"window to becoming a modern pharmaceutical company," Robertson said, but it was a long, difficult and costly project that required extraordinary patience. When Tambocor finally was introduced to the U.S. market in January 1986, 3M had invested 20 years and at least $50 million in Tambocor. Some observers say the cost was considerably higher than that estimate.

The story of Tambocor—one of the first of a class of drugs for treating irregular heartbeats—started in 1966 when 3M's Biomedical Group began exploring new applications for its proprietary fluorochemical technology. They succeeded in making a compound which was the forerunner to flecainide acetate. About the same time, Dr. Jack Schmid, who had done his Ph.D. work in cardiopulmonary research at the University of Arkansas, arrived at 3M. It was Schmid who

It's tremendously thrilling to make something useful, like Tambocor, that's never been made before. > **Elden Banitt** *research scientist,*

Pharmaceuticals Division

saw the link between the compound and controlling irregular heartbeats.

Schmid assembled a research team including a young research chemist, Elden Banitt, fresh from a research fellowship at the University of California-Berkeley, and Bill Bronn, a pre-med student at the University of Minnesota.

The compound was the "lead" molecule in the team's search for a drug to treat the heart, but it had a "tight therapeutic index," meaning that the margin between an effective dose and a toxic one was too narrow. So, the team continued looking.

The process is really slow. It was a matter of continually going back to the chalkboard and redesigning. > **Bill Bronn** *research scientist,*

Pharmaceuticals Division

The team tested more than 200 compounds in hope of finding a molecule that was effective, non-toxic and wouldn't cause serious side effects. "In this kind of work, you have to take the long view," Banitt said. "There were serious dead ends and a lot of frustration. We'd spend weeks synthesizing a compound and in 15 minutes, we'd discover it was completely inactive. We weren't shooting blindly though; we had a lead. It was an orderly process; we saw step-by-step improvements." While some compounds were inactive, some were so potent they could stop a heart.

It is also a characteristic of the drug discovery process that scientists don't know when to stop looking. The team found flecainide acetate before they reached the halfway point in their work. "You go along until you finally discover that you're not making anything better than you already have," Banitt said. It was 1971. Banitt and Bronn looked at the brown bottle of white powder

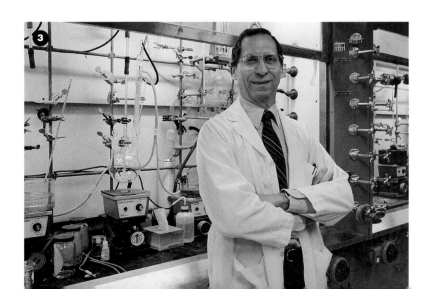

that showed great promise—at least on paper—in treating heart arrhythmias. Still, questions persisted. It would still take clinical trials to prove that Tambocor could be effective in humans.

By 1973, 3M was betting on the compound in the brown bottle. Trials with healthy human volunteers began two years later. 3M applied for patents on Tambocor in that same year, knowing that years of

> There were many people who felt this was not an area for 3M to get into. It was far away from the company's usual line of businesses.
>
> > **Elden Banitt**

testing leading up to FDA approval would erode its 17-year patent and competitors would quickly jump in with nearly identical compounds. Testing on healthy humans lasted for three years before the drug was given to ill patients in 1978. While 3M and Riker had other drugs in testing (an anti-inflammatory for arthritis and an analgesic for control of postsurgical pain), the company put those on the back burner in 1979 and focused its resources on Tambocor. "We leapfrogged over two or three competitors who were ahead of us in the research process," said Dr. Gary Grentzkow, retired director, medical affairs, Pharmaceuticals Division. 3M set a goal of preparing its new drug application for the FDA in about half the time it normally took.

> **The Story Continues**

By 1981, the U.S. Food and Drug Administration (FDA) decided that Tambocor was a significant enough drug that it received higher priority in the review process. The next year, Tambocor was sold in West Germany where the national drug approval process is shorter.

Determining which patients would benefit most from Tambocor without side effects was challenging. At one point, Grentzkow had to halt testing. A few days later, Grentzkow had to face his peers at an American Heart Association Annual Meeting. "I can remember so vividly people coming up to me on the convention floor and saying flecainide would never make it to market," he said.

But instead of giving up, 3M quickly started more testing. By November 1983, the test results showed that Tambocor could be used safely. The company's ultimate triumph came on October 31, 1985, when the FDA gave 3M approval to sell Tambocor.

> **Aldara: 'It's Not Over 'Til It's Over'**

The bomb dropped at a morning team meeting on January 6, 1983. The anti-viral research project, headed by Richard Miller, was a casualty of Tambocor. 3M had decided to put his team's work, and others, on hold in order to focus resources on the promising heart arrhythmia drug. "It was like getting punched in

1 Tambocor, a drug designed to control irregular heartbeats, was introduced in the U.S. in January 1986, after it won FDA approval. **2** Aldara (imiquimod) 5% cream, 3M's first approved immune response modifier drug, is sold worldwide. This packaging is for Greece.

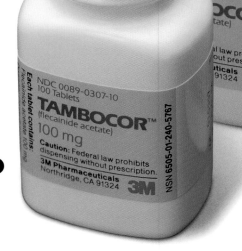

the stomach," Miller remembered, "but pharmaceuticals needed a success, and Tambocor had been the first product to come out of our drug discovery program. We needed to get it to market as fast as possible and having more money would speed that up."

Miller and the biologists who reported to him were put on 3M's "unassigned list." It was time to find another job in the company, his colleagues advised, and do it quickly. "Our management set up meetings with all of us to talk about networking to find new positions," Miller said.

But, Miller was either too stubborn or persistent to walk away from his promising project.

Miller, then a research scientist, had joined 3M in 1977 to lead a team with John Gerster that was exploring how drugs might fight off viruses in the human body. Miller had focused his doctoral and postdoctoral study on viruses, before anti-viral drugs even existed. He was excited about this new frontier, and the work consumed him.

The development time for pharmaceuticals is 10 to 15 years from discovery to FDA approval and it can cost as much as $300 million. Only one compound out of every 10,000 makes it to the market. **> Elden Banitt**

The research team's first challenge was to create a compound that would poison a virus without destroying healthy human cells. "Gerster made new compounds based on precursors for DNA or RNA," Miller said. "He made a novel combination that wasn't found in nature and we hoped it would selectively inhibit virus production. My lab tested the drugs that John made."

In 1982, Miller studied a promising compound supplied by Gerster and he decided to test it. "From the very first experiment, we were excited about the results," Miller said. "We repeated our experiments, and we knew

"He asked if it was hopeless," Miller's former supervisor, Ed Erickson recalled. "I said, 'Well, you're still here. And, it's not over until it's over.'"

> Minneapolis Star Tribune

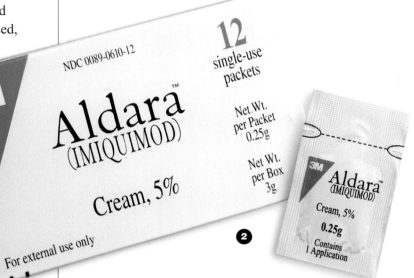

we had something totally new and different. We discovered later that our drugs stimulated the immune system to fight off a virus."

After being put on the unassigned list, Miller looked for a new position within 3M, but his heart wasn't in it. "I didn't do a very good job in my interviews," he said. "When they'd ask what I wanted most to be doing, I'd say, 'Go back and work on anti-viral drugs.'"

Some people felt it wasn't possible to create a drug that would inhibit a virus and not be toxic to cells. I didn't agree. **> Richard Miller**

And, so he did. New opportunities weren't knocking at Miller's door, so he went to his manager, Ed Erickson, and asked if he could continue working on the research project, at least until an offer came through. "Our team was paid as long as we were on the unassigned list," Miller said. "We just didn't have jobs. I told the team, 'It's going to be a while before we have jobs; in the meantime, let's continue the experiments.' Ed was very supportive and encouraged us to keep working; Gerster, who was a Ph.D. chemist, continued making compounds for us to test."

For six months, the team continued its experiments and the results were consistently good. Miller "shopped" the project around 3M looking for a permanent home for the research, but his desire was to remain in pharmaceuticals. The team brought in a nationally respected expert in anti-viral drugs to review the results. This expert confirmed that no other compound of its kind existed.

By July 1982, Miller and team members who hadn't gone on to other jobs were reinstated as a full-fledged research team. "It was great—like having a big weight lifted," Miller said. "By the end of the year, we selected the drug for development: imiquimod. By the end of

It's really important to keep management informed. Today, if I had a result like we had in 1982, I'd be at my manager's door insisting, 'Look at this!' > **Richard Miller**

1983, the team recommended the next steps—developing formulas for testing, analysis and toxicology—before human clinical trials could begin in 1989. We were fortunate to have a number of people in 3M management who had come through our division and supported our work, including Robertson, Baukol, Meredith and Erickson."

Three phases of clinical testing with humans con-

tinued through 1996, and imiquimod cream was shown to be effective in treating genital warts. Meanwhile, the challenges posed in manufacturing the drug on a large scale were significant, said Eric Jensen, manufacturing technical manager, Pharmaceuticals Division. "It was a very different product for 3M and even for our Pharmaceuticals Division," he said. "The drug itself has very complicated chemistry. It's produced in a cream that, in itself, is difficult to make. We made the drug in

Here was a brilliant scientist who knew that this drug had value. He wasn't going to let it die and he found a way to push it forward. Richard Miller embodies the entrepreneurial spirit of 3M: a person with passion who won't be stopped.

> **John Benson** executive vice president, Health Care Markets

France and the cream in the U.K. and, to accomplish that, we had to create a whole new center of manufacturing excellence. On top of that the cream had to be packaged in exact, small amounts in sachets made with a multilayer laminate, foil, paper and polyethylene. It took us nearly five years to get really good at the manufacturing process."

By mid-1996, 3M submitted its new drug application to the FDA and, in February 1997, the drug was approved for sale. Sold by prescription, Aldara cream applications cost about $20 a week for up to 16 weeks

1 Aldara, a highly effective treatment for genital warts, also shows promise in treating other viral infections and some forms of skin cancer.

of treatment. By contrast, surgery for genital warts costs hundreds of dollars and causes pain and scarring.

Miller's persistence over 15 years paid off and his interest in the subject has not waned. "Understanding the body's immune system is an exploding area of research," he said. "We're learning more about how to enhance immunity with drugs. Back in 1982, we knew about interferon and interlukin, but today there are as many as 70 different proteins that can affect the immune system. We hope to produce several generations of immune response modifiers."

Topically applied, Aldara also has shown promise in treating other viral infections and some forms of skin cancer, including basal cell carcinoma and actinic keratosis, a precancerous condition caused by too much exposure to sunlight. "Our drug enhances cellular immunity," Miller, now corporate scientist, Pharmaceuticals Division, said. "That's the part of the immune system that you need to get rid of virus infections and tumors. We think we have made a very important addition to the drugs doctors have to use."

Asked by a reporter if he would still be working on the drug years after approval of its initial introduction, Miller said, "It could take me to retirement. Physicians call and say they want to thank me. That's very satisfying. Most people in pharmaceuticals want to do research to create drugs that help people."

After the success of Aldara, 3M allocated an extra $100 million in corporate funding to the Pharmaceuticals Division in 1999 to accelerate research into the drug's other applications. Aldara's success required patience and persistence and, at times, stubborn people. Over time, the development of Aldara is the largest, single investment made in a pharmaceutical product in 3M's history.

time-tested truths

- **Product ideas that can change the basis of competition merit "patient money" and patient support from internal sponsors.**

- **The early stages of a new product or technology shouldn't be "over managed."**

- **Products that require years of attention and investment but will never blossom need to be "weeded" out as early as possible.**

- **Success separates the persistent from the simply stubborn.**

- **Ideas with the highest potential often require people to take the long view.**

- **Uninhibited research for uninhabited markets is a 3M tradition.**

STATES PATENT OFFIC

1,5

cKNIGHT, OF ST. PAUL, MINNESOTA, ASSIGNOR TO MINN
NUFACTURING COMPANY, OF ST. PAUL, MINNESOTA, A
NNESOTA.

HAND BLOCK FOR ABRASIVES, ETC.

Application filed November 14, 1922. Serial No. 600,831.

concern: that I, WILLIAM LESTER   like and characterized by the features of
a citizen of the United States,   proper weight, flexibility, if desired, and
a resident of St. Paul, in the county   shape rendering it convenient to be grasped
of Ramsey and State of Minnesota, have   for use; the provision of an improved hand
nvented certain new and useful Improve-   block for carrying and sustaining a sheet
ments in Hand Blocks for Abrasives, Etc.,   of abrasive material or the like, character-
f which the following is a specification.   ized by the provision of an improved hand
This invention relates broadly to support-   means actuated by the grip of the h
ng and sustaining means, more particularly   the provision of an improved hand
o an improved hand block for supporting   sustaining a sheet of abrasive
nd sustaining a sheet of abrasive material   the like, characteriz
r the like, and especially one characterized   hand-pressure
y the feature of retaining such sheet by   means'
e pressure of the hand grasping the b
d for tensioning the sheet
e block when in use.
in other features
after.

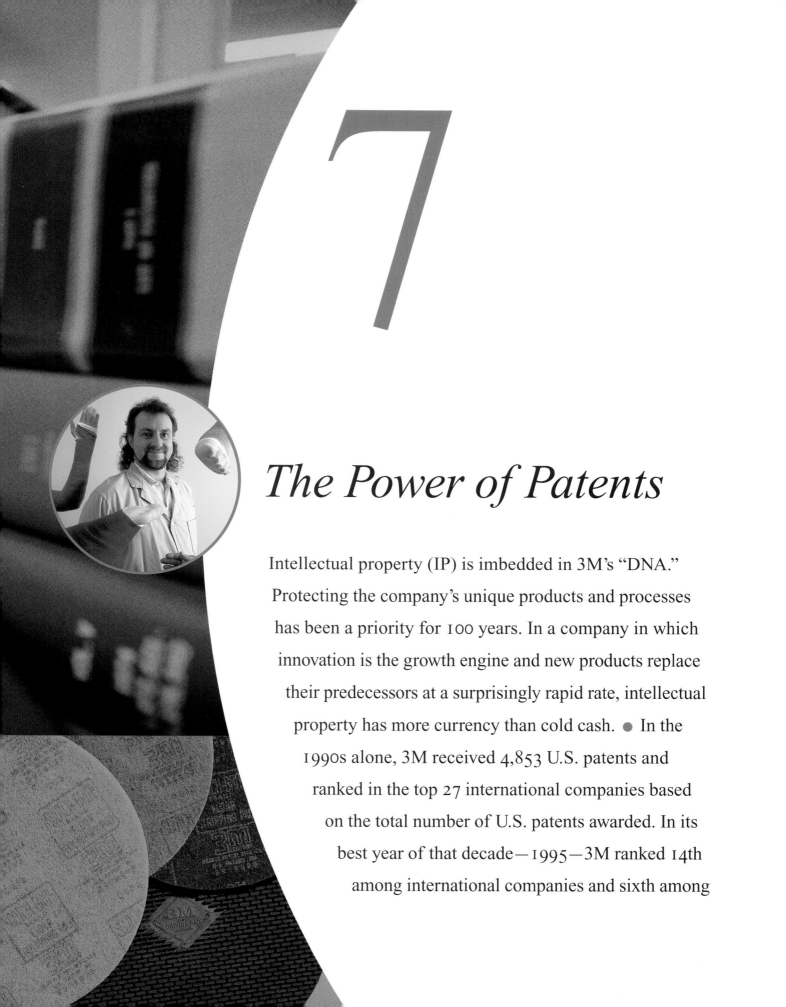

7

The Power of Patents

Intellectual property (IP) is imbedded in 3M's "DNA."
Protecting the company's unique products and processes
has been a priority for 100 years. In a company in which
innovation is the growth engine and new products replace
their predecessors at a surprisingly rapid rate, intellectual
property has more currency than cold cash. ● In the
1990s alone, 3M received 4,853 U.S. patents and
ranked in the top 27 international companies based
on the total number of U.S. patents awarded. In its
best year of that decade—1995—3M ranked 14th
among international companies and sixth among

U.S. companies receiving patents. These rankings put 3M in a league with other patent powerhouses such as IBM, NEC, Canon, Motorola, Toshiba, Mitsubishi and Hitachi.

> **'William's right smart, but . . . '**
William McKnight's introduction to the power of patents came early—and painfully. After 12 years without producing a really profitable product, 3M finally introduced

Vigorous defense of our patents and trademarks was crucial in 3M's early years. They were our franchises around the world: our capital.

> **Audun Fredriksen** *retired vice president,*

3M Health Care Division

❶

its Three-M-ite abrasive cloth in 1914 to the relief of everyone with a stake in the struggling company. The product sales took off as the United States' need for Army vehicles, airplanes and munitions increased. The flexible cloth was superior, particularly for workers who hand sanded around moldings and curved metal surfaces. Then bad news came in a sternly worded letter from 3M's rival, Carborundum Company, saying that 3M had infringed on Carborundum's patent for its abrasive, "Aloxite."

McKnight was visiting his boyhood home in Brookings, South Dakota, when the news of the potential Carborundum lawsuit broke. When the troubled general manager told his parents, Joseph and Cordelia, his father offered practical advice. "William's right smart, Mother, but he doesn't know anything about patents, and it would be a waste of time for him to become a patent expert in time to handle this. Get a good lawyer, son."

The singularly memorable lawyer, Paul Carpenter of Chicago, who was eventually hired by 3M, was a precursor to a staff of about 60 intellectual property lawyers at 3M in 2001. In addition, today 3M also has numerous other outside counsel. Working together, they obtain and defend the company's patents, trademarks and product brand names.

In this instance, Carpenter notified Carborundum that 3M would continue production, and the struggling company never heard from its competitor again. In fact, revenues generated by the flexible abrasive

All the time Paul Carpenter was checking patents, he wrote voluminous letters to Ober and McKnight . . . briefing them in the intricacies and value of patents . . . The Three-M-ite incident gave 3M its first real patent consciousness.

> **Virginia Huck** *author, "Brand of the Tartan"*

Chapter opening photos 3M's patent staff works diligently to protect the company's intellectual property; McKnight's patent for Hand Block for Abrasives was filed in 1922 and approved in 1925; Scotch-Brite floor pads, 1962; Colorful Scotchcast Plus casting tape.

❷

3

cloth grew from about $15,000 in 1914 to more than $600,000 by 1919. McKnight's education in patents made him a fierce defender of 3M's unique knowledge, and his philosophy guided the company's approach to patent and trademark defense into the 21st century.

3M's success was built on unique products— products that were protected by patents.

> **Carolyn Bates** *3M intellectual property counsel*

McKnight was convinced that patent protection was crucial because 3M's competitive advantage lay in the unique nature of its products. He was sure that the most effective patents would bolster a business objective. Though cash settlements could be lucrative and prove 3M was in the right, McKnight reasoned it was even better to use patent protection to keep competitors at bay and preserve the company's market share and profit margin.

> ### Bulldog with a Law Degree

Carpenter was a character—tall and slim, bordering on gaunt, and outspoken. "You never knew what he was going to do or say," McKnight recalled. "We were having this struggle with Johnson & Johnson (J&J) in a patent infringement. They had eight lawyers and one of them got up and preached a whole sermon. Carpenter finally got up and said, 'Do we have to listen to this crap?' Then we all walked out, leaving them sitting there."

1 This statue of McKnight shows him holding his own first patent for Hand Block for Abrasives. **2** Elek-Tro-Cut Three-M-Ite abrasive cloth was the company's first successful product. **3** Paul Carpenter, 3M's first patent attorney, became one of the company's most important counselors. **4** A 1925 Francis Okie patent application for an adhesive binder for sandpaper, with his handwritten comments.

McKnight soon hired Carpenter full time and moved him to St. Paul, reasoning that, in his words, "He charged so much, we thought we could get him cheaper if we hired him." Even as late as the 1970s, 3M's internal patent counsel still had its own separate name— Alexander, Sell, Steldt and DeLaHunt.

The Wetordry patent helped us get distribution in the automotive market. We had the top quality product and set the standard in the marketplace.

> **John F. Whitcomb** *retired group vice president,*

Coated Abrasives Group

But it wasn't just economics that moved McKnight to corner Carpenter's time. The patent attorney was an astute legal bulldog who was highly productive and shunned wasted time. "He had lots of statues in his office," said Bob Tucker, retired vice president, Legal Affairs. "When he thought you had been there long enough, he'd reach for his big feather duster and start dusting the statues. That was your signal to get out."

When Carpenter wrote and defended 3M's Wetordry abrasives patent, said Clarence "Sam" Sampair, retired

president, International Operations, "He gave us prestige in the sandpaper community. Before that, we were a poor third cousin of Carborundum and other big companies. Carpenter's patent group made all the people in 3M patent-minded."

> Getting Tough, Standing Firm

When 3M's unique Scotch brand cellophane tape was introduced in 1930, Americans found multiple uses for it—from mending torn book pages, ceiling plaster and sheet music to patching cracked turkey eggs on the farm. "Infringers were eager to get a share of the market," said Bob Wolfe, retired director and senior vice president, Engineering and Manufacturing. "William McKnight made one of the most significant decisions of his tenure when he insisted on defending Dick Drew's patent for cellophane tape."

The decision took nerve, Hugh Tierney, retired vice president, Reinforced Plastics Division, agreed. "Col. Johnson of Johnson & Johnson reared up and told Mr. McKnight that his father and his father before him had coated pressure-sensitive adhesive on any backing they cared to put it on and McKnight wasn't going to tell them they couldn't. 'You do,' McKnight said, 'and you'll be in a lawsuit.' Mr. McKnight made it stick."

Drew's original cellophane tape patent application was called "the grandfather application," Tierney said, because it contained broad claims of new and novel features. "We fought nine lawsuits in nine years, and those novel features gave us patent extensions for 17 more

DREW PATENT STRUCTURE

CLAIM 16:
AN ADHESIVE SHEET COMPRISING A NON-FIBROUS FLEXIBLE FILM BACKING HAVING NON-POROUS SURFACES,

A WATER-INSOLUBLE NORMALLY TACKY AND PRESSURE SENSITIVE FLEXIBLE ADHESIVE COATING,

AND AN INTERPOSED FLEXIBLE PRIMER COATING FIRMLY BONDING SAID ADHESIVE COATING TO THE BACKING,

THE ADHESIVE AND BACKING BEING OF SUCH KINDS THAT THE BACK SURFACE OF THE BACKING IS INACTIVE TO THE ADHESIVE COATING TO A DEGREE PERMITTING UNWINDING OF THE ADHESIVE SHEET FROM ROLLS THEREOF WITHOUT DELAMINATION OR OFFSETTING OF ADHESIVE,

SAID ADHESIVE SHEET TRANSMITTING LIGHT SO THAT THE SHEET WILL NOT CONCEAL THE COLORING OR MARKINGS OF SURFACES TO WHICH APPLIED.

ACCUSED STRUCTURES (AS REPRESENTED BY DEFENDANTS)

OUTSIDE NEGATIVE PRIMER

NOTE: THE "INTERPOSED" LAYER PUSHES THE ADHESIVE TO ONE SURFACE OF THE FILM BACKING, SECURING A PREFERENTIAL ADHESION A FULL FUNCTIONAL EQUIVALENT OF PATENTED STRUCTURE IN UNWINDING ROLLS.

years. Because of patent protection, 3M had time to learn to make its tape better than anybody else in the country."

With degrees in chemistry and library science, Harold Hughesdon was drawn to technical information and patent work in the 1950s. "My job was to walk around the 3M labs, be a sounding board and listen to people who thought they had inventions," said Hughesdon, who retired as director, Technical Contracts, International Lab Operations. He corralled all the experimental work available, talked to the inventors and patent lawyers, and identified what further experiments had to be done before a patent was filed. "McKnight's philosophy was clear," Hughesdon said. "I remember a Business Week magazine cover story on 3M in the 1950s. It said our strategy was to get strong patents and charge what the traffic would bear. When I describe 3M in a nutshell, I use three P's: patents, profits and paternalism."

In the United States, when 3M puts a new product on the market, there is a 12-month "grace period" to apply for the patent. In most other countries, there is no such allowance. "It was an uphill battle to try to convince 3M people there was more to patent protection than just in the United States," Hughesdon said. By the 1970s, however, 3M was taking no chances with its U.S. and international patents. They were filed before a new product was disclosed outside the company.

Even so, securing and defending a patent decades ago was tough, said Charlie Lauder, retired 3M patent counsel. "The antitrust supporters had taken over

Congress in the 1930s and they stifled all the patent coverage they could influence," he said. "Some courts said the only patents that were valid were the ones they hadn't gotten their hands on yet." McKnight wanted to protect every idea or technology that could be patented. "He didn't want anybody stealing anything that we had," Lauder said. But, that didn't stop competitors from trying.

> A Crimp in a Competitor's Plans

On the same day in 1959 that 3M introduced its new 16-inch circular floor pad for industrial cleaning, a customer of a major rival, Norton Company, shipped samples to Norton's lab for analysis. "Every company of any size keeps track of its competitors, but when you go to the other guy's backyard and pick up a product and analyze it, that's meaningful," said Stan DeLaHunt, who was part of the 3M team that defended the patent for 10 years. When Norton introduced a similar product a few months later, it claimed that 3M's Scotch-Brite floor pad couldn't be patented

4

1 A legal document produced for a 1945 cellophane tape patent case.
2 Law depositions in an early 1940s cellophane tape patent case.
3 An October 1958 article in Business Week magazine reported that 3M operated under the belief that "strong patents are the surest way to profits."
4 By 1960, Scotch-Brite floor pads were available to consumers for home use.

3 MANAGEMENT

3M's Way: Patents Plus Labs

Minnesota Mining & Mfg. builds on this formula: an unfilled market, a new product to fit it, a patent to protect position.

In an era when such phrases as market domination, price maintenance, monopoly, have become downright unfashionable, at least one company—Minnesota Mining & Mfg. Co., better known today as "3M"—not only uses them proudly, but as a very basis for its corporate existence.

To William L. McKnight, its chairman—who at 70 has largely delegated operating responsibility, but who shaped 3M into its current form and is still very much its voice—and to Herbert P. Buetow, its president, the legal monopoly provided by patents is a primary tenet of corporate life.

And at a time of rapidly advancing technology—when more and more U.S. companies are drifting away from reliance on patent protection into emphasis on cross-licensing and patent pools, counting on marketing strength and production knowhow to protect their positions—McKnight and Buetow (cover and pictures) plan to fight even more forcefully for "patent monopoly" on 3M's products.

• **Broad Field**—Minnesota Mining is perhaps best known for Scotch Tape—a brand name that has become almost generic for all pressure-sensitive cellophane tapes. Actually, it makes some

because of "prior art"—a combination of information and drawings of similar inventions that already had been published. Any person with reasonable imagination and skill could have come up with the same idea, Norton argued.

3M brought patent infringement suits against competitors in France, Germany, the United Kingdom and Australia, among others. Millions of dollars of sales were at stake, said DeLaHunt, not to mention a pivotal legal battle with Norton. 3M had successes in its foreign suits and DeLaHunt said this aggressive approach was crucial to 3M. "Our successes outside the United States put a crimp in our competitors' plans," he said.

> The Justice Department Calls

Antitrust issues made headlines in the 1960s, and 3M was not untouched. This was a decade of rapid growth for 3M, and the U.S. Justice Department argued that the company was monopolizing key businesses—including pressure-sensitive tape, magnetic tape and presensitized aluminum printing plates—beyond the scope of 3M's patents. 3M didn't contest the charges and entered into a consent decree in a companion civil case.

But, the outcome of that loss was long lasting and positive, said John Ursu, senior vice president, Legal Affairs and General Counsel. "The Danville case (so called because the court was in Danville, Illinois) caused us to pay attention to the practical limits of exploiting intellectual property," he said. "As a result, 3M developed a strong compliance program that is the best of any company in the world. That serious attention to compliance evolved into a strong corporate value. Integrity and reputation have always been important to 3M."

Without the patent system, 3M innovation would come to a screeching halt. > Carolyn Bates

When Gary Griswold, president and chief intellectual property counsel, 3M Innovative Properties Company, joined 3M in the early 1970s, 3M's patent staff was one-third the size it was by 2001. By the 1980s, the term intellectual property was in vogue. It was first used to describe that broad category of ideas, inventions, technologies and brands protected by patent, trademark, copyright and trade-secret law.

Griswold watched a shift occur—from an "anti-patent" attitude in government and the courts characteristic of earlier decades—to an environment in the 1980s where patents were more highly valued and protected. Traditionally, appeals in patent cases were heard in various circuit courts of appeal around the country. There was little uniformity in the decisions, Griswold said, and some of these courts consistently found patents invalid

or not infringed. In 1982, however, the U.S. Congress established a Court of Appeals for the Federal Circuit that would hear all patent appeals from across the country. The outcome was more uniformity and a more "patent-friendly" environment for patent owners.

In the 1980s and 1990s, the number of patent applications mushroomed as emerging high-tech companies multiplied in computer and software, medical devices, pharmaceutical, and telecommunications industries and "dot-coms" born of the World Wide Web. Not surprisingly, the number of patent infringement and piracy issues increased dramatically as the global economy defined itself and enjoyed robust years.

At 3M, three major intellectual property cases in the 1980s underscored the company's historically strong defense of its products and technologies. One case led to the largest cash settlement in 3M history. Another defended 3M's leadership in a business born decades earlier and the third case protected a new idea from a rush of "me-too" product copies.

> ### The Cast Worth $129 Million

By the 1970s, J&J had cornered the casting market with its plaster-of-paris bandage roll, but in 1980, 3M upstaged J&J with a superior alternative called Scotchcast orthopedic casting tape. For years, people with broken bones wore the heavy plaster casts that had to be kept dry (or the plaster would disintegrate) and wouldn't allow the skin to breathe. Scotchcast tape was polyurethane, but it could be used just like plaster. The

physician dipped the material in water and wrapped it around the broken bone, shaping it to fit. When the tape dried to a hard cast—much faster than plaster— it was stronger, lighter and far more comfortable than plaster. And, it breathed, allowing the skin underneath to stay dry. J&J was at risk of losing its domination of a $200 million market in the United States alone.

Two years after 3M introduced Scotchcast casting tape, J&J unveiled a look-alike product called Delta Lite casting tape. 3M offered to license its technology to J&J, said Carolyn Bates, intellectual property counsel, but the company rejected the offer. In 1985, the same year 3M was issued its Scotchcast patent, the company sued J&J for patent infringement. "With each successive Scotchcast improvement, J&J copied us," said Bates. "We kept applying for new patents on these improvements then suing J&J for patent infringement when their products showed the same improvements. It helped us build an even stronger case."

When the patent case was decided in 1991, the U.S. District Court in Minneapolis agreed that J&J had committed patent infringement and misappropriation of trade secrets. J&J was ordered to take the infringing casting products off the market. Ultimately, Bates said, damages and interest collected by 3M totaled

1 In response to the Danville case, 3M developed a strong compliance program.
2 As late as the 1970s, 3M's patent counsel operated under its own name— Alexander, Sell, Steldt and DeLaHunt. Pictured clockwise from lower left: Stanley DeLaHunt, Donald Sell, Cruzan Alexander and Frank Steldt.
3 About 60 intellectual property lawyers at 3M work to obtain and defend the company's patents, trademarks and brands.

$129 million, representing more than 30 times J&J's profits on the offending products and nearly twice as much as their total sales for those products. For 3M, it was the largest recovery in the company's history and, at that time, the fourth-largest patent infringement award in the United States. "3M has been very aggressive in enforcing its patent rights," Bates said. "We believe in respecting the intellectual property rights of others and this case reinforced the importance of that 3M policy."

For Bates, personally, who began her career at 3M in a lab, this was a legal assignment of a lifetime. "This case was a patent attorney's dream," Bates, who earned her law degree in 1976, said. "It was a fantastic learning experience."

Since resolving this case, 3M has worked closely with J&J and has developed some strong business relationships with the company.

> ### Keeping Infringers at Bay
About 1980, 3M introduced a new and improved version of its Scotchlite high-intensity reflective sheeting, a product with its "roots" in a material invented by Eugene McKenzie in the early 1960s. The new product was covered by a patent issued to a young 3M scientist, Joe McGrath. A few years after the introduction, Seibu, a Japanese company, began selling a competitive product and insisted that their Seibulite Ultralite sheeting did not infringe 3M's patent. After long negotiations that led to no resolution, Seibu began exporting its product to the United States. They must have known that 3M would call "foul." When the case went to trial in February 1987, the International Trade Commission decided in favor of 3M and U.S. customs officials were told to refuse to let in Seibu's product.

There was much at stake, said Roger Tamte, 3M intellectual property counsel. "High-intensity sheeting was a mainstay of our Traffic Control Materials Division. An earlier product had been subjected to tough pricing competition by Seibu and others," Tamte said. "3M was concerned that Seibu would drive down the price of this new product in the effort to sell their own product."

Ray Richelsen, who retired as executive vice president, Transportation, Graphics and Safety Markets, was the division's vice president at the time. He made the decision to defend the patent in the United States and abroad. "Patent enforcement is expensive," said Tamte. "You try to judge your chances of success. It was a gutsy move because the cost of litigation shows up on the division's bottom line, and it can cost millions." From 1987 until 1994, when 3M's U.S. patent expired, the company had no competition in the United States for Scotchlite high-intensity reflective sheeting, and 3M's successful enforcement of its patents in other countries limited competitors' sales around in the world.

> ### Protecting the Canary Yellow Notes
When 3M introduced its revolutionary Post-it notes in 1980, the little yellow notes changed the basis of competition and quickly became the highest value-added

1 Scotchcast Plus casting tape offers cast wearers colorful options.

product the paper industry had seen. "Naturally, there were a lot of companies looking for an adhesive to do the same thing," said Jerry Chernivec, 3M intellectual property counsel. At the time, the Post-it note adhesive was patented only in the United States and, although offshore competition had access to the published patent information, a strong competitor did not surface.

"We had some competitors in Japan," Chernivec said, "but their adhesive aged, making it difficult to pull a note off the pad. Then we ran into American Pad and Paper (AMPAD) in Massachusetts." AMPAD was a mature company with less than stellar growth whose major product was yellow legal pads. "They tried to structure an adhesive that would provide the same characteristics as those in Post-it notes but wouldn't infringe on our patent," Chernivec said. When AMPAD introduced its product in the mid-1980s, 3M decided AMPAD had, in fact, crossed the line.

3M sued AMPAD and the case went to trial in 1991. Two years before the trial, Mead Corporation—a 3M customer—acquired AMPAD. "Mead was a good friend of 3M," Chernivec said. "They bought our products, and we bought from them." Involving a customer in litigation was not what 3M wanted to do

but protecting Post-it notes from tough competition in the product's infancy was crucial. 3M won its patent case, and Mead and 3M negotiated a settlement. Most importantly, Mead got out of the repositionable notes business, Chernivec said: "That put teeth in our patents. Other competitors took a strong look at whether they should do anything that might infringe on our patent coverage."

In 2000, the U.S. Patent and Trademark Office registered 3M's famous canary yellow color trademark for Post-it notes. Soon afterward, 3M also registered the color blue used on its premium quality Scotch painters' tapes and 3M is pursuing the color purple for some of its sandpaper. "All three colors are clearly associated with 3M," said Robert Hoke, 3M intellectual property counsel. "We're not trying to exclude competition, but we're making sure that our competitors play fairly."

> **Where's the BEF? Defending a Market**

Protecting a strategic business with huge potential for growth was crucial to 3M in the 1990s when the company introduced Vikuiti brightness enhancement film

2 The September 1980 issue of The Office magazine featured newly introduced Post-it notes that changed communications forever.

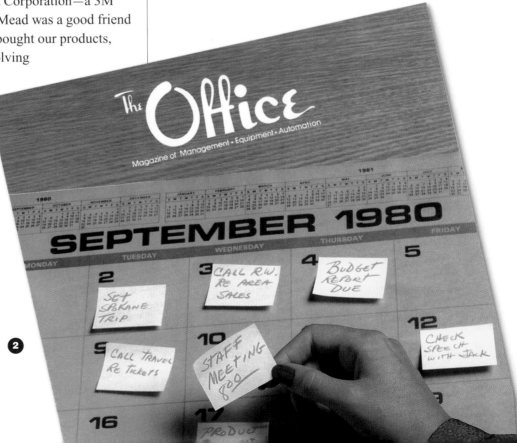

What's Your IP Quotient?

An intellectual property (IP) audit is like an insurance policy or an annual physical. When 3M develops a new product or technology that has strong market potential, the company needs to make sure that all patent and trademark protection is in place. IP counsel reviews the claims and looks for any gaps in patent coverage before a competitor can find a weak spot.

3Mers examined about 1,700 patents related to reclosable fastening methods—ranging from screws, buttons and clips to the well-known Velcro reclosable fasteners. As a result of this assessment, 3M realized that it had the technological heft to move from being a second-string player to a star in the reclosable fastener business, said Al Sipinen, senior specialist, intellectual property liaison. Sipinen and his team identified three fastening technologies that 3M should shore up and build upon. "Without this examination, we wouldn't have known how strong or weak we were compared to our competition," Sipinen said. The assess-

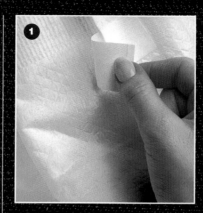

ment identified gaps in the marketplace. "Everybody was making hooks out of polypropylene and polyethylene, but they couldn't stand up to high temperatures, like the heat of a car engine," Sipinen said. 3M's Corporate Process Technology Center began exploring how to make a high temperature-resistant hook.

The assessment also identified areas where 3M had no competition. "We realized there was one type of hook that we produce for disposable diapers that no one else has. That moved 3M to strengthen its patents in that arena," Sipinen said. Sipinen and a 3M team were asked to

develop a template for conducting intellectual property assessments at 3M that can be used in connection with every important technology.

And, it's not just lawyers who find these IP Audits fascinating. One 3M scientist became so interested in patent protection that he took an intensive course in patent law in Washington, D.C. His intellectual curiosity surfaced in the most unlikely places.

"We both joined the same 3M-sponsored bowling league," said a 3M IP counsel. "We were at the alley and he came over and took me aside, looking puzzled. He said, 'We're studying section 102G of patent law and I don't quite understand this point . . .'" There was a brief, though educational, delay in league play that night.

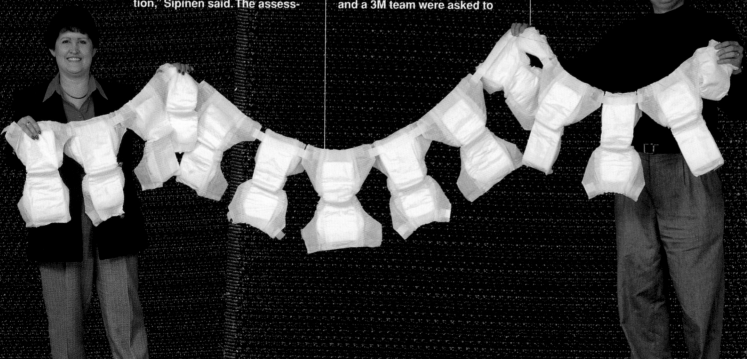

(BEF). The unique surface material with tiny "micro-replicated" structures was designed to enhance brightness and conserve battery power in computers, cellular phones and other devices that rely on liquid crystal displays (LCDs).

"3M got into this market at precisely the right time, when the sale of laptop computers was exploding in the early 1990s," said Steve Buckingham, 3M intellectual property counsel. "By that time, the size, weight and price of laptops were dropping. Our film made the LCD screens brighter and the batteries last longer." At first, 3M commanded the entire market, but within

In intellectual property law, our strategy is to map out and protect a key competitive product area. 3M has invested in the research to develop a new technology and the company needs to obtain a solid return on that investment.

> **Gary Griswold** *president and chief intellectual property counsel, 3M Innovative Properties Company*

a few years, several Japanese companies—including Sekisui Chemical, Dai Nippon Printing and Mitsubishi Rayon—introduced competitive products. 3M saw its market share decline through 1994 and drop significantly by 1995.

3M sold its brightness enhancement film to a number of backlighting manufacturers, primarily based in Japan.

Those companies then sold their backlighting modules to display manufacturers who, in turn, made liquid crystal displays for computer manufacturers. 3M had pending patent applications in Japan, but issued patents in the United States. "As far as the patents on our film were concerned," Buckingham said, "our competitors didn't infringe on our U.S. patents until the assembled products were imported into the United States by major computer

The power of our patents is the reason for the success of every division of our company. Patent protection gave 3M the time to develop markets that weren't developed and change the basis of competition. > **Ron Mitsch**

retired vice chairman and executive vice president

manufacturers. Those same companies were also buying 3M products."

"The question was, would we sue customers who were important to us," Buckingham said. "The answer was 'yes,' but it was not an easy

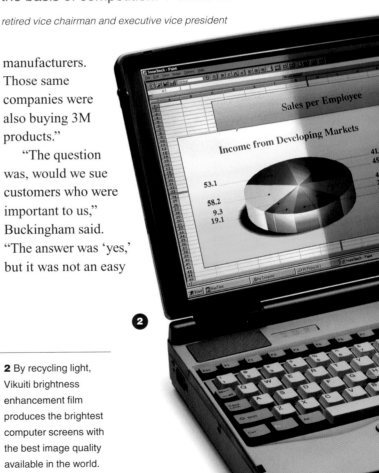

1 Because of technological expertise, 3M became the leader in closures for disposable diapers. Using the Scotchmate hook-and-loop fastening system, diaper closures hold securely even when lotions, oils and powders have been applied.

2 By recycling light, Vikuiti brightness enhancement film produces the brightest computer screens with the best image quality available in the world.

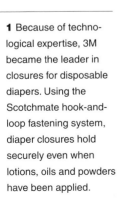

decision. If it hadn't been for our patents and our willingness to assert them, our competitors would have been willing to sell their films at a price we simply couldn't afford to match; they would have taken the market away from us."

3M took action in late 1995 and gave two of its most important customers an early warning. After about four months of negotiations, both companies agreed not to purchase products from film manufacturers that infringed on 3M's patents. Since then, 3M's patents on Vikuiti film have been respected, and 3M expects the film to continue to be an important product in the 21st century.

Fortunately, and perhaps surprisingly, 3M's relationship with its two customers became stronger, Buckingham said. "The experience opened up communication between us and the companies' design teams in Japan, for example," he said. "3M came to understand better what they were looking for and what was important to them."

> **Leveraging 3M's Intellectual Property**
The 1990s sparked an even greater emphasis on making the most of 3M's storehouse of discoveries, processes and technologies.

In 1990, 3M's Chairman of the Board and CEO Allen Jacobson asked Ron Mitsch to leave his position as group vice president temporarily and focus on how the company could accelerate its innovation rate. "I went through all of our technical audit reports, talked to a lot of people and listened

even more," Mitsch said. Six months later, Mitsch came back with a set of recommendations that he called the "Research and Development (R&D) Imperatives." Among 10 key strategies, one focused on 3M's knowledge base. "It was an unequivocal endorsement of intellectual property," he said. "It stressed the importance of an intellectual property training program in the company, a patent strategy based on being the 'first to file,'

No company can rest on its laurels—it either develops and improves or loses ground. Our company has adopted the policy 'Research in business pays.' > **Richard Carlton** *retired 3M president*

and an IP audit of our major technology programs." That greater emphasis kicked off an increase in patent applications that continued through the 1990s.

As part of those R&D imperatives, 3M developed a new Corporate Intellectual Property Policy in 1992 that asked every business unit and research and development group in the company to develop worldwide IP strategies and implementation plans. From 1992 on, technical people were expected to become familiar with the patent and nonpatent literature related to their areas. The policy further said that 3M would continue

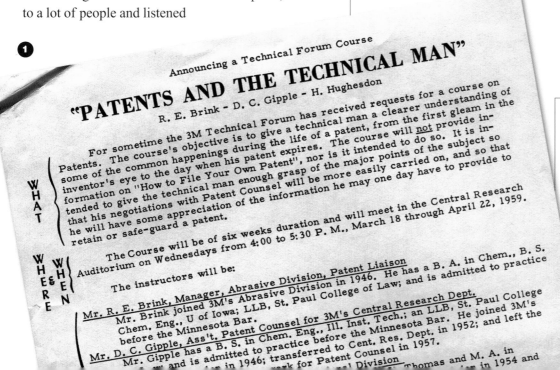

1 A 1959 Technical Forum course on patents gave 3M's technical community a better understanding of their importance.

to "protect its substantial investment in research and development by obtaining, maintaining and enforcing" patents and copyrights and by protecting trade secret rights. In addition, 3M underscored the importance of respecting the IP rights of others and committed to defending its "global brand assets," such as the 3M, Scotch and Post-it brands, in order to enhance the company's reputation and leverage product marketing.

> ### A Company Within a Company

3M took this focus on intellectual property to a new level in April 1999, when it created 3M Innovative Properties Company (3M IPC), a wholly owned subsidiary responsible for protecting and leveraging 3M's IP assets around the world. While not a novel idea—many companies including Lucent Technologies, DuPont and Toys "R" Us have done it—this development was new to 3M.

3M's innovative culture and our intellectual property are like motherhood and the American flag around here. > **Gary Griswold**

"We shifted our focus from solely protecting our businesses to trying to get more leverage out of our intellectual property," said Griswold. For example, 3M now has a Strategic Intellectual Asset Management (SIAM) group that is exploring ways to generate value from unused or underutilized intellectual property within the company.

In some cases, when a 3M technology has more applications within the company than anyone first imagined, 3M IPC helps identify new matches that can ultimately produce unique and marketable products.

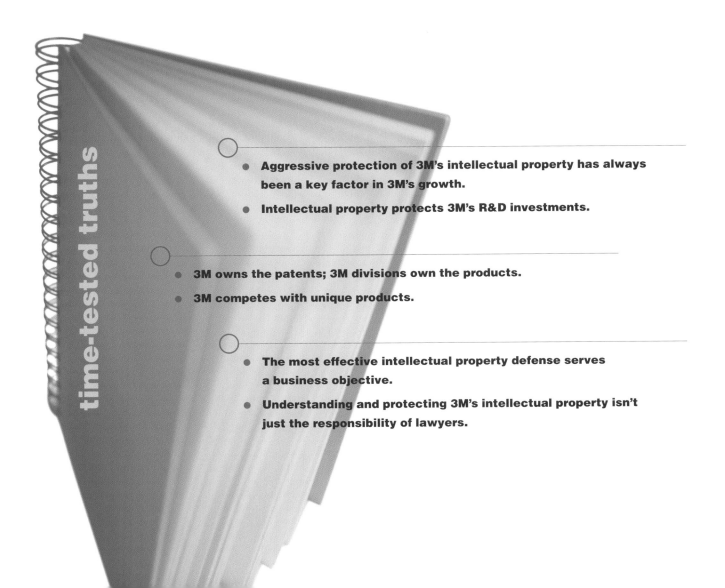

time-tested truths

- Aggressive protection of 3M's intellectual property has always been a key factor in 3M's growth.
- Intellectual property protects 3M's R&D investments.

- 3M owns the patents; 3M divisions own the products.
- 3M competes with unique products.

- The most effective intellectual property defense serves a business objective.
- Understanding and protecting 3M's intellectual property isn't just the responsibility of lawyers.

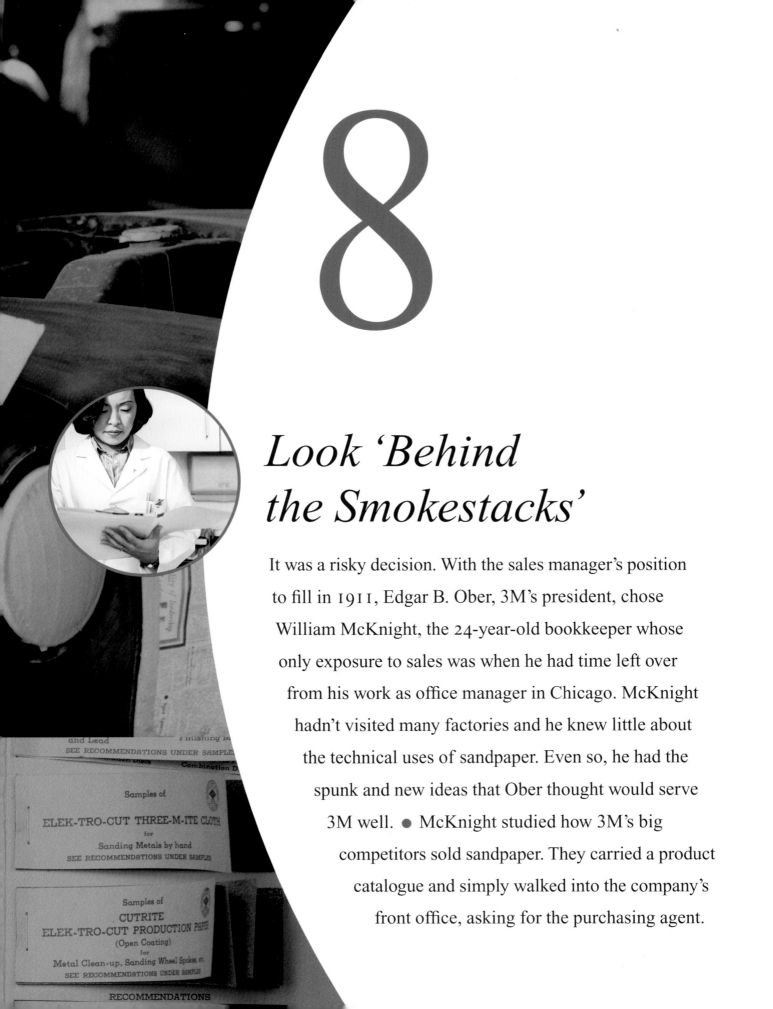

8

Look 'Behind the Smokestacks'

It was a risky decision. With the sales manager's position to fill in 1911, Edgar B. Ober, 3M's president, chose William McKnight, the 24-year-old bookkeeper whose only exposure to sales was when he had time left over from his work as office manager in Chicago. McKnight hadn't visited many factories and he knew little about the technical uses of sandpaper. Even so, he had the spunk and new ideas that Ober thought would serve 3M well. ● McKnight studied how 3M's big competitors sold sandpaper. They carried a product catalogue and simply walked into the company's front office, asking for the purchasing agent.

If they were lucky, they got an order. But, McKnight had a bold idea that took more initiative. It could have easily backfired, too.

McKnight knew that 3M's products were probably no better than its competitors', but he was ambitious enough to try his unconventional approach by calling on 29 Rockford, Illinois, furniture manufacturers in a single day. Those companies were the most important

His plan was to get into the back shop of a firm, talk with the workmen to learn whether or not they were satisfied with the product they were using. And, if they were willing, he demonstrated his own product from 3M right on the spot.

> **Mildred Houghton Comfort** *author of "William F. McKnight, Industrialist"*

sandpaper buyers, but they were a tough sell. The tall, thin young man with red hair asked if he could step into the back shop to talk to workers. The usual front office answer was, "What for?" When they asked the name of McKnight's company, most people had never heard of 3M. "We're new," he said, "that's why we're anxious to learn what you need." Grudgingly, the front

office "gatekeeper" let McKnight into the factory's inner sanctum and men on the production line told him what they thought, including how sub-par some 3M products they had tried actually were. Not only did McKnight have to insist on better quality back at home in St. Paul, Minnesota, but he faced a price war. McKnight and Ober agreed that 3M could win with better quality, but they wouldn't be victors on price alone.

During this era, McKnight expanded his philosophy of looking "behind the smokestacks," going right to the factory floor. As he rose in the company, he insisted that new salesmen go into the back shop of a factory, just as he had done. They must talk to workers and find out their problems, he said. On the spot, they must identify the abrasives the workers needed. They must demonstrate 3M products and follow up by bringing samples to the companies' factories. To ensure that 3M products were consistently of good quality, McKnight wrote to Ober suggesting that a general manager coordinate 3M factory output and field experience. Ober agreed and gave McKnight the job.

Chapter opening photos Scotch masking tape used in auto body shops in the 1920s; A carriage and auto painter praised Wetordry sandpaper in 1923; Wetordry sandpaper sample booklet; 3M worked closely with doctors and hospital staff to develop products for the health care industry.

1 A sketch from an early *Megaphone* newsletter for employees showed A.G. Bush delivering his instructions to salespeople: "Follow the trail of smokestacks to new customers." **2** People on production lines often know far more about a plant's needs than those in the front office.

> **Sparks, Sawdust and Inspiration**

While the product was created well before Richard McGrath's time, he remembers Stikit sanding discs with glue on the back so they could be easily attached to a sanding tool. "Before Stikit discs, people had disc adhesive that they applied to the sandpaper backing with a little brush, then they waited for it to dry before

I recall coming across historical records from abrasives that described McKnight's first sales meeting in the early 1920s. He said, 'Go and find out what the customers want . . . and come back and tell us what it is.' That was the founding philosophy of 3M. From that came huge advances . . . from our understanding of the marketplace we served. > **Richard McGrath**

retired vice president, Industrial Markets

starting their work," McGrath, retired vice president, Industrial Markets, said. "Initially, Stikit discs were created for automotive body shops. We understood the market well enough to see the customer's need. We captured market share like gangbusters and eliminated our biggest competition, Norton." Though not often mentioned as a groundbreaking product, McGrath said Stikit discs represented an early and successful combination of two of 3M's core technologies, abrasives and adhesives, in a never-before-seen product that changed the basis of competition and spawned many product offspring.

McKnight's philosophy of looking behind the smokestacks has been a key factor in 3M's major product developments. John Benson, executive vice president,

3M has to look big to our competitors and to our investors. It has to look small, nimble and fast to our customers. Those two things are not dichotomous; they can play together.

> **W. James McNerney, Jr.** *chairman of the board and chief executive officer*

Health Care Markets, said, "I remember hearing that if you were to succeed as a sales rep in abrasives at 3M, you had to go to the back of the shop and throw sparks. It meant putting a new belt on the equipment, picking up a piece of metal, grinding it and throwing sparks. If it was a woodworking customer, it meant making sawdust. The idea was to get out with the customers; live with them; see what they see."

On Benson's first day at 3M in 1968, he saw this principle in action. "Ron Baukol (then working in the health care area of 3M, now retired executive vice president, International Operations) hired me," Benson said. "He wanted me to work with anesthesiologists to understand their needs. 3M had never worked with them before, but it seemed that some of

❷

our products ought to be useful." Baukol and Benson set off for Northwestern Hospital in Minneapolis (now part of Abbot-Northwestern) that same day. "We were sitting in the surgeons' lounge. The anesthesiologist tried to describe his work and he finally said, 'Look, I can't do it here. You've got to come into the operating room and see it firsthand.'"

I used to define innovation as something that happened in the lab, but our customers don't see it that way. We're innovative when we help them. We're innovative when we give them solutions.

> **Katja Finger** *communications manager, 3M Public Relations and Communications, Latin America and Africa*

Benson was invited to witness an open-heart procedure the next morning at 6 a.m. "I didn't sleep a wink," Benson said. "I was excited and scared. The experience drove the point home. I think our very best ideas come from people who spend time with our customers on their turf."

Lew Lehr, the "father" of 3M's medical business and later chairman of the board and chief executive officer, went on grand rounds in the early 1950s with local doctors, especially surgeons, to understand how 3M products and

technologies could be of value to them. Since 1999, 3M has collaborated with United Hospitals in St. Paul in a program called Partnership in Patient Care in which 3M employees meet with medical staff to gather feedback on existing products and prototypes in conferences and focus group panels. Originally created as a way for 3M technical employees to gain a closer understanding of the customer's environment, the program has been expanded to include anyone in the division. The goal is to understand medical staff and patient needs by learning together, sharing information about 3M technologies, and developing personal working relationships with staff.

In a similar partnership with Woodwinds Health Campus in Woodbury, Minnesota, 3M developed a new medical tape by asking nurses to test the tape and offer feedback. At the Mayo Clinic in Rochester, Minnesota, 3M is working with the world renowned medical center to learn more about the issue of preventing infection during hospital stays.

When Gary Pint participated in the start up of 3M's Telecom Business Unit in 1968, the team's role was to build the business from an embryonic idea to a leading, worldwide business group. The smokestack lesson was part of their strategic thinking. "To start and build the Telecom business, we had to listen carefully to customers and be as responsive as possible," said Pint. "We followed Mr. McKnight's philosophy

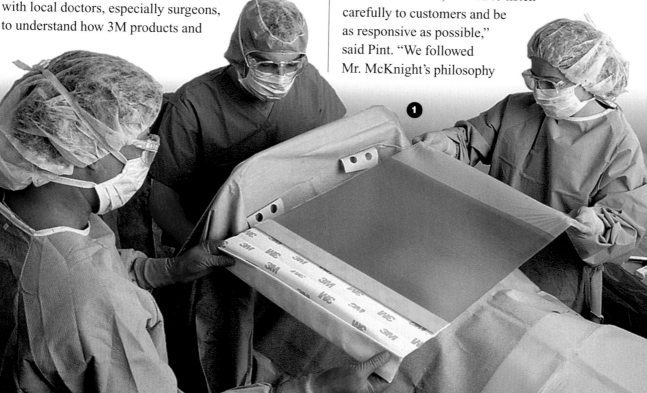

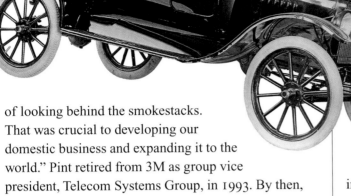

of looking behind the smokestacks. That was crucial to developing our domestic business and expanding it to the world." Pint retired from 3M as group vice president, Telecom Systems Group, in 1993. By then, the business had grown from virtually zero sales to several hundred million dollars.

We call it being 'customer intimate.' If we're going to develop new and better products to help improve the practice of medicine and advance human health, we better be out there with the practitioners—the doctors, the nurses, the anesthesiologists. > **John Benson** *executive vice president, Health Care Markets*

> Eons in Automotive

Very few companies can claim a nearly 90-year relationship with the same customers, but this is how long 3M has served the automotive industry. It began in 1914, when 3M's Three-M-ite abrasive cloth proved to be the superior product for finishing metal; just as

Henry Ford's unique mass production methods caught on and a legion of car manufacturers produced more cars, faster, with diverse brand names such as Locomobile, Crestmobile, Pierce Arrow, Packard, Cadillac and Buick. Every car maker needed miles of sandpaper to smooth wooden and metal parts and to refine body finishes.

Seven years later, in 1921, 3M introduced another innovation when Eastern salesman Joe Duke called on Philadelphia auto painting shops to demonstrate Wetordry sandpaper, the first waterproof sandpaper. After overcoming some skepticism from painters accustomed to using pumice, Duke knew he had an unqualified success in his product satchel. Wetordry sandpaper reduced the excess heat caused by dry sanding; it produced a smoother finish; and it worked well with fast-drying lacquer, a superior coating compared to slow-drying varnish. When car makers discovered that 3M's waterproof sandpaper dulled the natural shine of the lacquer surface, Francis Okie—the creator of Wetordry sandpaper—quickly concocted Retsul (luster spelled backward) polish. While it never rivaled

1 Disposable surgical drapes were the first product in the 3M Health Care product line. **2** Wetordry sandpaper found success in both automotive manufacturing and repair shops. It provided a smoother finish and worked faster than competitors' products.

the more successful Simoniz polish, Retsul polish—sold with Wetordry sandpaper—demonstrated 3M's eagerness to solve customers' problems, while preserving the market for Wetordry sandpaper.

Dick Drew, the affable, maverick inventor, followed McKnight's advice to get onto the factory floor and talk to the production people. He had exceptional results. Drew's innovative Scotch masking tape, introduced in 1925, gave automobile painters razor sharp separations in two-tone paint jobs and made Drew a legend around 3M.

> When I was a kid, I remember a Christmas package from 3M. My dad was an engineer at Cadillac in Detroit and he later became president of General Motors. I especially remember the sandpaper. Dad always used it in his shop. > **David Cole** director, Office of the Study of Automotive Transportation, University of Michigan

When all-steel cars emerged in the 1930s, manufacturers needed adhesives to attach upholstery, trim and sound-deadening materials to soften the noise of reverberating steel bouncing over rough roads and potholes. 3M's solution was a spray rubber adhesive, also called rubber cement, made from re-claimed rubber. "General Motors and Chrysler were big customers in Detroit and so was Briggs, an auto body manufacturer," said Jim Hendricks, founder and first chairman of 3M's Technical Forum, who spent 16 years in Central Research and served as manager, Tape Research.

"I moved to Detroit right after joining 3M in 1936 to work with our auto customers," Hendricks explained. "Our adhesive was better than the competition's because it was flexible and it wouldn't harden in lower temperatures." 3M's spray adhesive sales grew quickly and soon demand exceeded supply. The company financed a special plant devoted to the new adhesive, rather than settling for an improvised wagon shed-turned-manufacturing-plant where the product's raw materials were stored in converted horse stalls.

When 3M introduced Scotchlite reflective sheeting for highway markings in 1939, automotive uses again surfaced quickly with applications for cars and semi-trailer trucks. Until the early 1960s, however, masking tape and abrasives were 3M's entree into the auto industry. With the acquisition of Dynoc Company, a maker of decorative wood grain for cars, a new product line emerged; 3M created the first vinyl film that replaced paint for automotive graphics in 1964. This breakthrough gave 3M a major boost in its automotive business and manufacturers had more colorful and elaborate graphics to attract consumers. 3M's glass bead technology used in reflective products made these graphics even more sophisticated.

The 1964 Ford Mustang was the first car to sport 3M Scotchcal film graphics, followed by a majority of American "muscle cars," popular in the 1960s and 1970s. Screen printing soon replaced vinyl and more intricate designs—notably those on the 1976 Pontiac Firebird—became the ultimate example of customized graphics.

By the late 1960s, when the Decorative Products Division was formed, those products became the cornerstone of our automotive business. It meant we were dealing with materials that were going on the finished car versus only materials used in the production of cars. > **David Brown**

business director, Automotive Division

Also in the late 1960s, 3M introduced fluoroelastomers, compounds that could tolerate wide temperature ranges and exposure to fluids like fuel, gear lubricants, engine oils and rust inhibitors, making them ideal for automotive gaskets, seals and tubing. Scotchgard fabric protectors, first used by Ford in 1968, helped interior cloth seats, door panels and carpets resist oil, water and soil. 3M Interam mount, designed for catalytic converters in 1976, solved multiple problems for car manufacturers. Interam mount looked like a felt blanket that cushioned the converter inside its metal housing. It held the converter in place and prevented excess heat from escaping into the car.

> **The Tape That Binds**

But, it was 1978 when a major 3M breakthrough transformed car manufacturing. Art de St. Aubin, then a 3M marketer, led a new project that ultimately evolved into the Industrial Specialties Division with global implications. The innovation driving this new business was double-coated foam tape, a first in the industry. It replaced mechanical attachment of body side moldings and weatherstrips. This revolutionary product changed the basis of competition. With taped—instead of mechanical—attachments on cars, there were no more unnecessary holes, fewer screws or bolts and less rust, the byproduct of punching holes in metal.

De St. Aubin, who retired as executive director, 3M Automotive Center, credits Joe Abere, a 3M corporate scientist, with development of the improved technology, and Gordon Engdahl, then division vice president, Industrial Specialties Division, with the support needed to see the project through. They called it Isotak tape in 1978, but it had its start nearly 10 years earlier with the original two-sided neoprene tape developed by Scientist Ed Lavigne. Neoprene tape had the durability to per-

1 Grit samples of Wetordry Tri-M-ite sandpaper in the 1920s. **2** Wetordry sandpaper was also sold to consumers in the 1920s. People found many uses for the paper in their homes. **3** Scotchcal high performance graphic films, developed in the 1960s, were used extensively on the "muscle cars" of the 1970s. **4** 3M dimensional graphics used on a Toyota Supra.

form on the outside of a car, and it gave 3M the chance to demonstrate how it could attach moldings and ornamentation for Ford, Chrysler and later General Motors. Neoprene tape was generating approximately $16 million in sales by the late 1970s, but the tape's holding power wasn't consistent. It worked with car moldings that were engineered to accommodate tape instead of screws and rivets. But, moldings that weren't designed for tape often failed. Parts started dropping off cars.

"We had the chance to develop products for bonding trim to the new, flexible bumpers that were coming out on the 1979 Monte Carlo," said David Brown, business director, 3M Automotive, "but General Motors' body side moldings attached with neoprene tape weren't holding. That drove us to find something new that could outperform neoprene tape, even though the performance requirements were still not clear."

We must understand the requirements of 3M products better than our customers do.

> **David Brown**

It was a defining moment for 3M Automotive when Brown and Joe Jones visited the GM production facility that made flexible bumpers for the 1979 Monte Carlo. "When we arrived, we found thousands of moldings on the floor," Brown said. "None of them adhered. It was breathtaking. Why 3M's tape failed was, at first, a mystery. 3M later learned that General Motors' supplier of car moldings—in preparation for a potential union

We operated more like commandos than a big army. I think a lot of the small projects that got started at 3M operated like that. It was hard to draw the line between marketing, sales and technical. Everybody did a little bit of everything.

> **Art de St. Aubin** retired executive director, Automotive Innovation Center

strike in its plant—had shipped two months' of inventory to GM in the hot summer months. As the moldings sat stored in semitrailer trucks, the heat caused an oily material called a "plasticizer" to migrate from the moldings and seep into 3M's neoprene. As a result, the tape couldn't do what it was designed to do.

"General Motors didn't know that we'd developed Isotak acrylic foam tape because it was still in testing. But, General Motors needed a solution, fast,"

1 CIFERAL, a bus manufacturer in Brazil, used 3M VHB (very high bond) tape to attach aluminum exterior side panels to the vehicles' frames.

Brown said. "We flew in Gordy Engdahl, our vice president, and we presented the product. We promised to ship the new tape within a week.

"Gordy believed in the people who worked for him and he gave us opportunities," said Brown. "He knew about the Isotak technology and he supported investments in our pilot work. He was a strong advocate of technical innovation."

> When you're dedicated to the success of a project, you can't get it out of your head. It isn't a six- or eight-hour job. It has to involve your psyche . . . It's a 'practical obsession.'
>
> **> Joseph Abere** *3M corporate scientist*

> Adversity is the Mother of Invention

The Isotak tape that set an industry standard in 1978 was based on a 3M technology that—at the time—was earmarked for extinction because it couldn't meet extraordinarily high cold weather specifications. "But, we kept working to prove that our product was suitable for the automotive environment," said de St. Aubin.

The project had its start in the middle of a national economic recession. "We went to Allen Jacobson, who was then vice president, Tape and Allied Products Group, and he supported us," said de St. Aubin. Jacobson, who

later became 3M chairman and CEO, cut the product development team slack. "He told me I hadn't filled out any new-product forms in six months. He said, 'I don't want you to stop what you're doing, but once in a while, fill out some of the forms.'"

"We simply called our new product 'two-sided sticky tapes,' but they were very sophisticated," Abere said. "We could see their immediate application in automotive but also in general industry, for example, in office furniture. We devoted all our time to developing that technology."

> 3M took initiative in understanding the potential of creating a high-performance tape that was capable of providing fastening without drilling holes. Others tried it, but 3M was the best at it.
>
> **> David Cole**

"Adversity led us to develop this new generation of tape products," said Brown, "including acrylic foam tape and what is known today as VHB (very high bond) tape."

About the same time 3M introduced the new double-coated tape, others in the auto industry were replacing metal moldings with plastic. As plastic became a more acceptable alternative, de St. Aubin said, "We started

2 VHB tapes have added benefits of vibration dampening and reduced corrosion. **3** VHB tapes have replaced labor intensive riveting and reduced rusting in many applications, including trucks and cars.

No 'Lone Ranger'

Back in the mid-1980s, the Ford Ranger had a prosaic image. "It was a little work truck and the most affordable of our truck products," said Robert Aikins, design executive, Ford Motor Company. "It appealed to young people or those in their mid-40s who wanted a second, utility vehicle."

But, Ford wanted to alter the little truck's image. It could become a truck with a positive, upbeat "attitude" — fun to drive with a sense of style. "That's when we enlisted 3M," said Aikins. "We wanted to put more excitement into the Ranger line, and 3M had long experience with supplying Ford with decorative stripes and ornamentation." 3M Automotive employees in St. Paul and Detroit developed several potential designs using many decorative tapes. "We tried translucent tapes, tapes that allowed the body color of the truck to show through, high gloss tapes and metallics," Aikins said. "It wasn't enough to go with standard colors. We needed new and unique ideas and 3M gave us the innovative applications." Not only did the designs have to look good, they also had to pass Ford's rigorous climate testing.

After developing design sketches using several options, 3M built a mock-up of the Ranger to illustrate how the applications would look on a real truck. "That helped us get final approval," said Aikins.

"We went from being just a player in the compact pickup business in 1987 to Ranger becoming number one among more than half a dozen competitors," Aikins said. "3M's involvement in changing the Ranger's image contributed to making it the leader. We began selling about 300,000 Rangers in North America each year."

When Ford explored replacing structural steel with aluminum to reduce the weight of its trucks and increase fuel efficiency, 3M worked with Ford's Research and Vehicle Technology Lab in the mid-1990s to invent a superior "two component" adhesive to bond large, metal sections without welding. "3M's lab people, application engineers, marketing support in St. Paul and sales people did an outstanding job of working with Ford and responding to their needs in a short time — less than 14 months from the idea to the production line," said Kevin McKenna, director, 3M Ford key account. "Our job is to look out to 2006 and match Ford's needs," said McKenna.

Speed at DaimlerChrysler

John Herlitz was 21 when he joined Chrysler as a product designer in 1964. Along with 3M's innovative reflective graphics and first-to-market acrylic tapes, Herlitz remembered being a wide-eyed, young designer visiting the 3M campus in St. Paul. "Seeing the full range of 3M activities fascinated me because they were active in so many fields other than automotive," said Herlitz, senior vice president/product design, DaimlerChrysler Corp. "There was tremendous energy generated between 3M's creative people and ours. We even saw automotive application. That's why the interchange has been so valuable over the years."

Today, when DaimlerChrysler designers are addressing ornamentation, graphics and badging (the last phase of new vehicle design development), they send their ideas to 3M's Detroit-based Automotive Center electronically. "3M has the equipment to receive our graphic interpretations and make prototypes very, very quickly," said Herlitz. "That high-speed link is all-important in our business."

Problem Solving at GM

Whether a car is on the production line or in development, 3M has proven to be an agile and well-versed problem solver for General Motors (GM). "Let's say we have difficulty with a part adhering to the car or some difficult adhesive condition," said Ray Bierzynski, director, functional vehicle design. "We call 3M and ask them to come here, or go to the plant, analyze the process and come up with ideas. That's when 3M's responsiveness has come in handy. Speed is crucial because GM builds about 50 to 75 cars an hour."

A new design is likely to require more attention. Bierzynski, for example, wrestled

coming through the center-mounted brake light. "Even though it had nothing to do with their adhesive expertise, 3M helped us analyze the foam gasket material that caused the leak. They even helped our supplier find a better material."

Intense competition has led GM to rely more heavily on 3M and its other suppliers: "We have to use more 'best practices' and proven methods," said Bierzynski, "and—at the same time—take mass and costs out of our processes. That means we have to lean on our sources for new ideas, generated at a faster rate, and for applications that are the most consistent and efficient they can be.

"When I worked most closely with 3M people, to their credit, I had the pager and phone numbers for every key person. I always knew they'd get back to me right away."

attaching everything—nameplates, moldings around bumpers, the drip rail around doors with our new tape."

Not only did the tape reduce manufacturing costs by eliminating metal holes and welding studs, it also reduced rust, made it possible to use fewer parts in assembly, shut out moisture and dust and helped vehicles last well beyond warranty limits.

"At first, we had no competition," said de St. Aubin. "It was a complicated application because the tape had to perform in extreme variations of hot and cold weather. The technology allowed us to expand and serve automakers around the world. By the 21st century, 3M had tape plants in Japan, Europe and the United States. It is a testimony to fulfilling a customer need and seeing an opportunity for which we had high hopes."

"Japan has more than 250 acrylic foam tapes used in their automotive market," said Brown. "We have 75 in America. Europe has about 50. Few are the same. Because we can customize our products, we can be far more responsive to individual customer needs."

By 2000, sales of 3M's line of acrylic foam tape exceeded $1 billion around the world and it had been used on more than 500 million vehicles. Innovation continues with the next generation of tape that will provide even stronger bonding power.

3M has helped us stay ahead of the game with ideas that push the design envelope. > **Don Brown**

national product planning manager, Toyota Motor Sales

In the new century, 3M is producing more than 1,000 different automotive products for uses as broad as bonding, acoustical insulation, fastening, air filtration, decorative trim and graphics, fabric protectors, electrical and lighting components and security labeling. 3M automotive customers can tap into more than 20 global automotive centers, dubbed "answer centers," where the staff is focused on pinpointing solutions to specific customer needs.

Background: Scotchcal paint protector film

> **Pursuing a Plethora of New Customers**

It wasn't until the early 1980s that 3M looked beyond its traditional, industrial roots and explored the global potential for its consumer business. The impetus started with Lehr, then chairman of the board and chief executive officer, who reorganized the company into business "sectors" and carved out the consumer business to report directly to him.

"Consumer had grown almost by sheer accident until Lew Lehr's decision," said Moe Nozari, executive vice president, Consumer and Office Markets. "If we made sandpaper and tape for industrial customers, we said, 'Why not sell it in grocery or hardware stores?' We'd start with a product, then go with it, wherever it fit. We'd find our way into new markets. Lew's decision to let consumer stand alone

1

gave the business sharper focus, as well as more visibility and legitimacy in 3M's internal world of product innovation and profit centers."

A recession in the United States during the early 1980s actually worked in favor of building the consumer business. Nozari put it this way: "When General Motors sells fewer cars, it needs fewer products from 3M, but consumers don't stop eating or washing their dishes with Scotch-Brite cleaning products. An economic downturn affects our consumer business less—especially if the

Our goal is to give people a product that's better than what they have today . . . or a brand new product they didn't know they needed.

> **Moe Nozari** executive vice president, Consumer and Office Markets

product is lower cost, like cleaning sponges, Scotch Magic tape, 3M mounting products with Command adhesive, sandpaper and Filtrete filters for furnaces.

"When Ernie Moffet became group vice president, Consumer Group, some people felt it was a hollow title," Nozari said. "He had only one division and a small project reporting to him." By the late 1990s, however, that one division had grown to five—Commercial Care, Construction and Home Improvement Markets, Home Care, Office Supplies, and Stationery Products divisions—generating nearly 20 percent of the company's total revenues from about 12,000 consumer products. Today, Consumer and Office Markets is one of the six 3M Market Centers.

"A key success factor for Consumer and Office Markets has been our ability to outpace the industries we're in by creating new-to-the-world products and getting them established rapidly," said Nozari. "In three years, Post-it flags grew to $100 million in sales. Command adhesives, which adhere to most flat surfaces, then release without damage when properly removed, will be to hammers and nails what the Post-it note was to scratch paper, paper clips and staples.

"We want to be the first to make our own best products obsolete; that way, it's difficult for the competition to catch up."

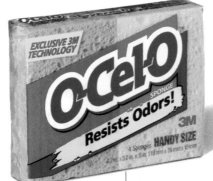

> You're a Great Company, But . . .

Taken alone, unique products aren't the only big factors in successful customer relations.

"In the early 1990s, our customers told us that 3M was a great company, it had wonderful products and people," said Ron Mitsch, retired vice chairman of the board and executive vice president, "but they also said we were difficult to do business with. We had 10 to 20 divisions calling on the same customer. It wasn't unusual to have a customer reach into his desk, pull out a stack of business cards and ask, with obvious frustration, 'Whom do I call?'" That's when 3M inaugurated "integrated solutions." Key account people are assigned to customers. "3M's consumer and office businesses were most successful," said Mitsch. "In seven years from 1992 to 1999, they grew 15 to 20 percent annually with their key account focus. It meant doing business in a different way and working across divisional lines. It involved giving up some power if you were a general manager or group vice president."

> Growing Market Share at Target

In the world of major discount stores, Target appeals to upscale consumers, typically women in their 30s and 40s, with family incomes around $55,000 a year. Given this profile, it wasn't surprising when Target chose to eliminate its lesser quality cleaning sponges and stock only cellulose versions, including 3M's O-Cel-O and Scotch-Brite brands. Megan Tucci, senior buyer, said, "3M was our best supplier with the most creative ideas and a willingness to invest in the program. Walk into Target today and we're proud to say that we carry top brands and top quality." Tucci said that 3M took the initiative to help Target enhance its business by suggesting new, bonus pack promotions, as well as more effective product displays. "3M helped us design a new vertical display that made the sponges more visually appealing. They also helped fund the effort and they showed us how to grow our business," Tucci said. "Our sponge sales increased 20 percent two years in a row."

> Lew Lehr wanted 3M to be a bigger player in the consumer market and it happened because of our key accounts focus. Now we have an 'audience' at the top of each company.
>
> **> Ron Mitsch** *retired vice chairman and executive vice president*

1 3M Consumer and Office Markets features some of the world's best-known brands including Scotch, Post-it, Scotch-Brite, Command, Filtrete and O-Cel-O. **2** The Scotch-Brite microfiber cloth is a multipurpose, reusable cleaning cloth designed for dusting and cleaning mirrors and windows.

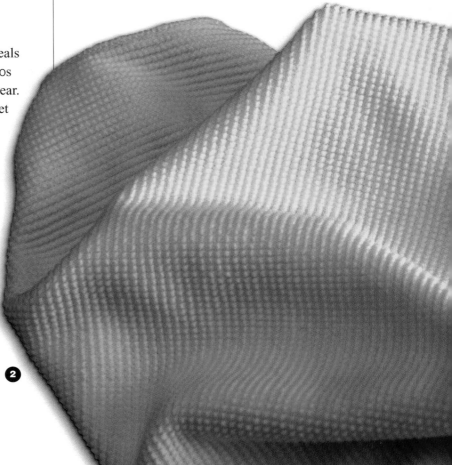

2

> **We Have This New Idea . . .**

It was a win-win-win opportunity for Sam's Club, Costco and 3M. The idea emerged at "top to top" meetings in which executives from each company met with their 3M peers to share ideas and mutual marketing strategies. 3M had a new cleaning product informally called "wipes" that had just emerged from a company lab in October 1998. "We said, 'We've got this material, it's unique and here's what it can do," said Bill Banholzer, director of club trade at 3M. "We'd like to see if your members are attracted to it and, at the same time, bring value to you."

Brad Feagans, vice president and divisional merchandise manager for Sam's 465 discount retail clubs in the United States, suggested introducing the cloth in 3M's own "backyard" in Minnesota.

Less than eight weeks after that initial discussion, the new Scotch-Brite microfiber cleaning cloth was stocked in five Sam's stores. "A new product needs awareness and sampling," said Banholzer. "Within three weeks, we had a success on our hands."

"Next it was Florida," Feagans said, "and once the sales took off, we went to all of our stores." In fact, in an annual event at which Sam's executives each select a new product to promote, Jim Haworth, senior vice president of operations, singled out 3M's new product. "The idea is to promote that item and build sales," said Feagans. "3M's wipes started the year generating about $450,000 a week in our stores and we aimed to double that."

"3M looks at what products are right for our customers," said Feagans. "We've worked with 3M since 1986. They have a strong work ethic, they're fair, honest and do what they say they'll do. Our company cultures are similar. They bring us new product ideas and we can help test how successful they might be. It gives our cus-

tomers access to the newest products. They're not all 'home runs,' but many are."

Costco, a customer since 1975, gave 3M access to one of its 35-store regions to test the new cleaning cloth. "We put together customer focus groups to find out what they liked about the wipes," Banholzer said. "Our market research is valuable to Costco and Sam's because they don't always have the time to do it. From that research, we developed a display for Costco that was highly visible and displayed the product's benefits."

"3M works hard at listening to us, creating better product presentations in our clubs, and offering attractive, value-added promotional ideas," said Steve Messmer, assistant general manager, Costco Wholesale. "They'll include a Post-it note holder in a pack of 5- by 7-inch Post-it notes or a dispenser, valued at $7 to $10, with six rolls of packaging tape. We work diligently with 3M to create packages that display well in our clubs and cost less to produce so we can pass those savings on."

We buy the cream of the crop. We shop from the top two to three vendors in a product category. With 3M, quality has never been an issue.

> **Steve Messmer** *assistant general manager, Costco Wholesale*

Pennies saved matter a lot when the volume purchased is so large. "We sell about 173 million yards of 3M premium packaging tape a year at our 254 clubs in the United States," said Messmer, "693 million sheets of Post-it notes, 3- by 3-inch size, and 10 billion inches of Scotch Magic tape."

Since 1994, when Nozari developed the key accounts

program for 3M consumer and office markets, the company's business with the country's major buying clubs has doubled, said Banholzer. "We have a good understanding of each other's businesses," he said. "We share our corporate strategies. Our goals are the same—to grow our businesses."

> Lifetime Lighters

Zippo Manufacturing Company—the largest manufacturer of lighters in the world—had a huge problem in 1997. Of the more than 14 million lighters the company produced in a typical year, about 1 million were losing their custom emblems. "We were getting calls from customers," said Fred Atherton, senior buyer for Zippo, based in Bradford, Pennsylvania. "People said, 'Gee, your lighter works great, but our logo fell off. That's where 3M came in. It took a lot of research and a couple years to develop an adhesive that could withstand extreme humidity and temperature conditions as well as repeated shock."

Zippo couldn't take any chances—the company, founded in 1932, had a long tradition of offering lifetime guarantees for its products. "Although Zippo doesn't guarantee the various finishes, we treated this problem with the utmost urgency. We put on a full court press to find a solution," said Atherton.

3M developed a very high bond (VHB) tape that is only .010 of an inch thick. "It was a long time in development," said Paul Smithmyer, senior product/process engineer for Zippo. "A lot of testing had to be done,

including dropping the lighter repeatedly from 8 feet off the ground and exposing it to cycles of extreme heat and cold over eight hours."

But, that wasn't the only production issue Zippo faced. When the company exposed a lighter to an acid bath to stencil a customer logo on its product, the chance of that acid damaging other surfaces was high. "There were times," said Atherton, "when 100 percent of the manufacturing run was scrap. The acid leaked and contaminated the rest of the lighter in the process. This was at the end of our manufacturing process and we were left with nothing. It cost us a lot of money."

3M created a special "masking" tape that covers the surface and won't allow the acid to damage the surface. "It's like a window frame that we place over the lighters and it allows only the exposed area to get the acid," Atherton said. "That product reduced our rejected lighters to virtually zero."

> The Customer in the Next Cubicle

3M's new business in ergonomics had its start in no less than the chief executive officer's office. "Desi (L.D. DeSimone) had always been extremely vocal about the importance of health and safety for employees," said Claude Denais, now managing director, 3M Venezuela, formerly business unit director, Office Supplies Division. In 1989, 3M examined the source of computer-related injuries and illnesses, and found that nearly half were related to ergonomic issues. The study also indicated that over a decade the average cost of all lost time inci-

1 Costco Wholesale alone sells about 10 billion inches of Scotch Magic tape a year. **2** 3M's line of ergonomic products includes computer keyboards, wrist rests, mousepads, document holders, polarizing task lights, even office air cleaners.

dents at 3M were—at a minimum—$28,000 to $42,000 per person.

3M focused first on muscular skeletal cases that show up in plant activities. A training program reduced the number of lost-time cases related to ergonomics by 70 percent. Before long, attention expanded to the entire company, said Tom Albin, retired manager, Ergonomics Services, Office Supplies Division. "The same injuries can occur in offices and industrial settings," he said. "Someone doing data entry at a desk can develop wrist problems; someone in a plant who assembles a product uses repetitive motion. Injuries related to ergonomics can also come from too much exertion or working in an awkward position."

By 1993, there were about 30,000 3M people who routinely used computers for as long as eight hours each workday. 3M's corporate ergonomics group worked with engineering to develop a company-wide training program, called Turbo Ergo. Albin and his colleague, Nancy Larson, applied for a 3M Alpha Grant to develop educational materials focused on computer ergonomics for employees, including an informational Web site.

Ultimately, this focus on healthy environments for 3M office and plant workers spawned the company's new line of specially designed gel-filled wrist rests for computer keyboards and mouse platforms, document holders and stands, foot rests, polarizing task lights, office air cleaners, safety mats, and computer filters to reduce eye strain. It had become evident that a business opportunity was ripe for picking. "When we looked at the products available," Albin said, "either they didn't do what we thought they should do or they only addressed a few ergonomic issues."

It was an unlikely new business for the then Commercial Office Supply Division. "When Chuck Harstad, now staff vice president, Corporate Marketing, was division vice president," said Denais, who ran 3M's office and stationery businesses in France and later managed the embryonic ergonomics business, "most of the products in our division were sticky products—Post-it notes and Post-it flags, for instance. Chuck wanted us to think outside the box. He said, 'It doesn't have to stick to anything.' "

Denais' team looked outside their division to find 3M technologies. For example, the gel used in the wrist rests was first developed by 3M Health Care for other medical needs. His team had built in "consumer focus groups" of 3M employees who gave them feedback on their early product designs. The team even videotaped people at their work stations to understand how they worked. "We noticed people massaging their wrists without even thinking about it," Denais said. "We had videoconferences with our peers in Europe, Canada and Japan to review our product concept drawings. It was important to have international involvement early."

Harstad, the team's sponsor, "sheltered us from the skeptics" as the project evolved, Denais said. He provided resources without expecting immediate, tangible results. "We were the equivalent of a small, start-up company. Our team had the imagination, creativity

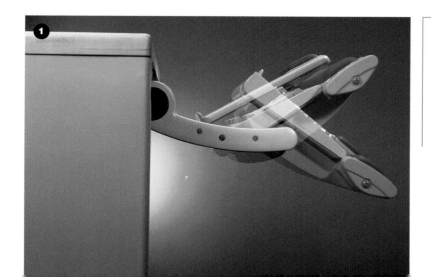

1 Patented gel-filled wrist rests contain a compound originally developed for medical needs. 3M's adjustable keyboard also helps reduce ergonomic injuries.

and speed of a new venture. Chuck protected us from the bureaucracy that's inevitable in a big company. We also had an advantage over our competition. We started with a clean sheet of paper, rather than trying to modify existing products to make them more ergonomic."

After three years of work, beginning in 1992, 3M introduced its first four products in July 1995—a wrist rest, document holder, foot rest and air cleaner. "We continued to add new products each year," Denais said. "We want to be the leading provider of ergonomic solu-

tions—wherever people work, in offices, plants, at home, in hotel rooms, on airplanes." By 2000, 3M's ergonomics business had an annual growth rate of 50 percent. "What we're most proud of is that 55 percent of our customers are outside the United States," said Denais. "People in Europe, Scandinavia, Canada, Australia and New Zealand are very savvy about ergonomics." And, in the categories in which 3M has ergonomic products, the little start-up business—that learned from its internal customers first—now has significant worldwide sales.

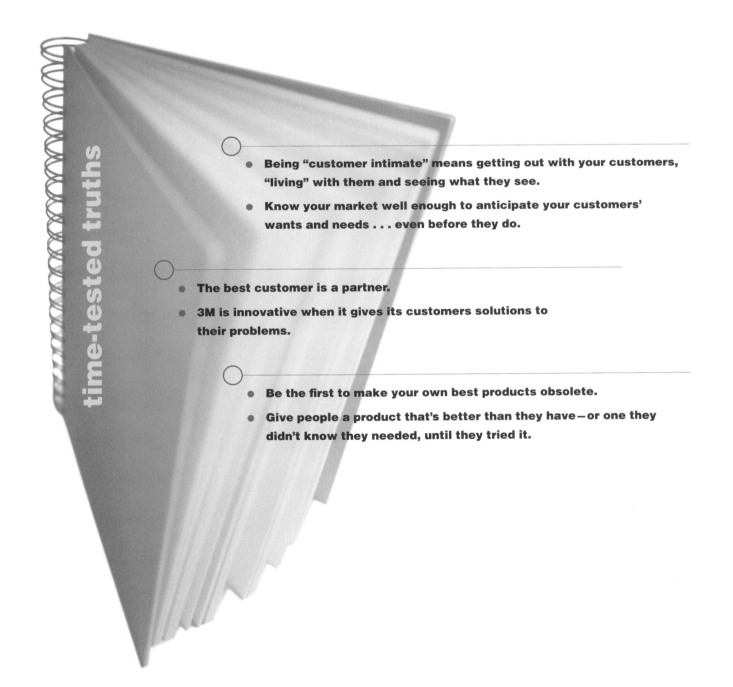

time-tested truths

- Being "customer intimate" means getting out with your customers, "living" with them and seeing what they see.
- Know your market well enough to anticipate your customers' wants and needs . . . even before they do.

- The best customer is a partner.
- 3M is innovative when it gives its customers solutions to their problems.

- Be the first to make your own best products obsolete.
- Give people a product that's better than they have—or one they didn't know they needed, until they tried it.

1900s

1910s

3M Events

1902 3M founded in Two Harbors, Minn., on June 13 when five founders sign articles of incorporation.

1903 Harriet (Hattie) Swailes, 3M's first female employee, hired.

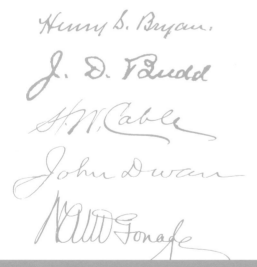

1904 3M has its first and only sale of Crystal Bay corundum.

1905 3M moves to Duluth, Minn.

Lucius Ordway invests in the company.

1906 First sandpaper sale to South Bend Toy Co. totals $2.

1907 William F. McKnight hired as assistant bookkeeper for $11.55 per week.

1910 3M moves manufacturing operations to St. Paul; first factory built.

1912 3M pioneers method of screening abrasive grit to maintain consistent size.

1913 Company profitable for first time.

1914 Oil soaked garnet produces flawed sandpaper; 3M begins its first quality control program.

Three-M-ite abrasive cloth introduced.

1916 First 3M laboratory established; 3M headquarters moves to St. Paul.

3M pays its first dividend— 6 cents a share on August 11. (3M has paid quarterly dividends on common stock without interruption since then.)

1919 Annual sales exceed $1 million.

Board approves 2-for-1 stock split.

Building No. 1 in St. Paul

World Events

1902 Enrico Caruso makes his first phonograph recording.

1903 Henry Ford founds the Ford Motor Co.

1904 Theodore Roosevelt wins U.S. presidential election.

London Symphony Orchestra gives its first concert.

1905 Albert Einstein formulates his Theory of Relativity.

1906 San Francisco earthquake kills 700; $400 million property loss.

1907 Robert Baden-Powell founds Boy Scout movement in Great Britain.

1908 General Motors Corp. formed.

Ford Motor Co. produces the first mass-produced car, the Model T.

1911 Marie Curie is awarded the Nobel Prize in chemistry.

1912 Woodrow Wilson wins U.S. presidential election.

S.S. Titanic sinks on her maiden voyage after colliding with an iceberg.

1913 Federal income tax introduced in the United States through the 16th Amendment.

1914 WW I begins.

1915 First transcontinental telephone call between Alexander Graham Bell in New York and Thomas A. Watson in San Francisco.

1916 Woodrow Wilson is re-elected president.

1919 WW I Peace Conference begins at Versailles.

1920s

St. Paul office in 1926

1925 Scotch masking tape introduced.

1928 3M Engineering Department organized.

1929 McKnight succeeds Edgar Ober as president.

3M and eight other U.S. abrasives manufacturers form Durex, a joint venture holding company in England, to conduct European business.

Shareholders approve incorporation of 3M as a Delaware company; 3M stock first traded over the counter.

3M buys Wausau Abrasives, its first acquisition, for $260,000.

1921 Wetordry waterproof sandpaper— the world's first water-resistant coated abrasive— patented and introduced.

Richard P. Carlton hired as a $65-a-month lab assistant.

1922 Board approves 2-for-1 stock split.

Robert Skillman makes 3M's first business trip to Europe.

1924 First formal product research begins.

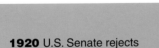

1920 U.S. Senate rejects League of Nations.

19th Amendment gives American women the right to vote.

1921 Former President William Howard Taft named chief justice of the United States.

1922 Soviet states form U.S.S.R.

1923 Popular songs include George Gershwin's "Rhapsody in Blue."

U.S. President Warren G. Harding dies in office; Vice President Calvin Coolidge succeeds him.

1924 Ford Motor Co. produces 10 millionth car.

J. Edgar Hoover named director of the FBI.

1925 "The Great Gatsby," authored by St. Paul native, F. Scott Fitzgerald, published.

Madison Square Garden opens in New York City.

1926 Kodak produces the first 16mm movie film.

1927 Holland Tunnel opens, linking New York and New Jersey.

Charles Lindbergh makes first solo nonstop flight across the Atlantic Ocean.

1928 Herbert Hoover elected U.S. president.

1929 "Black Friday" as U.S. Stock Exchange collapses on Oct. 28.

Construction begins on Empire State Building.

1930s

1930 3M buys Baeder-Adamson Co.

Pension plan established for 3M employees.

Scotch cellophane tape introduced.

1931 3M begins producing Colorquartz roofing granules.

1932 3M "monkey business" ad campaign begins, created by British cartoonist Lawson Woods.

1935 3M's first automotive under-seal coating products introduced.

Sandpaper packages featured illustrations of Sandy Smooth. The name originated with 3M employees, who affectionately called McKnight "Sandy Smooth."

1936 Adhesives Division established in Detroit; adhesives plant and laboratory opened.

Sales hit $10 million.

1937 Central Research Laboratory established.

First successful test of reflective tape coated with glass beads.

1938 Scotchlite reflective sheeting introduced commercially.

1939 Cornerstone laid for new St. Paul headquarters building (#21).

First traffic sign featuring Scotchlite reflective sheeting erected in Minneapolis.

3-M

Company picnic in 1934

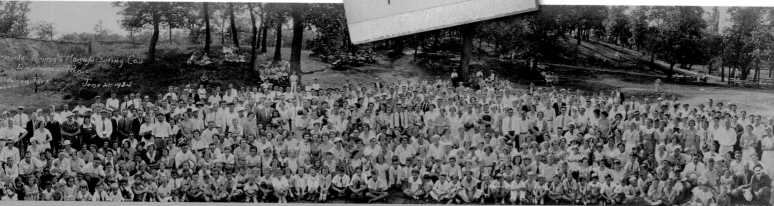

1930 South African micro-biologist Max Theiler develops a yellow fever vaccine.

1931 "Star Spangled Banner" becomes official U.S. national anthem.

1932 Franklin D. Roosevelt wins U.S. presidential election in Democratic landslide.

The Lindbergh baby is kidnapped.

The Lambeth Bridge in London and the Harbour Bridge in Sydney open.

1933 21st Amendment to U.S. Constitution repeals prohibition.

1935 President Roosevelt signs U.S. Social Security Act.

"Porgy and Bess" opera by George Gershwin opens in New York.

1936 Roosevelt is re-elected U.S. president.

Margaret Mitchell's "Gone With the Wind" wins Pulitzer Prize.

Henry Luce begins publication of Life magazine.

1937 Amelia Earhart lost on solo Pacific flight.

London bus drivers strike.

1938 President Roosevelt sends appeal to Hitler and Mussolini to settle European problems amicably.

Lajos Biró of Hungary invents the ballpoint pen.

1939 First baseball game is televised in the United States.

1940s

1942 Inland Rubber Corp. acquired.

1945 More than 2,000 3M employees are on military leave.

Scotch vinyl electrical tape introduced.

1946 3M listed on the New York Stock Exchange on Jan. 14.

1948 3M's first nonwoven product— decorative ribbon for gifts introduced.

3M organized along divisional lines.

Sales top $100 million.

3M debuts its first surgical drape.

1949 McKnight becomes chairman of the board; Carlton named president.

Employee stock purchase plan introduced.

SCOTCH BRAND
Sound Recording
TAPE

1947 Scotch magnetic audiotape introduced.

3M acquires five companies, forms National Outdoor Advertising.

New plants opened in Hutchinson, Minn. (tape); Los Angeles, Calif. (adhesives); and Little Rock, Ark. (roofing granules).

Forty acres of 3M's original Crystal Bay mine site are donated to the state of Minnesota for Tettagouche State Park.

Open house at the Hutchinson plant, 1948

1940 Winston Churchill becomes British prime minister.

Roosevelt re-elected to third term as U.S. president.

1941 Japanese bomb Pearl Harbor on December 7.

Joe DiMaggio successfully hits in 56 consecutive games to establish record.

1942 Enrico Fermi of the United States splits the atom.

1944 D-Day in WW II, the Normandy Invasion.

President Roosevelt re-elected to a fourth term.

1945 Roosevelt dies; Harry Truman becomes president.

WW II ends in Europe.

United States drops atomic bombs on Hiroshima and on Nagasaki; Japan surrenders; war ends.

1946 U.N. General Assembly holds its first session in London.

1947 Jackie Robinson becomes first black to sign a major league baseball contract.

1948 Indian leader Mahatma Ghandi is assassinated.

U.S. Congress passes the Marshall Plan Act providing $17 billion in aid for Europe.

Harry Truman elected U.S. president.

1949 Apartheid begins in South Africa.

1950s

3M Events

1951 3M establishes its International Division, after the dissolution of Durex; international sales reach $20 million in first year; new international companies are created in Australia, Brazil, Canada, France, Germany, Mexico and the United Kingdom.

Explosion in minerals building kills 15 employees, injures 49.

3M announces first 4-for-1 stock split.

Thermo-Fax copier introduced.

3M's Technical Forum established.

1952 Guy Lombardo plays at 3M's 50th anniversary celebration attended by 11,000 St. Paul employees and guests.

Scotchlok electrical connectors and Scotchkote insulation introduced.

1953 Herb Buetow succeeds Carlton as president.

3M breaks ground for first new corporate headquarters (3M Center), building on a 325-acre site east of St. Paul.

1954 RCA uses Scotch magnetic tape to record TV programs for the first time.

The American Institute of Management names 3M one of the five best managed companies in the United States and includes it among the top 12 growth stocks.

U.S. Post Office fleet vehicles carry Scotchlite reflective decals.

1955 Central Research Laboratory moves into the first research facility at 3M Center, the new corporate headquarters. The building, #201, is the first of many new lab buildings.

1956 3M introduces Scotchgard fabric and upholstery protector to the textile industry.

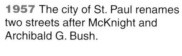

1957 The city of St. Paul renames two streets after McKnight and Archibald G. Bush.

1958 Scotch-Brite cleaning pads marketed for industrial use.

1959 Worldwide results are consolidated and sales exceed $500 million.

World Events

1950 Record crowd of 199,854 attends World Cup soccer game in Rio de Janeiro.

1951 "I Love Lucy" TV comedy debuts.

North Korean forces take Seoul and reject American truce offers.

Color television introduced.

1953 Queen Elizabeth II crowned.

Nobel Prize in literature is awarded to Winston S. Churchill.

Ben Hogan wins Masters, U.S. Open and British Open golf championships.

Edmund Hillary of New Zealand becomes first man to climb Mount Everest.

1954 Dr. Jonas Salk develops polio vaccine.

1956 Prince Rainier of Monaco and Grace Kelley are married.

1957 U.S.S.R. launches Sputnik I and II, the first satellites.

Mackinac Straits Bridge, Michigan—world's longest suspension bridge—opens.

1958 European Common Market established.

Governor Orval Faubus of Arkansas defies Supreme Court integration order by closing schools in Little Rock.

United States establishes National Aeronautics and Space Administration (NASA).

1959 Fidel Castro becomes premier of Cuba.

1960s

1960 Scotch Brand Magic transparent tape introduced.

Micropore surgical tape, the first hypoallergenic tape, introduced. It is a key to success of 3M Health Care business.

Sumitomo 3M joint venture created in Japan.

3M announces 3-for-1 stock split.

1961 3M subsidiaries established in Austria, Colombia, Denmark, Hong Kong and Norway.

International sales increase nearly sevenfold in one decade: from $20 million in 1951 to $136 million in 1961.

Manufacturing plants established in 12 countries: Argentina, Australia, Brazil, Canada, Colombia, United Kingdom, France, Germany, Japan, South Africa, Spain and Mexico.

1962 Building 220, the first of 3M Center's administration buildings, completed.

Tartan Turf, the first synthetic grass surface, introduced.

1963 Bert Cross named 3M's seventh president, succeeding Buetow.

3M's first research lab outside of the United States is completed in Harlow, England, near London.

The Carlton Society is created to honor career technical contributions.

1964 3M acquires Ferrania S.p.A., an Italian manufacturer of photographic products for professional, industrial and consumer markets.

1965 3M sales exceed $1 billion.

1966 McKnight steps down as board chair and becomes honorary chairman after 60 years with 3M; Cross named board chairman and CEO.

1967 3M develops the first disposable facemasks and respiratory protection products.

1969 3M products are used in the first moon walk on July 20, 1968. Astronaut Neil Armstrong leaves a footprint on lunar dust in boots made from Fluorel synthetic rubber from 3M.

Photo courtesy of NASA

1961 John F. Kennedy inaugurated as 35th U.S. president; establishes Peace Corps.

Yuri Gagarin (U.S.S.R.) orbits the earth in 6-ton satellite.

Alan Shepard makes first U.S. space flight.

1963 President Kennedy assassinated in Dallas, Tex.; Lyndon B. Johnson becomes president.

Dr. Michael DeBakey uses first artificial heart to take over the circulation of a patient's blood during heart surgery.

1964 Martin Luther King Jr. wins Nobel Peace Prize.

1965 Lyndon B. Johnson inaugurated as 36th president of the United States.

U.S. astronaut Edward White completes first space walk.

1966 Indira Gandhi becomes prime minister of India.

1967 Thurgood Marshall appointed to the U.S. Supreme Court.

Dr. Christiaan N. Barnard performs the world's first human heart transplant in South Africa.

1968 Martin Luther King is assassinated.

Sen. Robert Kennedy assassinated in Los Angeles.

1969 Richard M. Nixon inaugurated as 37th U.S. president.

Golda Meir named prime minister of Israel.

Apollo 11 lands on the moon's surface on July 20; Neil Armstrong walks on the moon.

1970s

3M Events

1970 New products include Scotchban paper treatment to protect food packaging and 3M box sealing tapes.

Riker Laboratories acquired.

Harry Heltzer succeeds Cross as chairman of the board and CEO.

1971 New medical products plant opens in Brookings, S.D.; decorative products plant opens in Nevada, Mo.

1972 Board of Directors recommends 2-for-1 stock split.

1973 First 11 Golden Step team winners honored.

McKnight retires from the Board of Directors, ending 66 years of service to 3M.

3M creates the first van-pooling program in the United States.

1974 Ray Herzog named CEO to succeed Heltzer.

1975 Pollution Prevention Pays (3P) program introduced.

3M Riker introduces Buf-Puf skin products.

1976 3M becomes one of 30 companies included in Dow Jones industrial average.

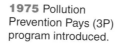

1977 3M Consumer Products Group established.

1978 Red 3M logo introduced.

McKnight, the architect and builder of 3M, dies.

1979 Lew Lehr succeeds Herzog as CEO and becomes chairman of the board in 1980.

3M annual sales top $5 billion.

New products include Thinsulate thermal insulation.

World Events

1971 The 26th Amendment to the U.S. Constitution, allowing 18-year-olds to vote, is ratified.

1972 Arab terrorists kill two Israeli Olympic athletes and nine other hostages in Munich.

1973 In a tennis match billed as the "battle of the sexes," Billie Jean King defeats Bobby Riggs, 6-4, 6-3, 6-3.

1974 Richard Nixon resigns; Vice President Gerald Ford becomes 38th U.S. president.

1976 North and South Vietnam are reunited as one country after 22 years of separation, with Hanoi as its capital.

Jimmy Carter is elected 39th U.S. president.

1977 Massive blackout in New York City leaves 9 million people without electricity for up to 25 hours.

1978 The first "test-tube baby" is born in England.

U.S. President Carter, Israeli Premier Menachem Begin and Egyptian President Anwar Sadat agree on a Camp David peace accord.

1979 The Shah of Iran is forced into exile and is replaced as Iranian leader by Ayatollah Khomeini; nearly 100 U.S. Embassy staff and Marines are taken hostage.

Conservative Margaret Thatcher becomes prime minister of Great Britain.

Disaster is narrowly averted at U.S. Three-Mile Island nuclear power plant.

1980s

1980 Post-it notes and Scotchcast casting tape introduced.

1984 3M reaches an agreement with China to establish a wholly owned company there.

3M and NASA announce joint research program exploring manufacturing in space. In November, first 3M research experiments are conducted on space shuttle Discovery.

Plans for new administrative offices and laboratories in Austin, Tex., announced.

Genesis program announced to encourage technical entrepreneurship in research and new product development.

1985 First refastenable diaper tapes introduced by 3M.

3M and Harris Corp. form a joint venture for worldwide marketing, sales and service of copiers and facsimile machines.

Academy of Motion Picture Arts and Sciences gives 3M a Scientific Engineering Award for magnetic film that improves audio capabilities of movie sound tracks.

3M becomes the 14th U.S. company to have its stock listed on Tokyo Stock Exchange.

The U.S. Food and Drug Administration approves the sale of 3M's Tambocor, a drug that controls irregular heartbeats.

1986 Lehr retires; Allen Jacobson succeeds him as chairman of the board and CEO.

3M ranks second on Fortune magazine's list of the most admired U.S. companies.

Scotchcal drag reduction tape, based on microreplication technology, helps the Stars & Stripes yacht win the America's Cup competition.

3M establishes six major technology centers in Europe to meet the special needs of European customers.

1987 M.J. Monteiro introduces 50/50 objective—50 percent of total revenue generated by international sales.

3M announces a 2-for-1 stock split.

3M acquires Unitek Corp., a worldwide supplier of orthodontic products.

1988 3M is worldwide sponsor of the Olympic Games.

3M global sales top $10 billion.

1980 The World Health Organization formally announces the global eradication of smallpox.

John Lennon is shot and killed in New York City.

Ronald Reagan is elected the 40th U.S. president.

1981 Iran releases all hostages.

Egyptian President Anwar Sadat is assassinated.

1982 The Vietnam Veterans' War Memorial is dedicated in Washington, D.C.; the names of more than 58,000 dead are inscribed.

1983 U.S. space shuttle Challenger is launched on its maiden flight and completes three missions in 1983.

1984 A silicon microchip that stores four times more data than previously possible is developed.

1985 President Ronald Reagan begins second term in office.

1986 The world's worst nuclear accident takes place when a reactor blows up at Chernobyl power station, Kiev, U.S.S.R.

The U.S. space shuttle Challenger explodes, killing all seven crew members.

1989 The Exxon Valdez causes the world's largest oil spill.

The Berlin Wall is opened by East Germany and eventually torn down.

George Bush becomes the 41st president of the United States.

1990s

1990 More than 30 percent of 3M's sales come from products introduced within the last five years.

3M introduces Pacing Plus product development programs that receive priority funding to speed product development.

1991 U.S. District Court of Minnesota enters a judgment in favor of 3M for $129 million against Johnson & Johnson for patent infringement of Scotchcast casting tape.

3M introduces Scotchshield window film, shatter-resistant, heat- and cold-resistant window protection.

Sales in Japan top $1 billion.

Jacobson retires and is succeeded by L.D. DeSimone as chairman of the board and CEO.

1992 For the first time, 50 percent of 3M sales come from international, reaching $7 billion.

1993 A toll free number, 1-800-3M HELPS, answers product inquiries from customers and 3Mers in the United States.

1994 Post-it easel pads introduced.

3M announces 2-for-1 stock split.

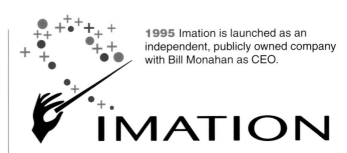

1995 Imation is launched as an independent, publicly owned company with Bill Monahan as CEO.

3M receives the National Medal of Technology—the highest award bestowed by the U.S. president for technological achievement.

3M debuts an Internet site giving its customers links to thousands of pages of information on 3M programs, products and technologies.

Junior Achievement posthumously inducts McKnight into its National Business Hall of Fame.

3M introduces the first metered dose asthma inhaler, free of ozone depleting chlorofluorocarbons.

1990 The first edition of Microsoft Windows 3.0 software is shipped to consumers.

The Hubble space telescope is placed into orbit by the U.S. space shuttle Discovery.

1991 Operation Desert Storm begins in response to the Iraqi army seizing of Kuwait.

1992 President George Bush and Russian President Boris Yeltsin proclaim a formal end to the Cold War.

The Mall of America, the largest shopping complex in the United States, opens in Bloomington, Minn.

Ten thousand cellular phones sold in the United States.

1993 William Clinton becomes the 42nd U.S. president.

A bomb explodes in the basement garage of the World Trade Center in New York City.

Martin Luther King national holiday is observed for the first time in all 50 states.

1995 A bomb explodes outside the Alfred P. Murrah Federal Building in Oklahoma City, killing 168 people.

1996 President Clinton appoints Madeline Albright the first female secretary of state.

AT&T introduces Internet access service.

2000

1996 New products include flexible circuits for electronic products and HFEs (hydroflouroethers), replacing ozone depleting chloro-fluorocarbons.

1997 Dental Products Division receives the Malcolm Baldrige National Quality Award, the most coveted quality award in American business.

National Ad Co., now known as 3M Media, sold.

Aldara (imiquimod) approved by the U.S. Food and Drug Administration.

1999 3M reorganizes into six business segments: Industrial; Transportation, Graphics and Safety; Health Care; Consumer and Office; Electro and Communications; and Specialty Material.

3M acquires the outstanding minority interest in Dyneon.

2000 For the first time, nearly 35 percent of sales come from products introduced in the previous four years.

3M introduces the Vikuiti brand for light management products that make electronic displays easier to read.

Michael Johnson wins gold in the 2000 Olympics' 400-meter sprint wearing shoes made from 24-carat gold Scotchlite fabric developed by 3M.

Restored 3M/Dwan Museum reopens in Two Harbors, Minnesota.

2001 DeSimone retires; W. James McNerney, Jr. named new chairman of the board and CEO.

Six Sigma quality improvement tools introduced at 3M.

3M Acceleration Program introduced to generate greater returns from R&D; significant additional corporate resources go to Pharmaceutical Division to speed research and development on immune response modifiers that have major market potential.

Cream, 5%
Aldara™
(IMIQUIMOD)

In response to Sept. 11th attacks on America, 3M and its employees and retirees donate more than $2 million in cash and products.

1998 The Dow Jones industrial average hits 9,000 for the first time in a single day's trading.

The Associated Press celebrates its 150th anniversary.

President Clinton names Eileen M. Collins the first woman to lead a U.S. space mission.

1999 The Senate fails to convict President Clinton on two articles of impeachment.

Scientists from the United States, Japan and England announce the first mapping of an entire human genome, part of the Human Genome Project.

2000 Dot.com companies proliferate, but the bubble bursts in spring 2001.

George W. Bush wins the U.S. presidential race after a lengthy recount in Florida.

2001 Three hijacked commercial jetliners destroy World Trade Center towers in New York City and hit the U.S. Pentagon, killing more

than 4,000. A fourth hijacked plane crashes in a field in Pennsylvania.

U.S. Congress approves military action in retaliation for "acts of war" and nations around the world join this "War on Terrorism."

2002 12 European nations start using the Euro, a common unit of monetary exchange.

1951 France   1951 Canada   1951

9

Going Global—
The Formative Years

Wetordry sandpaper was William McKnight's ticket to
Europe in the 1920s. Finally, his company had a hot
product that could compete with the best abroad. In those
days, only 4 percent of 3M's sales came from outside
the United States, but the number was certain to grow.
After all, in one country, human life was at stake.
England was desperate for an alternative to traditional
dry sanding because terrible evidence was accum-
ulating. Workers who dry-sanded paint finishes in
multiple industries were dying of lead poisoning
caused by the paint they used. Wet sanding
would keep the poisonous dust at bay.

While Britain's Parliament considered banning lead paint altogether, McKnight wrote to major companies suggesting the Wetordry sandpaper solution. Brimsdown Lead Co. Ltd. of Brimsdown, Middlesex, contacted McKnight immediately and 3M shipped off samples. Meanwhile, McKnight also dispatched Robert Skillman, 3M's Eastern Division sales manager, to Europe in 1922 to search for distributors who would handle 3M products, especially Wetordry sandpaper. Skillman's efforts paid off—in one year, sales of 3M's waterproof sandpaper in Britain jumped from less than $200 to more than $68,000 with a majority of the orders coming from auto manufacturers, wood workers and the railroads.

William McKnight had a wide vision in the 1930s. America was in a depression and Europe was in turmoil. It wasn't a time when a person would eagerly say, 'Let's go for it.' But, he did. > **John Marshall** *retired director, International Operations*

Understanding the potential of global expansion, McKnight made a compelling case to his board to budget $75,000 for manufacturing plants "across the pond." But, building a business in Europe wasn't like expanding in the United States. 3M needed foreign patents to cover its products. And, in several countries, products for sale could only be manufactured in the home country, not imported. Competition also was growing. American companies wanted a piece of the global business and they formed an export venture to promote U.S. abrasives in Europe, Africa and South America. In 1923, 3M joined that association (called the American Surface Abrasive Export Corporation) along with eight major competitors.

But, McKnight had more ambitious plans than export trade alone. He believed that 3M's global future would be based on strong patents around the world, strategic manufacturing sites chosen to serve international markets, a global sales and marketing network and—eventually—3M Research and Development labs in many countries.

> **McKnight: All Business in France**
McKnight made his first Atlantic crossing in 1924 to explore what it would take to secure foreign patents and begin manufacturing outside the United States, including acquiring other existing abrasives plants. Although he was 36 years old and on his first trip to Paris, the all-business McKnight took almost no time off to see the sights. When he finally convinced his boss to visit the Louvre Museum, Skillman complained that McKnight raced past miles of extraordinary art in 20 minutes.

After his first trip to Europe, McKnight decided to learn at least one language before he returned, said Virginia Huck, author of "The Brand of the Tartan" and 3M historian. "He asked his secretary, who spoke French fluently, if she would give him a lesson each morning,"

Chapter opening photos The International Department staff in 1944 consisted of three Millies: left to right, Mildred Jacobson, Mildred Berg and Mildred Alvig; Flags representing early 3M international companies hang in the Innovation Center at corporate headquarters in St. Paul; Language dictionaries served as a source of preparation for international recruits from St. Paul.

Huck wrote. "McKnight's spirit was willing, but his tongue was inept. He gave up and decided to depend on interpreters."

As 3M expanded its international reach in the 1950s, the company recognized that technology wasn't just being developed in the United States. New businesses overseas needed technical service support, just as 3M had always done in America. **> Geoff Nicholson** *retired staff vice president, Corporate Technical Planning and International Technical Operations*

McKnight's first attempts to acquire abrasives operations in France and Germany failed. His first try at manufacturing Wetordry sandpaper in England, in a shared patent arrangement with two British companies, also failed when 3M's major rival, Carborundum Company, threatened to build its own manufacturing operation on British soil. They predicted that more American competitors would surely follow.

The year was 1928. McKnight took a step back. He believed that the British market only could support one American abrasives operation. If the Americans were going to gain a foothold in Europe, they would either swim together or sink separately. That's why Durex Corporation—the company that ultimately propelled 3M into global

business—was formed in 1929. The U.S. Congress had passed a law that allowed American companies to pool their interests in order to compete in foreign trade. 3M and eight North American competitors created Durex, a holding company based in England, that could acquire stock in foreign ventures and manufacture abrasives and other patented products overseas. The partners also created Durex Abrasives Corporation, an organization that would sell a single line of coated abrasives all over the world using one sales force, instead of nine, and one brand, Durex, instead of many. In its first decade, however, Durex lacked focus and momentum.

After Armistice Day in 1945, McKnight stepped in and turned to Clarence Sampair, vice president, Manufacturing: "Mr. McKnight said, 'Our foreign operations are dying on the vine,'" Sampair recalled. "'If we're going to develop our overseas business, we've got to have people in the Durex operation to help develop new products and manufacturing ideas.'"

1 Robert Skillman, 3M's Eastern Division sales manager (left), with William McKnight. He was the first 3Mer to investigate potential international sales. **2** Durex Abrasives Corporation was formed in 1929 by 3M and eight competitors to sell a single line of coated abrasives to international markets.

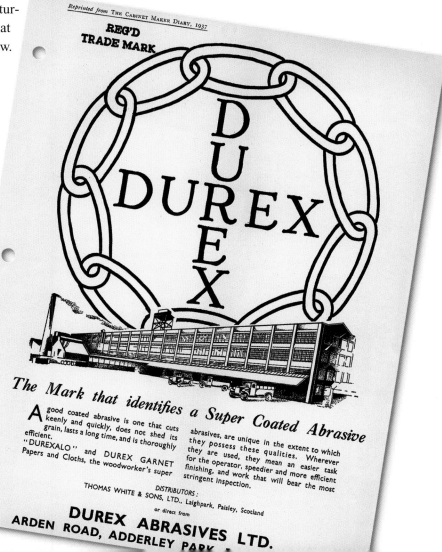

Reprinted from THE CABINET MAKER DIARY, 1937

REG'D TRADE MARK

DUREX

The Mark that identifies a Super Coated Abrasive

A good coated abrasive is one that cuts keenly and quickly, does not shed its grain, lasts a long time, and is thoroughly efficient. "DUREXALO" and DUREX GARNET Papers and Cloths, the woodworker's super abrasives, are unique in the extent to which they possess these qualities. Wherever they are used, they mean an easier task for the operator, speedier and more efficient finishing, and work that will bear the most stringent inspection.

DISTRIBUTORS:
THOMAS WHITE & SONS, LTD., Laighpark, Paisley, Scotland
or direct from

DUREX ABRASIVES LTD.
ARDEN ROAD, ADDERLEY PARK

'Please Write Soon'

Clarence Sampair bounced around Minnesota and South Dakota before he joined 3M in 1927. Though he studied mechanical engineering for two years, he graduated from the University of Minnesota with a liberal arts degree. "The engineering school was pretty narrow in those days," he said, "and I always liked English and history."

Sampair sold reference books to country school teachers and then started his own business with three derelict trucks. "It was the era when some of the first cement highways were built in Minnesota," he said. "I drove one of the trucks, hauling gravel, and I had a couple of drivers for the other two. We worked hard all day and I fixed the trucks by night. The longer the road crews worked, the more I thought I made. But, it all went back into keeping the trucks repaired."

By late summer 1927, Sampair's trucks were ready for the junk heap. He didn't have any other prospects, so he searched the help wanted ads and found this one: "Technical man or man with some technical experience wanted, please write soon." Although he was a St. Paul native, Sampair had never heard of Minnesota Mining and Manufacturing Company.

Sampair went to work for Richard Carlton. "We haven't had any real quality control in our factory," Carlton told Sampair, "but we think we need some. I don't know exactly what this job will turn out to be, but it's probably going to be whatever you make it."

And, make it, Sampair did. During his 43-year career at 3M, Sampair became president, Manufacturing. Seven years later, McKnight chose him to lead 3M into the global marketplace. Sampair retired as president, International Division.

> **The Demise of Durex**

Sampair recruited 3M people to join Durex. They became plant managers or started new Durex operations in Canada, Brazil and Australia. They became directors of engineering and research: "We were well represented," said Sampair, retired president, International Division. "That was important because 3M was supplying more new products to Durex than any of the other partners."

But, McKnight's international ambition seemed inhibited by Durex, and the political winds from Washington suggested that antitrust and Durex were certain to collide in the courts. McKnight also wanted to secure a reliable source of raw materials. In 1950, 3M bought more than 85 percent of the materials it

It had been operating as a guess and by-God thing. By the time World War II came, Durex hadn't made much progress. > **Clarence Sampair**

retired president, International Division

needed to make coated abrasives from other companies. The best solution was a merger with Carborundum with 3M as the majority owner.

About the time that merger was announced, a bill authored by Senator Estes Kefauver was passed by Congress and found its way to President Harry Truman's

1 3M's St. Paul Commercial League Golf team won the championship in 1937. The team included Herb Buetow (standing, second from left) and Clarence Sampair (seated, right).

*Background:
3M purple sanding belt*

desk. This "anti-merger" bill took a rifle shot at mergers and acquisitions that hinted of monopoly and 3M scrapped a plan to merge with Carborundum.

The U.S. Justice Department also took direct aim at Durex and argued that the holding company was in violation of the Sherman Antitrust Act. "We weren't too unhappy with the breakup of Durex. It left us free to go our own way and Mr. McKnight had great intuition for international business," said Sampair, "but we were very disappointed in losing Carborundum. It was a coincidence that both events happened at the same time."

During the Durex years, 3M had invested about $875,000 in its foreign operations and the returns hadn't met McKnight's expectations.

There were only four partners left in Durex when it was dissolved: 3M, Behr-Manning, Carborundum and Armour. When they divided up the company's assets in 1951, 3M inherited a sandpaper plant in England, a small plant in France, an office in Germany and a tape factory in Brazil. They agreed that top managers from Durex could choose where they wanted to go. "We got a good cross section of the top people," Sampair said. "In fact, we probably got more than our share." 3M's total international sales in its first year reached $20 million.

> Frame that Judge!

Fifty years later, people who experienced the breakup of Durex and others—who only heard about it—agree that it was one of the most important events in the life of 3M. John Whitcomb, retired group vice president, Abrasives,

Adhesives, Building Services and Chemicals Group, quipped that a portrait of Judge Charles Wyzanski, who ordered Durex's dissolution, should have been framed and hung in 3M's boardroom to honor his "jump start" of 3M's International Operations.

Instead of participating in joint ventures and coalitions, 3M created one of the most significant, competitive advantages in the world: a long-standing, strong, international presence.

> **John Ursu** *senior vice president, Legal Affairs and General Counsel*

But, the choice to pursue international growth was not an obvious one. In the early 1950s, most American companies were focused on domestic growth and few had the international ambitions of McKnight and his entrepreneurial sidekicks, Sampair and Maynard Patterson, who later retired as group vice president, International Division. There were few global trade models to follow so 3M, in characteristic fashion, invented its own.

"American companies had the advantage of an industrial and research base largely in place and a large home market in the United States, while Europe and Asia were rebuilding after the war," said Harry Hammerly, retired executive vice president, 3M International Operations.

3M got a head start in developing its European business because Jack Davies, the former sales manager for Durex, joined 3M and brought 60 percent of Durex's

2 A 1955 meeting of 3M's International managing directors, standing left to right: Bill Winslow, Brazil; Clarence Sampair, president of 3M International Division; Jack MacKenzie, England; Lou Spiess, Mexico; and Maynard Patterson, Canada. Seated left to right: Werner Herold, France; Dick Priebe, Australia; and Robert Scarlett, Germany.

35 Companies in 20 Years

These 3M international companies began operations in the 1950s:

1951 Australia, Brazil, Canada, France, Germany, Mexico, United Kingdom
1952 Argentina
1953 South Africa
1956 Netherlands
1957 Spain
1959 Italy

These 3M international companies had their start in the 1960s:

1960 Japan (Sumitomo 3M), Puerto Rico
1961 Austria, Colombia, Denmark, Hong Kong, Norway
1962 Belgium, Sweden, Zimbabwe
1963 Peru, Switzerland-Zurich
1964 Philippines
1965 Lebanon, Venezuela
1966 Panama, Portugal, Singapore
1967 Malaysia, Thailand
1969 Finland, Switzerland-East, Taiwan

European distributor network with him, as well as sales managers who were natives of Switzerland, the Netherlands, France and Italy. Other people who made up 3M's international "A team" included Bob Scarlett, Andy Donaldson, Al Butz, Werner Herold, Cal Corwin, Bob Young, Dick Priebe, Audun Fredriksen and Jim Thwaits.

> **The Advantages of Building from Scratch**

It took almost 15 years in England and eight years in Brazil before 3M had the right combination of people and operations, Sampair said. "The two we inherited

> 3M was in the top 20 U.S. companies with international operations in the 1950s. We reached our goal of 25 percent of sales overseas early and there weren't many that did it. We were ahead of the curve. > **Maynard Patterson**
>
> *retired group vice president, International Division*

from Durex took a long while to make over, but the businesses we built from scratch developed more rapidly. I think our standards were higher and we were never satisfied with what we took over."

There were two notable exceptions, however: CETA in Paris and Carstens in Germany. "CETA gave us our first

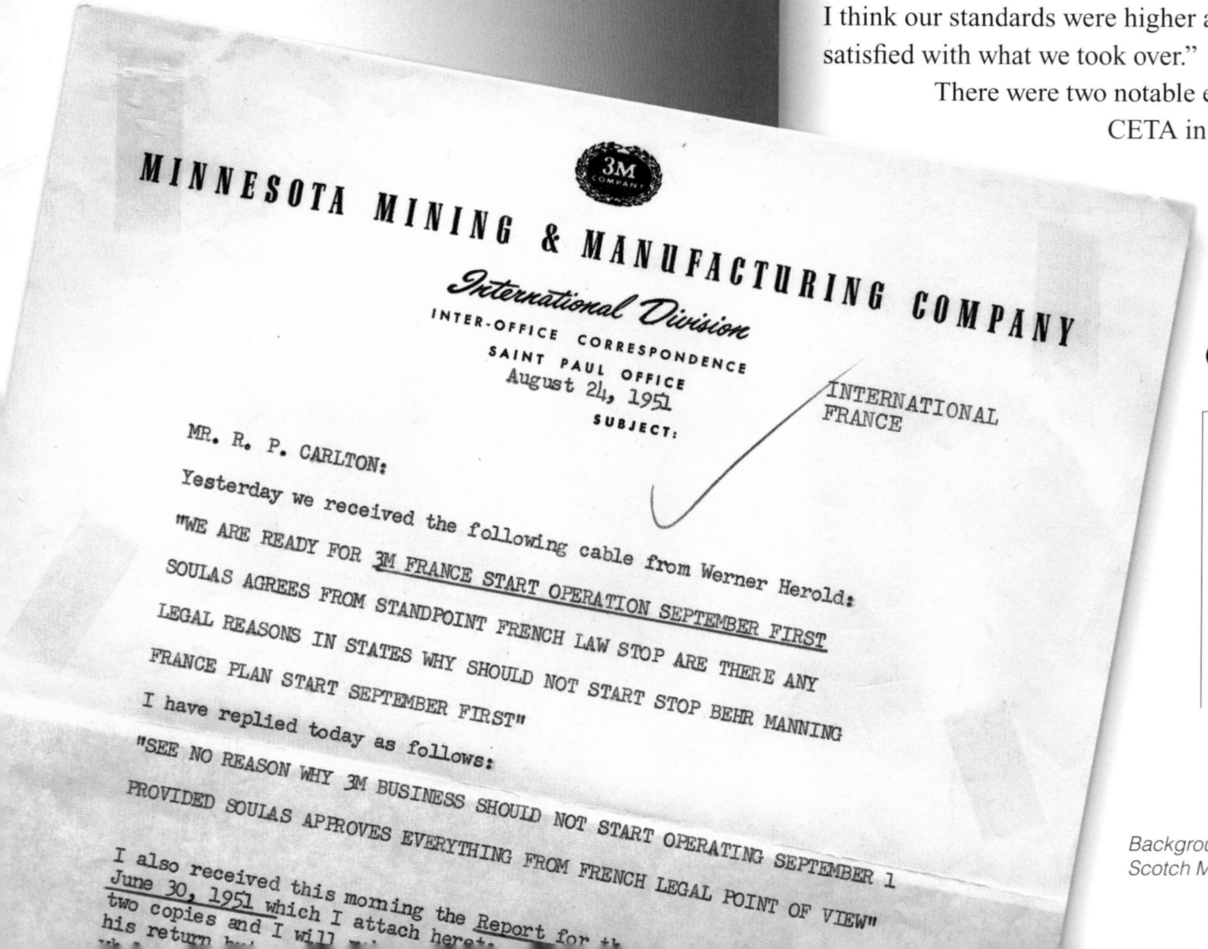

MINNESOTA MINING & MANUFACTURING COMPANY

International Division

INTER-OFFICE CORRESPONDENCE
SAINT PAUL OFFICE
August 24, 1951
SUBJECT:

INTERNATIONAL
FRANCE

MR. R. P. CARLTON:

Yesterday we received the following cable from Werner Herold:

"WE ARE READY FOR 3M FRANCE START OPERATION SEPTEMBER FIRST SOULAS AGREES FROM STANDPOINT FRENCH LAW STOP ARE THERE ANY LEGAL REASONS IN STATES WHY SHOULD NOT START STOP BEHR MANNING FRANCE PLAN START SEPTEMBER FIRST"

I have replied today as follows:

"SEE NO REASON WHY 3M BUSINESS SHOULD NOT START OPERATING SEPTEMBER 1 PROVIDED SOULAS APPROVES EVERYTHING FROM FRENCH LEGAL POINT OF VIEW"

I also received this morning the Report for th June 30, 1951 which I attach heret two copies and I will al his return

1 Memo to 3M President Dick Carlton confirming the opening of 3M France operations. **2** A 1958 French television commercial for Sasheen ribbon and Scotch cellophane and gift wrap tapes.

Background: Scotch Magic tape

home in France and an office and address we could be proud of—something we didn't have before," Sampair said. To help finance growth in that country, 3M also borrowed against CETA's valuable real estate—an asset that meant more to French bankers than sales and prof-

The timing was right. 3M got off to a fast start at a time when world trade was expanding.

> **Jim Thwaits** *retired president, International Operations*

its. 3M did the same in Germany in which the old and respected Carstens name matched with prime property in Hamburg. It helped them avoid running to St. Paul for a cash infusion.

From the start of 3M's international business, the company insisted that foreign ventures pay their own way. In addition, 3M's international companies were expected to pay St. Paul a 5 percent to 10 percent royalty, first. "Our biggest problem was providing ourselves with working capital because we were expanding so rapidly," Sampair said. "Royalties had to be authorized by the governments of the countries in which we operated, and we had to pay them promptly to St. Paul. Our borrowing base in France and Germany gave us a tremendous financial boost."

In its formative years, the International Division was viewed by many in the company as an entrepreneurial venture run by a band of mavericks who had broad freedom to do what they needed to help their embryonic

companies survive and thrive. "It was an adrenaline rush, day after day," said Patterson. "My feet weren't even touching the ground. We were dealing with big decisions and big numbers. I built a strong fence around International Division to keep most everybody out. If we got caught up in all the red tape of a big corporation, we were sure to drown.

"Let's say the Australia factory needed a new boiler house. We couldn't afford to send 15 different people to Australia to build it." Instead, Patterson had his own, small engineering team. They picked the brains of 3M experts in St. Paul and used that reservoir of knowledge to get the job done quickly.

Until the late 1960s, the International Division was separate. Management basically said, 'You guys go out there and see what you can do.' Then, all of a sudden, it was a big business.

> **Harry Hammerly** *retired vice president, International Operations*

To unburden new managing directors from well-meaning help offered by headquarters, Patterson protected them. "I asked Em Monteiro to start a small company in Colombia," Patterson said. "I told him to pick the key person he wanted to take with him. 'Go start a company,' I said, 'and no one from St. Paul is going to visit you unless you ask for them. We'll stay out of your way and if someone sticks his nose in your business,

you call me.'" It was the same way Richard Carlton counseled Patterson when he joined 3M and took the assignment to start 3M Canada. "My job was to keep all those helpful folks away," said Patterson.

3M's strategy is global, but implementation has to be local. > **Giulio Agostini** *retired senior vice president, Finance and Administrative Services*

> **Gaining a Strong Footing**

As soon as possible, the International Division bought out its distributors. "Distributors didn't spend money developing our new products," Sampair said. "They saw it as a losing proposition, even though the new product might be a big money maker in future years." Some distributors resisted being acquired and, when negotiations came to a standstill, 3M started new operations independently. "In Italy, we gave our distributors notice and

You can't secure a great deal of foreign business by sending a salesman out with a bag of samples of our 40,000 products and an order pad.

> **Jim Thwaits**

set up shop in about three days in Milan," Sampair said. "The same thing happened in Switzerland." By 1962, 3M had either acquired all of its European distributors or gone into business on its own.

3M's international growth occurred in stages, said John McDevitt, retired 3M corporate economist. "We started out exporting to a country and working through

3M's decision to establish wholly owned foreign companies after 1950 will prove to be the most significant organizational step ever taken.

> **Lew Lehr** *retired chairman of the board and CEO*

sales subsidiaries. In that way, we began to understand the country, the business community and the needs of the marketplace." After that step, 3M established warehouse operations to stock goods and paid for those goods in local currency. "The next phase was converting products locally to the sizes that the market, custom and culture dictated," McDevitt said. "3M shipped jumbo rolls of products from St. Paul to each country

1 International ads from 1959 showed that the appeal of Scotch brand tapes translates into any language. **2** By 1956, Clarence Sampair (left) and Maynard Patterson were regular passengers on TWA flights.

Background:
3M purple sanding belt

where they were converted and packaged in the local language. The last stage was designing and building plants, buying machinery, and getting them up and running. It was a relatively low cost, affordable approach."

> ### International: Creator of Champions

From the start of the International business, Sampair believed that overseas management was the training ground for 3M's future leaders, even though some viewed the assignment as a career-breaker.

Managing directors of international companies ranked considerably lower than U.S. group vice presidents, even though Sampair believed they had equal or

Some of us still remember seeing the crate stamped 'Reject, Ship to International' in 3M European warehouses in the 1960s. Come to think of it, maybe that's how I got into international . . . > **Harry Hammerly**

even greater responsibility. "International is the place to train future 3M presidents," Sampair argued forcefully. "If we give those jobs the recognition they deserve, we could interest some of our new group vice presidents and they'd get a lot more education than they do in the United States. We should have ambitious people in those leadership positions and they should have staff people of their own to

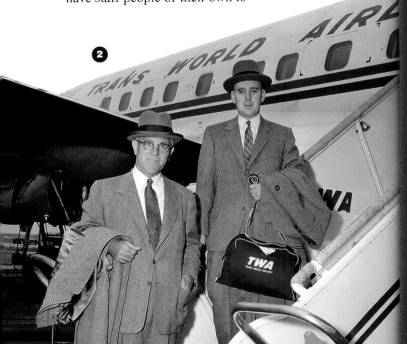

2

The Bootstrap Kid

The choice was easy for Maynard Patterson. When Durex disappeared, he picked 3M. "They had more products," he said, "and more diversity."

Patterson was a native of the Gaspe region of Quebec, Canada, whose family moved to New Jersey when he was a boy. After graduating from high school, Patterson found work as a messenger at AT&T headquarters in New York. He became a "page" (a glorified errand boy) for the chairman of the company and the top man took an interest in the hard working teen-ager.

"What are you doing in a job like this?" he asked Patterson. " 'I've got to work, Mr. Gifford,' " Patterson answered. "Ever thought of going to college?" the CEO asked. Patterson had no resources, so Gifford arranged a full scholarship through AT&T. The page became a metallurgical engineer at Lehigh University and enlisted in the U.S. Army only a few months after the bombing of Pearl Harbor. Patterson was assigned to a colonel who, in his civilian life, was a Durex executive.

In 1951, in his first assignment for 3M, Patterson returned to his home country to organize the company's Canadian subsidiary in London, Ontario, with a check for $5,000.

"Although global expansion probably would have occurred even if Canada wasn't here, we are the granddaddy of the international companies," said Ian Service, senior specialist, Environmental & Regulatory Affairs, 3M Canada. "Many other international companies still come to 3M Canada to find out how we get things done."

In its first nine months, 3M Canada generated $284,000 in revenues. Just five years later, Clarence Sampair chose Patterson as his successor to run the International Division. With the help of Patterson's leadership, 3M's global sales rose from $54 million in 1956 to more than $675 million in 1970 with operations on six continents. By 2001, international sales would account for 53 percent of global sales.

give them the counsel they need." Time would prove Sampair right.

"Sampair and Patterson established an environment in which people in each country could grow," said Jim Thwaits, retired president, International Operations. "They gathered together a lean and hungry team and they pinned the rose of responsibility on the line management in each country. They had the U.S. company to draw from, but they didn't have it trying to run everything around the world. They were flexible enough to marry a solid business philosophy with local customs and patterns. 3M was able to be first with the most in many places."

> **Voices from the Field**

'Trust Me, Please Accept' It wasn't an easy assignment, but it wasn't meant to be. Thwaits was chief engineer of 3M Canada in 1955 when Sampair asked him to go to Brazil for three years and become chief engineer there. "Anyone who went to Brazil got a phrase book and learned some sledgehammer Portuguese," Thwaits said. "That was the preparation."

3M's young tape and abrasives plant in Brazil had some big challenges. The plant only ran two or three days a week. Why? There was no water. To solve that fundamental problem, 3M purchased more than 700 acres of land south of Campinas, Brazil—enough for the plant and a big reservoir on the property to catch water during the rainy season. That "lake water" lasted the

whole year. Equally challenging, the plant didn't have electrical power, so 3M shipped a big, second-hand diesel generator to Brazil from the United States.

The trouble was, Thwaits said, "It only worked a couple days a week and no one knew how to fix or maintain it." Tariffs and stiff regulations made importing engine parts to Brazil virtually impossible, so—on a brief return to the States—Thwaits visited the

When I began with 3M in 1954, I didn't believe how that small beginning was the start of a successful, multimillion-dollar company. There was a spirit of pitching in, being in a big family and working together to solve problems, no matter what your position was. > **Bruce Chapman**

retired managing director, 3M Australia

diesel engine manufacturer. He spent a week studying the engine, taking notes and drawing schematics. Then he found a small job shop in Rio de Janeiro that could make spare parts.

Communication, in those days, was terrible, Thwaits said. "We'd wait for days to get a telephone call. Airmail letters took a week and cable was fast, about three days, but very expensive.

"We got the generator going, the plant running, and we had water. I trained in the new engineer and I was ready to go back to Canada," said Thwaits. That is,

AUSTRALIA
St. Marys

BRASIL
Campinas

CANADA
London

FRANCE
Beauchamp
Pantin

GERMANY
Düsseldorf

St. Paul, Minn.

GREAT BRITAIN
ENGLAND
Birmingham
Slough
WALES
Gorseinon
Tredegar

MEXICO
Mexico City

UNITED STATES
New York

3M COMPANY INTERNATIONAL

until Sampair asked him to go to 3M England, instead. No way, thought Thwaits, and he said so. "But, you just don't understand," Sampair said in a return cable. "We need you in England. I'll guarantee that you'll be back in North America in three years. We'll send you over first class with your family. We'll take care of everything. Trust me. Please accept."

"I cabled back and said, 'Mr. Sampair, I got the message. I trust you,'" Thwaits said. "3M expected everything from you, but they wouldn't shortchange you, if you didn't shortchange them. Anyone who got the job done went on to another country."

Woody on the Fly Woody Woods started 3M South Africa in his Johannesburg home in 1953. "My wife was the typist on an old manual typewriter," he said. "We ran the company for two years like that." Woods said 3M soon outstripped its competitors and claimed a major share of the market. "We moved from importing tapes, and then abrasives, to manufacturing them around 1960," he said. "3M gave us the area not just in South Africa, but everywhere about 10 degrees north of the equator."

Because communication was poor, Woods covered his territory piloting a small plane on a circular route from Kenya to Ethiopia, Ghana, Nigeria and the Congo. "My wife kept things going while I was away," he said. "She had a thick book that described every 3M product in detail and she booked appointments for clients on my return several weeks later. She played a big part in the growth of the company."

Gilhespy in the Eastern Bloc Brayshaw (Bob) Gilhespy, a native of the United Kingdom, was part of the original team that founded Minnesota/Europa (later called 3M East) in Switzerland in the late 1960s with the aim of building business for 3M in the Eastern Bloc Communist countries of Europe. The assignment required patience. Each country worked on a five-year plan and imbedded in that plan were the clues about what 3M products would be most saleable.

In Belfast, I knew and worked with no one else but Irishmen. Then I came to New Zealand and joined 3M. Straight-away, I found I was working in a real United Nations. There were 12 different nationalities, not just in 3M as a whole, but in my department! > **Ian Mackay** *tape factory production foreman, 3M United Kingdom*

"First, we'd have to get them interested," Gilhespy said, "then we'd have to show the governments how our products fit their plans." Fortunately, he said, the leaders of 3M international businesses were successful in selling St. Paul on a long-term investment in Eastern Europe. "We prepared five-year forecasts to show how the business would grow if 3M had a company, starting with sales, moving to converting, then manufacturing," he said. "We tried to nail down all costs, all investments needed, price increases, whether the Communists would

1 A special international issue of the *Megaphone,* 3M's employee publication, in 1954. **2** Jim Thwaits (center) pictured in 1972 with Woody Woods, managing director, 3M South Africa, and Woods' wife.

still be in charge. If we could break even in three years, the returns would rise sharply after that— once we were established." The projections were solid and support came from St. Paul. Through its existence, Gilhespy said 3M East never lost money.

"Some of our sales were bartered—goods for goods—involving two transactions and sometimes three or four; we called those four-cornered shots," he said. Regardless of the goods, Gilhespy had to find the country that could pay cash. "Sometimes it would be scrap iron, paper, packaging products," he said. "I distinctly remember 20 railway cars of scrap iron coming out of Bulgaria and we decided to check one. We found a foot layer of stones below the iron. That took a little discussion."

Anyone who joined 3M East as a sales representative received a letter outlining dos and don'ts in the Eastern Bloc. "They included currency transactions, under-the-counter deals," Gilhespy said, "and proper behavior." Everyone had to sign, showing that they understood.

Gilhespy spent 70 percent of his time traveling in the Eastern Bloc. In those days, Westerners were not allowed to live in the East and that meant thousands of passport stamps and checkpoints.

Losing Mr. McKnight and Other Travel Tales

In the early years of the International Division, travel was arduous, often unpredictable and life in global outposts required flexibility.

Clarence Sampair estimated that half of his international working time was spent commuting from one country or city to another by train or propeller airplanes. One of those planes carried William McKnight to Sweden when a major distributor insisted on talking to the head man. "We got very concerned because Mr. McKnight wasn't at the airport and we couldn't get any word from the airline," Sampair said. "He had been delayed almost 24 hours. While we comforted his wife, Maude, we started making long-distance calls. The plane had left New York all right, but he never landed in Copenhagen."

1 William McKnight's briefcase traveled the world on 3M International business. **2** Georgette and Clarence Sampair (left) and Maude and William McKnight set sail on a European trip in 1955. **3** Jeahette Spiess (far right), with sons Duane (left) and Gerry and two stewards, sailed to Australia in 1946.
4 Em Monteiro and his wife, Maddie, were en route to Brazil in 1957 with their five children, left to right: Warren, Mark, Marguerite, Marilyn and John.

Finally, Sampair, who retired as president, International Division, learned that McKnight's plane had run into a storm over the North Sea and the pilot had landed in a remote Danish village. McKnight spent a sleepless night in a tiny, country inn. "McKnight was more than 70 years old at the time. It was an unforgettable experience for him—and us," said Sampair.

On another early occasion, McKnight, Sampair, Richard Carlton and a few colleagues chartered a single engine biplane to visit 3M's Gorseinon plant in the United Kingdom. Carlton, a former World War I pilot, was comfortable in the old planes, but others were leery. "Don't worry," Carlton said, "this is an all metal plane. It's one of the most stable." As it turned out, some of the plane's fuselage was actually made of fabric. When they arrived in Gorseinon, Wales, the pilot gamely buzzed the landing strip a few times to clear the sheep off the grass runways.

"I can't imagine what it must have been like for them to jump on an airplane or a boat and be gone for 12 to 13 weeks," said Ray Richelsen, retired executive vice president, Transportation, Graphics and Safety Markets. "They didn't have an infrastructure. They had nothing."

Jeanette Spiess moved to Australia to join her husband, Lou, in 1946, with their two children, ages 6 and 9. The trio traversed half the world on a troop ship converted to a passenger vessel with nothing but sleeping bunks. When she arrived, longshoremen were striking in

Australia and all of the Spiess family's household goods were sent right back to America. The family camped out, Lou Spiess said, until their belongings made the return trip. While Spiess supervised construction of a Durex tape plant (that later became 3M Australia), his wife adjusted to boiling clothes to clean them and regular visits from a horsedrawn milk cart that deposited their order in a Billy Can.

Madelyn (Maddie) Monteiro traveled to Campinas, Brazil, in 1957 when her husband, Manuel, took over operation of 3M's small plant while his predecessor spent a year at 3M in St. Paul. With their five children, the Monteiros boarded a ship traveling from New York to Santos, Brazil, because there was no reliable airline connection. "We sailed for 17 days with two of our kids in diapers and no air conditioning," she said. Children were expected to eat separately from adults (who wore formal dress in the evenings), so the Monteiros took turns escorting their children to meals.

The trip from Santos to Campinas was 90 miles on rough country roads. When Maddie Monteiro shopped at a nearby market, most food was fresh and little was canned, there was no prepared baby food and no ground coffee. "It was like stepping back in time, but I'd grown up in the Depression and I remembered similar days in America," she said. By writing grocery lists in Portuguese, Monteiro learned the local

language and, by shopping, she mastered Brazilian currency.

The pioneering families of 3M International were a fraternity. "The women were very resourceful and helpful," Monteiro said. "When I arrived, they showed me the ropes. They knew the doctors and dentists because they raised their children there. We always had someone else to help out and our friendships lasted for years, long after our overseas assignments." Em Monteiro eventually retired as vice president, International Operations.

Those years left lasting memories and a magnetic attraction for some. In his adult life, one member of the Monteiro family, John Manuel, returned to Brazil to teach history and anthropology in Campinas.

Fredriksen: Relentless Pursuit Audun Fredriksen remembers 3M "inheriting the remnants" of Durex when he traveled to Europe in the early 1950s to do research on a reflective sheeting. (He'd wind up becoming managing director, 3M Germany, five years later.) "Some of the operations were up-to-date but, in other cases, they were virtually nonexistent. Basically, we had to start from scratch. The drive and motivation to build International came only after 3M controlled its own future."

I met a gentleman recently in 3M Thailand. He said, 'Let me tell you what just happened. My new neighbor introduced himself and asked me where I worked. I said, 'I work for 3M' and he said, 'That's a very fine company.' It made me proud.' We want our people to be proud to be a part of 3M. **> Ron Baukol** *retired executive*

vice president, International Operations

The opportunities, Fredriksen said, seemed limitless. "There were still enormous wounds and destruction from World War II, but there was a terrific work ethic in Europe because people were very grateful to have a job." 3M tapes, adhesives, Scotchlite reflective sheeting and abrasives were the best selling products and 3M had tough competition in abrasives from German and other American competitors. "We were

relentless in our pursuit of higher quality and leading edge products," Fredriksen said. "We believed we could outperform our competitors at any time and we had an inventive campus back in St. Paul that supported us."

But, not always. 3M products made in America were not one-size-fits-all. Because it had a different format, for example, European letterhead was a different size so it couldn't be used with 3M's American overhead projectors. And, because electrical cables were larger in Europe than the United States, the American molds for making splicing products were useless overseas. "We had a tough time convincing headquarters that we needed product adaptations," Fredriksen said. "We just did it ourselves, but it wasn't always approved. That was our version of bootlegging. Sampair and Patterson covered our flanks back home."

Spiess: South of the Border Lou Spiess spent 15 years in Mexico, later retiring as vice president, Manufacturing and Engineering, after 40 years with 3M. His career began in 1952 when 3M rented an old tannery and bought a $25,000 coating machine. "It may sound unbelievable, but we turned it into a nice plant that, incidentally, had the lowest factory cost of any 3M international company at the time," Spiess said. "I was devoted to 3M and I liked the challenges I was given. Everyone I worked with seemed to feel the same way. If 3M succeeded, we would too.

"We imported all our raw materials, and our biggest product was masking tape because GM, Ford and

MINNESOTA MANUFACTURERA DE MEXICO, S. A. DE C. V.

CALZ. SN. JUAN DE ARAGON Nº 516   FCA. 17-82-10

MEXICO 14, D. F.   RESIDENCIA 20-50-76

3M

LOUIS S. SPIESS

GERENTE DE LA PLANTA Y V. PRES. DE PROD.

4

Chrysler were all assembling cars in Mexico," Spiess said. As good fortune would have it, the government of Mexico closed its borders to imported finished goods, so 3M Mexico dominated the tape market in its earliest years there. Mexico also granted 3M a five-year tax exemption.

Spiess was a progressive manager. In the early 1950s, he hired a blind Mexican worker who helped plant production by unwinding defective rolls of product and saving the tape cores. He hired buses to pick up people

> I entered 3M when I was 15 years old, on April 4, 1951. We lived happy lives and many marriages started here. I felt the company's goals were like my own. **> Rita Alvarez** *production line worker for 40 years, 3M Argentina*

and bring them to work. "They were lucky," Spiess said, "if they had a bicycle." Spiess planned holiday parties for the plant staff. "We had a Santa Claus and a Christmas tree, and we'd give gifts to all the kids," Spiess said. "Most of our employees' families were poor, but they brought their little girls in fancy dresses." When the 3M

Mexico plant was dedicated, it was customary to have it blessed by a local priest. And, when factory workers decided to plan a pilgrimage to the Catholic shrine of Guadelupe, Spiess accompanied them. "I always believed that if I treated our employees with respect," he said, "they would respect me in return."

Guion: Nix the Penthouse When Vern Guion, a multilingual Minnesotan, joined the International Division in 1950, the operation was called the Foreign Department and it was run by Mildred Jacobson and a handful of other women. "I had my desk right behind hers while I was working in the Tape Division," he said. "She asked me to translate letters in German, French and Spanish." Guion was named vice president and managing director, 3M Mexico, in 1962.

The downtown office of 3M Mexico had an elevator, a terrace and a penthouse. "I told management that I felt guilty about the luxurious layout and they agreed it was not in good taste," Guion said. "I made it my priority to get out of there. That's how we generated more profits, by cutting costs." Community service was also a priority. "We sponsored a Little League baseball club, bought the uniforms, provided the dugouts and equipment," said Guion. "It was the first time, and maybe the only time, some of those kids had shoes on.

"We worked closely with the local police and safety officials and made our conference room and equipment available to them for meetings," he said. "I even became an honorary lieutenant."

3

1 An employee at 3M Mexico fabricated Scotchlite road signs in 1958. **2** Vern Guion (left) with employees involved in a Little League club sponsored by 3M Mexico in 1962. **3** 3M Mexico's Little League club. **4** Lou Spiess, who later retired as vice president, Manufacturing and Engineering, spent 15 years in Mexico.

> **Japan: A Frontier with High Potential**
After World War II ended, 3M created a task
force to examine the opportunities in Japan, but
there was some resistance in St. Paul. Dennis
Maher, who rose from a 3M office boy to managing director, 3M Germany, was part of that task
force, which also included 3M's future CEO,
Harry Heltzer: "We went back and forth to
Japan two or three times in 1958 and 1959,"
Maher said. "We explored markets for
our product lines, laid out a strategy and put
together presentations to convince the Japanese that
we should be allowed in their country. That's when
I really became enamoured with International."

"There were still anti-Japanese feelings right after
the war," said Patterson, not to mention a touch of
American provincialism in St. Paul. But, Sampair
backed Patterson and told him to get McKnight's blessing, which he did.

"When Sumitomo 3M was established, Japanese
companies were not very competitive," said Hiroshi
Kurosaki, technical service, Electrical Specialties and
Electronic Products Divisions, Sumitomo 3M. "Even
just importing U.S. products and selling them 'as is' was
better than what Japanese manufacturers could offer.
The very mention of 3M entering the Japanese market
caused an uproar from local corporations and it was
compounded because 3M was in a joint venture with
very powerful and well-known corporations—Sumitomo
Electric and NEC. It scared the competition."

The negotiations in Japan were
long and hard, but 3M was able to
craft a very unusual 50/50 ownership
arrangement that was a first in 3M

At most Japanese companies, you're told
to do just as your superiors instruct. At
Sumitomo 3M, within two months I was
entrusted with my own customers and
territory and encouraged to take responsibility
and make decisions on my own. At first it was
difficult, but I came to appreciate the freedom
to think on my own. > **Yoshiharu Maeda** *salesman,
Industrial Tape Division, Sumitomo 3M*

history. 3M had always insisted on 100 percent ownership of any international subsidiary, perhaps harkening
back to the Durex days when 3M was only one voice
among many. "Sumitomo 3M Limited was formed in
1960," said Shigeru ("Lefty") Sato, retired director,
Public Relations and Government Affairs, a native of
Osaka who joined Sumitomo Corp. after his college
graduation. "There were 14 companies in the Sumitomo
Group and the joint venture was designed to import,
manufacture and market 3M products to the Japanese.
The first year we only had 18 employees and sales of
about $2,000."

1 Employees and their families enjoyed a company picnic in 1961, just one year after Sumitomo 3M was established in Japan.

Today, Sumitomo 3M has about 3,000 employees and the largest Research and Development lab outside of the United States, housing more than 500 scientists and technical people. "3M had a policy about going abroad and Japan was no exception," said Sato, who spent 36 years with 3M. "3M believed that overseas companies should be run chiefly by local people who understood the language, culture and business practices," he said. "I think that philosophy goes right back to McKnight's belief in respecting the individual and trusting people. Out of 36,000 overseas employees today, there are only about 200 from St. Paul in management. The second important principle was being a good corporate citizen in every country 3M entered.

We speak the same language around the world. Not the English language, but the language of our company. **> Giulio Agostini**

That was long before people in business talked about it. These two philosophies have been strong over the years."

3M devoted 1951 to organizing the International Division and the resulting growth spurt started and continued unabated. International revenues leaped from $18 million in 1951 to $136 million in 1960 and finally $552 million by the decade's end, generated by 35 companies around the world.

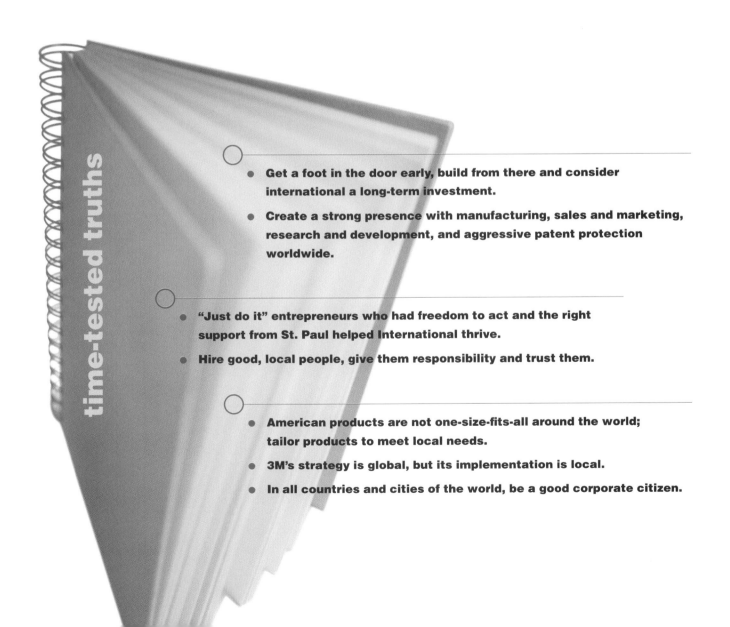

time-tested truths

- Get a foot in the door early, build from there and consider international a long-term investment.
- Create a strong presence with manufacturing, sales and marketing, research and development, and aggressive patent protection worldwide.

- "Just do it" entrepreneurs who had freedom to act and the right support from St. Paul helped International thrive.
- Hire good, local people, give them responsibility and trust them.

- American products are not one-size-fits-all around the world; tailor products to meet local needs.
- 3M's strategy is global, but its implementation is local.
- In all countries and cities of the world, be a good corporate citizen.

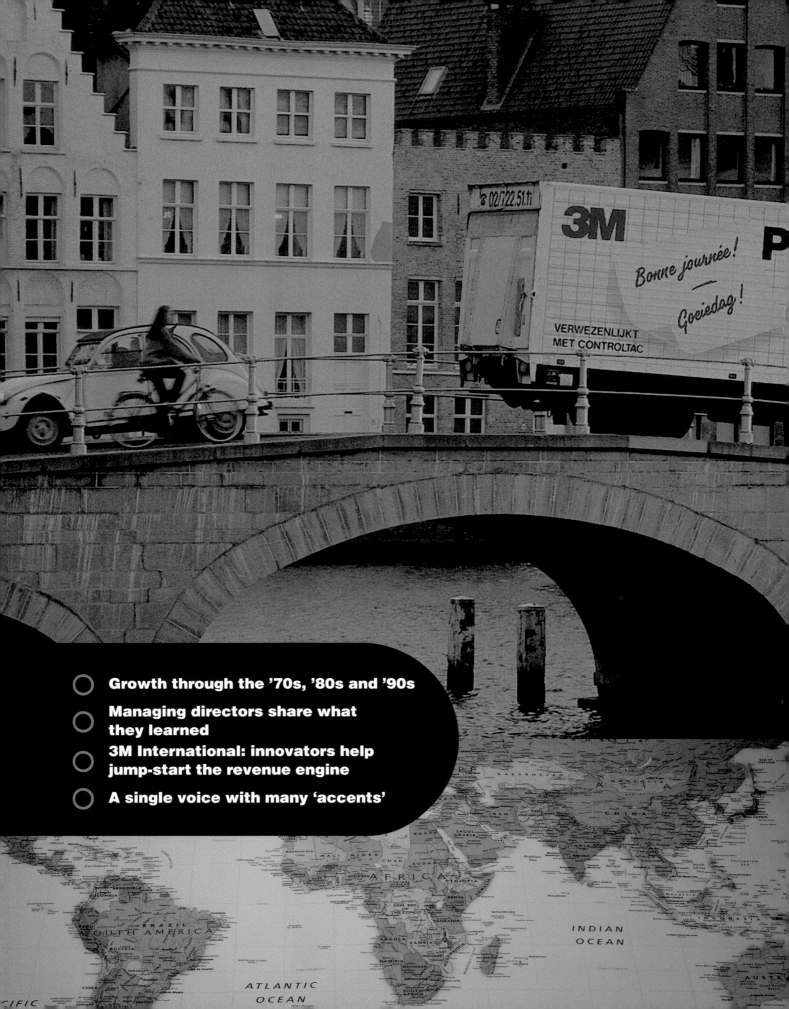

- Growth through the '70s, '80s and '90s
- Managing directors share what they learned
- 3M International: innovators help jump-start the revenue engine
- A single voice with many 'accents'

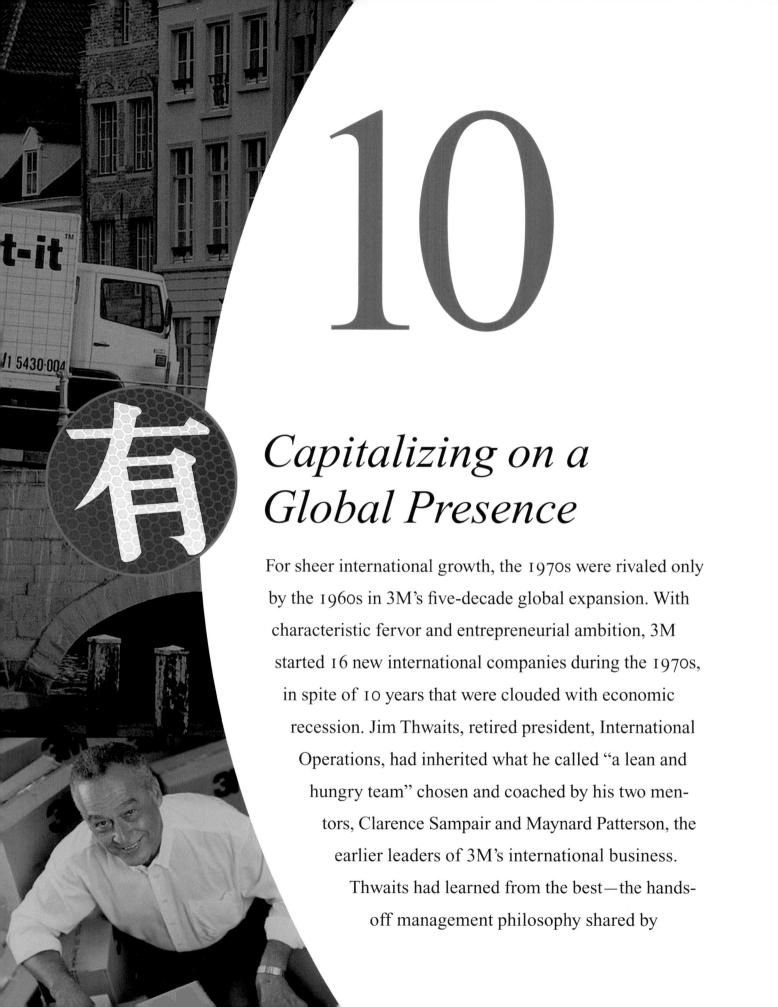

10

Capitalizing on a Global Presence

For sheer international growth, the 1970s were rivaled only by the 1960s in 3M's five-decade global expansion. With characteristic fervor and entrepreneurial ambition, 3M started 16 new international companies during the 1970s, in spite of 10 years that were clouded with economic recession. Jim Thwaits, retired president, International Operations, had inherited what he called "a lean and hungry team" chosen and coached by his two mentors, Clarence Sampair and Maynard Patterson, the earlier leaders of 3M's international business. Thwaits had learned from the best—the hands-off management philosophy shared by

Sampair and Patterson fueled 3M's international growth from the 1950s onward. "It's the troops who run the business," Thwaits said, "not the generals. You can't have people sitting in their jobs waiting for the command to come down from on high. All that top management can do is provide the climate for people in the business to run it in the best possible way."

> ### No 'Cookie Cutter' Companies

Thwaits believed in giving overall direction and then having faith in 3M people. "Outline the challenges and the tasks and ask them to set their eyes on the heights," he said. "It's important to be available for support and counsel, but never—ever—tell them how to get the job done. That's up to them." Thwaits defended the uniqueness of 3M's international business. "I made it quite clear," he said, "that I did not expect them to be stamped out of the same 'cookie cutter' as 3M U.S.A. I wanted them to have their own goals and ambitions. We had no right to stifle the creativity of our people in other countries."

By 1979, 3M's international business had grown from virtually zero sales in 1951 to a whopping 42 percent of the company's total revenues. Some observers wondered out loud if the early years had been easier—after all, the company was filling a marketplace vacuum. While that was true, the challenging aspect of international growth had been entering those first 35 countries in the 1950s and 1960s; building sound companies that could sustain themselves; developing professional management by finding, hiring and training local people;

and—perhaps most importantly—having the patience to wait for profitability. From the start, 3M's approach took the long view.

The 1970s' challenge was to build market share in every international location—a network that by the decade's end grew to 51 companies in as many countries which were sprinkled all over the world map. In most cases, it was expedient to exploit an existing product or technology in global locations, but by the end of the 1970s, 3M's international companies were not only producing solid financial results, they were also innovators in marketing, product adaptations and operations.

We were flexible enough to marry our business philosophy with local customs and patterns; we were able to be the first with the most in many places. > **Jim Thwaits** *retired president, International Operations*

"These ideas have spilled over to other international companies as well as 3M U.S.A.," Thwaits said. He believed that the international growth curve would be steeper than its U.S. counterpart. This prediction was fueled by Thwaits' own drive to succeed. "We have an absolute need—a duty—to do much better," he said. "We're an elite company. Any limitations on our growth are strictly the limitations of our own imaginations. I personally feel we can always do better."

Chapter opening photos A truck in Bruges, Belgium, uses Controltac fleet-marking film from 3M to advertise one of the company's best known products, Post-it notes; As of 2002, 3M has operations in 64 countries around the world; Antonio Mario Colombo packages products in Brazil; Scotchlite reflective sheeting is popular all over the world.

Thwaits, the consummate "cheerleader," helped International Operations prosper while riding through two serious economic recessions in the 1970s. The keys were to step up marketing; introduce new products faster around the world; and use those new products to increase market share, while weathering inevitable currency fluctuations. In smaller economies, the strategy was simple—establish a presence and expand when the timing was right. "This was true for the three new companies in Indonesia, Korea and Ecuador," Thwaits said. "We had the right people there, and we developed a nucleus of 3Mers from the country's population." In the so-called "Third World nations," 3M looked for government policies that welcomed long-term foreign investment.

> **Dismantling 'Silos'**

It became apparent in the 1970s that 3M's U.S. and International Operations should work more closely together. Given the size of its revenues, 3M International had a right to shed what some called its "second-class citizen" status. In addition, Thwaits and 3M CEOs Harry Heltzer and his successor, Ray Herzog, were convinced that International would flourish even more if 3M's domestic and global businesses were integrated as equals. "The gates were open," Thwaits said, "and there was a flow of people, information and assistance." Group vice presidents began working with the international companies to refine their business strategies. Some of those companies started developing their own new products. More international people were invited to St. Paul

31 Companies in 30 Years

These 3M international companies were established in the 1970s:

1970 Greece, Kenya
1971 El Salvador, Guatemala, Jamaica
1973 Costa Rica, New Zealand, Trinidad
1974 Dominican Republic
1975 Chile, Indonesia, Ireland, Nigeria
1977 Ecuador, Korea
1979 Uruguay

These 3M companies began operating in the 1980s:

1981 3M Gulf (United Arab Emirates)
1984 China
1988 India, Turkey

These international companies began operating in the 1990s:

1991 Czech Republic, Hungary, Poland
1992 Russia
1993 Pakistan
1994 Egypt, Sri Lanka, Vietnam
1995 Israel, Morocco
1997 Romania

1 In Bangkok, Thailand, a woman sells Scotch-Brite products from her sampan. 3M international companies find ways to marry their business to local customs. **2** 3M Vietnam was established in 1994.

to participate in meetings on business strategy and new products. Because international sales and marketing people needed more technical support, they called on 3M's stateside technical community more frequently. Plans were made to expand lab facilities around the world.

I came to 3M after toiling for six years to obtain a Ph.D. and nobody addressed me as 'Dr. Nicholson' or even 'Dr. Geoff.' I was 'Geoff' and I quickly came to appreciate that informality. It exemplified a climate of close, friendly and encouraging cooperation. **> Geoff Nicholson**

retired staff vice president, Corporate Technical Planning and

International Technical Operations

Integrating U.S. and "OUS" (outside the U.S.) operations, as it was called, wasn't easy. "When we first started to talk about manufacturing overseas, we got lip service," said Heltzer, 3M's chairman of the board and CEO in the early 1970s. "People went to meetings and said, 'Yes,' and then did exactly as they pleased. Gradually, they understood that because a plant was located in a country, the managing director had responsibility for that plant, but he was also responsible to the head of production in St. Paul. Over time, 3M managers began to think of management on a global basis." They began to see the advantages of worldwide cooperation in sell-

ing and distributing 3M products. But, in the words of retired Chairman of the Board and CEO Lew Lehr, "The integration process could best be described as evolution, not a revolution."

> **Overseas Innovation**

By the 1980s, 3M was benefiting in tangible ways from its Pathfinder Program, started in 1978, to encourage new products and new business initiatives born outside the United States. By 1983, winning Pathfinder teams had generated $153 million in new sales since the program began. 3M Brazil invented a low cost, hot-melt adhesive from local raw materials; an adhesive transfer tape designed for local car manufacturers; and a low cost microfilm reader for their local market. To complement 3M's line of audio and videotape products, 3M Germany marketed compatible hardware purchased from outside 3M to serve the growing broadcast industry. 3M Germany also teamed up with Sumitomo 3M to develop electronic connectors with new features for the worldwide electronics industry. 3M Philippines designed a Scotch-Brite cleaning pad shaped like a foot after learning that Filipinos polished floors with their feet. 3M Sweden discovered a new application for packaging tape when it persuaded the Swedish Postal Service to use the tape instead of sealing wax on registered mail.

Recognition formerly reserved only for Americans finally began including the accomplishments of international employees, too. International researchers were elected to the company's prestigious Circle of Technical

1 3M international employee publications from the mid-1970s played a key role in developing companies that share 3M's culture.

Most veterans of 3M International learned on the job, and the lessons are still useful to employees heading to international assignments.

Among many, major assignments, Josef Kuhn, who joined 3M in 1952, became managing director, Sumitomo 3M, in 1972 when its sales were about $300 million. "I learned a lot from the Japanese," said Kuhn, who spent much of his career in manufacturing. "Back in the early 1970s, they were already using methods that later became world manufacturing standards. One of them involved employees in what were later called 'quality circles.' Groups of employees got together to brainstorm how to improve plant productivity and reduce costs."

Kuhn, retired senior vice president, Engineering, Quality and Manufacturing Services, also recalled learning patience and negotiating discipline in Japan. "In those long meetings," he said, "we'd sit around the table and the Japanese would remain silent. Meanwhile, Westerners like me were uncomfortable with the silence and we'd talk too soon and too much."

Ken Schoen became managing director, 3M Italy, in the 1970s when the business was struggling. About three weeks into Schoen's assignment, Maynard Patterson, then vice president, International, paid him a visit and delivered "a lecture." "He talked for three hours, almost without stopping," Schoen, retired executive vice president, Information and Imaging Technologies Sector, said. "He told me Americans in International have to change their mindset. They have to understand there is more than one way to get things done. He talked about listening and learning more before making decisions. He emphasized how important it was to appreciate the local customs, to get to know the people. That's the miracle of International. We've blended many cultures with our 3M philosophy of doing business. In the end, everyone around the world says, 'I'm a 3Mer.'"

Vince Ruane was 22 years old when he went to work in 3M's export office in New York. "Al Butz often came in from St. Paul on his way to Europe and he told us about the companies that were being established," said Ruane who, in 40 years with 3M, worked all over the world. "It was a great event when Al visited, because it made me understand, in a very personal way, what William McKnight was trying to do with our international business." Ruane trained young people in preparation for their overseas assignments. "They'd come from good schools and we'd prepare them," Ruane, retired division vice president, 3M Traffic Control Materials Division, said. "We'd give them their one-way ticket to Colombia, Peru, Venezuela, Ecuador and I'd say, 'Good luck. Build a good business and you'll be successful.' I remember Em Monteiro, who later became executive vice president, 3M International, heading off to Colombia, and L.D. DeSimone, later 3M chairman of the board and CEO, as a young engineer on his way to Brazil. What they all had in common was the desire to seize an opportunity."

When Fred Harris Jr. became managing director, 3M Thailand, in 1975, he was glad to have an overseas assignment even though that region was still unsettled after the Vietnam War. "There was no formal coach," said Harris, "Nobody in 3M who said, 'I'm your Thailand expert.' But, like a lot of new experiences, sometimes the best thing to do is just plunge in when you hit the ground." Harris had considerable independence, which he preferred. "I was 10,000 miles away," he said. "The phones worked, sometimes; and the Telex worked, sometimes. I had to make most decisions on my own." Harris, whose 3M career began in 1971, used the experience he gained in Thailand when he became division vice president for several 3M businesses and, most recently, staff vice president, Community Affairs and Workforce Diversity.

Excellence, among them Helmut Karrasch at 3M's electrical lab in Hamburg, Germany, who developed a resin splicing system for crucial submarine equipment that withstood high pressure underwater. The first two international companies to receive Genesis grants to support entrepreneurial product development were 3M Canada and 3M Italy. Canada earned a grant for a bone growth stimulator program that delivers an electric current across

> ### The United States accounts for less than 5 percent of the world's population, so the other 95 percent became our marketplace to pursue. Expanding globally was a business-driven decision. > **John McDevitt** *retired 3M corporate economist*

fractured bones to promote healing. Italy's Ferrania research lab used a grant to work on an X-ray dosimeter program to measure radiation.

Other new product innovations with broad, international applications also began attracting stateside attention. When a Canadian marketer, Robin Pitman, came up with a product idea to clean ships underwater, he was invited to St. Paul to work with 3M lab people. From that collaboration came the Scotch-Brite marine cleaning disc. 3M Switzerland designed a smaller, hand-held dispenser for tape that other 3M companies, including the United States, adopted. In several rounds of friendly, intracompany competition, 3M U.K. and

3M in the United States each topped the other with improvements to the Stickit coated abrasive disc.

By the 1980s, lab operations outside the United States were also becoming notable contributors to corporate-wide product research and development. More than 1,200 technical employees worked on product and process development across the oceans. 3M's Hamburg, Germany, lab focused on electrical innovation. Labs in Gorseinon, Wales, and Caserta, Italy, honed in on recording materials. 3M France explored new tape applications and the Antwerp, Belgium, lab studied specialty chemicals. The Sumitomo 3M lab worked hard to stay on top of rigid standards set by Japan's high-tech manufacturers. 3M's European companies as well as 3M Japan, Brazil and Colombia took part in a global effort to accelerate automation in abrasives manufacturing. Other international companies studied ways to improve product packaging, make warehousing more efficient and conserve energy and reduce pollution—not just in their own locations, but with valuable implications for 3M worldwide.

Recognizing the intensity of global competition in the 1980s, Thwaits appealed to 3M to examine its marketing. "We have to approach this from a global perspective and not from a national perspective expanded globally," he cautioned. "We must have accurate local intelligence about markets. With all of the variables in market characteristics, manufacturing, distribution, communications and pricing, it can be bewildering. But, it can also be quite satisfying and profitable . . .

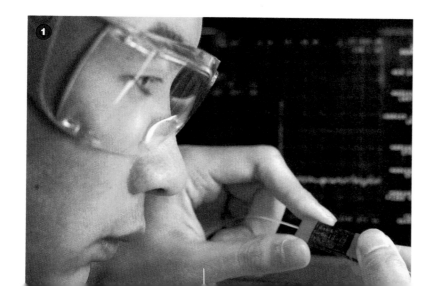

1 A scientist in the Telecom Lab at Sumitomo 3M works to adapt 3M technology to meet the needs of Japanese customers. **2** In 1997, 3M expanded production at the tape manufacturing plant in Itapetiniga, Brazil. **3** The operator of a film slitting machine in Hilden, Germany, separated waste for reuse. **4** Scotch-Brite sponges were among the most popular 3M products in emerging markets in the mid-1990s.

as we know." Thwaits said it was crucial to know the difference between a 3M product with universal appeal versus one that needed modifications to fit a country's particular wants or needs. And, he said, as some 3M products moved from proprietary positions to commodity status, 3M marketers had to be creative and successful in "distinguishing us from our competitors and making us unique in the eyes of our customers."

With each new international company created through the 1980s, 3M made a modest investment to get started, promoted basic products such as reflective sheeting and scouring pads to build a customer base, and then added products to build the business. "We don't have a lot of brain surgeons," Greg Lewis, department manager, Post-it flags and commercial print market, Office Supplies Division, told *The Wall Street Journal.* "We have well-rounded individuals who care about the business." Allen Jacobson, who succeeded Lehr as chairman of the board and CEO in the mid-1980s, told the *Journal* that 3M keeps its approach elegantly simple. After all, it had worked well for more than 30 years. There were some refinements in that simple strategy in the 1980s, however. Jacobson called on leaders in 3M's product groups to identify those among

3M's 50,000 products that had the highest potential for sales outside the United States. The top product areas, in keeping with Thwait's worldwide marketing "call to arms," developed global strategic plans. In addition, under Jacobson's leadership, 3M made dramatic gains in plant efficiencies all over the world so that 3M had the wherewithal to compete in any geographic location on price. From 1985 to 1989, 3M cut the labor needed to make its products by 35 percent and the manufacturing time required by 21 percent.

> **Let's Hear it for 50/50**

The impetus behind International Operation's stretch goals in the 1980s came from Manuel (Em) Monteiro, who joined the company in 1950 as a cost analyst but spent virtually all of his career overseas. Monteiro became executive vice president, International Operations, in 1981, working closely with Thwaits. By 1987, when international revenues had been riveted at the same 40 percent level for several years, he wasn't satisfied. "I want us to reach 50 percent of the sales of 3M products worldwide, and I'm confident we can reach it in the next five years," Monteiro said. "To do it, international sales will need to nearly double the U.S. growth rate."

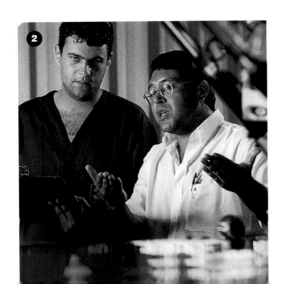

Speaking from experience, Monteiro knew why this goal could be achieved. "Considering that our penetration overseas is typically half that of the United States," he said. "I know the opportunity is there." Monteiro predicted that his 50/50 plan could be achieved by converting 3M technologies into unique, high-quality products faster, selling those products at a profit and providing customers with value that they could find nowhere else. He set up management action teams on each continent to develop growth strategies that the teams coordinated with divisional global strategies and local company plans. In 1992, International Operations contributed 50 percent of the company's total revenues for the first time.

We've been through hyperinflation, we've been through military governments, coups and tremendous political upheaval. 3M has a lot of staying power. > **John McDevitt**

> **Enter the 'Transnational' Company**

Just five days short of having 41 years with 3M, Monteiro retired with a statement that most people in 3M International probably echo in their careers. "I'll never like anything better than this," he said in 1991. "I'd like to do it all over again." Harry Hammerly, who succeeded him, felt the same. Like Monteiro, Hammerly emphasized the long view for 3M International. "One of our

hallmarks has been our financial strength that enables us to take that long-term view," Hammerly said and then smiled. "However, I like what Em Monteiro said, 'We want to maximize the short-term results indefinitely.'"

By the early 1990s, international business processes had changed dramatically. Market "windows" closed sooner than ever. There would be shifts away from 3M's methods of running international businesses. Given its sheer size and scope—57 countries by 1991—Hammerly said there would be a gradual move away from country-by-country management to more regional management. That's why the first European Business Center (EBC) was created in 1991 to manage 3M's chemical business across Europe. The EBC was charged with product development, manufacturing, sales and marketing, as well as paying attention to local country requirements. EBCs for the Disposable Products business and Pharmaceuticals as well as other EBCs soon followed. But, even with broader, geographic management, Hammerly—like Thwaits—emphasized that 3M International would never be a "cookie cutter" organization. Instead, it would continue to rely on informal organization.

"We're moving into a new kind of global management structure," Hammerly said. "It's called 'transnational' and, unlike more centralized organizations, a transnational corporation depends on an integrated network and teamwork. It's driven by the needs of the marketplace and the need to be competitive. For each business, we have to create the right mix of global,

1 Em Monteiro served as vice president, International Operations, from 1981–1991. 2 He was succeeded by Harry Hammerly who held the same position from 1991–1995 until he was succeeded by Ron Baukol. 3 John Marshall, retired director, International Operations, shown near the Great Wall of China, met regularly with Chinese officials during the 1970s and early 1980s, encouraging them to allow 3M to open a company there. 4 By 1994, 10 years after 3M opened its Chinese company with a handful of employees, 3M was selling more than 2,000 products in 20 of 29 Chinese provinces.

John Marshall, retired director, International Operations, understands long-term investment, perseverance and stretch goals. When he joined 3M in 1968, the company was busy establishing more international companies than it ever had in a single decade, 23 in all. As early as 1973, he traveled to China to explore what it would mean to do business there.

That was uncharted territory for 3M and every other U.S. company. "The Cultural Revolution was in its final stages, and most Chinese didn't want us there," Marshall said. "The only point of contact was the Chinese Export Commodities Fair, held twice a year in Canton. Seventy percent of China's foreign trade was conducted at the fair." While Europeans had been visiting China for years, he said, Americans were totally new to the vast country.

Through the 1970s, Marshall developed contacts in China and acquired more knowledge. When Deng Xiao Peng regained power in 1978, he put a program in place to make China a leading industrialized nation by 2000. "He knew he had to open doors to the West to achieve his goal," Marshall said, "and that's when our real opportunity emerged." Jim Thwaits, who later retired as president, International Operations, told Marshall to explore the details of starting a business in China with 100 percent ownership.

Given the conventional 3M freedom to succeed or fail on your own, Marshall set out solo

to answer four questions. "Should we be in China at all?" Marshall mused. "Yes," he answered himself, "because of the potential offered by a nation of more than a billion people." How would 3M win 100 percent ownership? The answer was to offer something of value—local manufacturing, technology or both. What products would 3M offer? Marshall narrowed the list to basic products that a developing country needs for better electrical generation and distribution and improved telecommunications. Where would 3M locate its operation? Shanghai, right in the center of the geographic region that produced 70 percent of China's gross national product.

The answers came a lot easier than the ultimate business deal. It took 12 long years of making contacts, strategizing, selling, facing dead ends and regrouping for 3M to open the first wholly owned foreign company in modern China. This included four years of negotiating to win China's approval to do business in the country. Finally, in November 1984, 3M was granted a license to operate a business in China. The first installation was an electrical tape converting plant.

After that international baptism of fire, Marshall was assigned to travel the world and look for places that 3M should be—and wasn't. He had a hand in establishing 3M Russia in 1992, 3M Pakistan in 1993 and 3M Vietnam in 1994. In each case, Marshall assuaged concerns in those countries about foreign exploitation. Marshall could say, with certainty, that 3M's presence in their countries would create well-paid, safe jobs; enlarge the tax base; and contribute to local knowledge of environmental protection, worker safety and management skills.

优 质 名 牌

John Marshall—Moving into Uncharted Territory

regional and local components—and that mix will differ by business." Eastern European nations were a good case in point in 1991. That's where 3M would continue to use its FIDO strategy (First In Defeats Others) in the Czech Republic, Hungary, Poland and Russia.

> **A Single Voice with 'Accents'**

As the 1990s progressed and 3M added even more countries to its international roster, speaking in one voice, worldwide, became a high priority. That effort was linked directly to the company's emphasis on a new identity strategy, introduced in 1993, that focused on creating a consistent, positive image of 3M around the world. With so many products to sell, the company had presented many "voices" to customers in the past and research showed that 3M could be much better known. Applied on the international level, the company's new voice would not have a single "accent," however. Instead, the voice would have many accents to acknowledge the diversity of cultures, languages and customers it served.

The continued potential for 3M International business was clear to Ron Baukol, who succeeded Hammerly as executive vice president, International Operations, and retired in 2002. By 1996, more than 80 percent of the world's gross domestic product (GDP) growth occurred outside the United States. "We had better be there," Baukol said, "and be a vital part of that growth." In its own analysis of how the world was swiftly changing, the World Bank compared the top economies in the year 2000 to the year 2020 with some astonishing changes. In 2000, the top five economies were the United States, Japan, China, Germany and France, in that order. But, in 2020, the economic map is expected to shift dramatically. The top five will likely be China, the United States, Japan, India and Indonesia.

By 1996, 3M International's penetration of its markets was 50 percent of U.S. levels and Baukol was convinced the percentage could increase by focusing on the company's three growth initiatives—Supply Chain Excellence, Earning Customer Loyalty and Pacing Plus Programs. While they were expressed in capital letters, these initiatives weren't new or revolutionary to 3M.

In 1995, more than 70 percent of 3M's total growth was achieved outside the United States. We have tremendous opportunities open to us.

> **Ron Baukol** *retired executive vice president,*

International Operations

They echoed what the architects of 3M International espoused five decades earlier: produce innovative products that our customers need, do it quickly and efficiently, then deliver their orders complete and on time. By the 1990s, the pace had accelerated considerably and the stakes were higher for 3M. "In both developed and emerging countries, we need to be very nimble," Baukol said. "The pace of change is fast and dynamic. If you can't respond quickly, you miss many opportunities."

1 The first global, corporate advertising campaign in the mid-1990s was designed to remind customers and potential customers of 3M's emphasis on innovation. The print advertisements were created for use in any culture and appeared in Europe, North America, Latin America and Asia. **2** A 3M Dominican Republic location where Rose Kopras served as the company's first female managing director. **3** A friendly receptionist at 3M Philippines, where Rosa Miller was managing director.

Rose Kopras was accustomed to firsts. She was the first woman to become a production department superintendent at 3M. She was also 3M's first female plant manager. But, becoming the company's first female managing director of an international company was a big breakthrough in 1990. "Em Monteiro was determined to see a woman leading an international company before he retired," said Kopras. The manager of the Cynthiana, Kentucky, manufacturing plant said Monteiro called, and "he asked me to fly to St. Paul the same day. I had no idea why, but I was uneasy—what if we'd shipped bad products to Japan?" When she arrived at the meeting, Monteiro asked her to be managing director, 3M Dominicana and Haiti. "He knew I had a lot to learn," Kopras said, "so he picked what he thought was a small, safe, nice place."

Three months after Kopras arrived at her new post in the Caribbean, hyperinflation socked those countries and Haiti's government dissolved. One year later, America was at war in the Persian Gulf, limiting the amount of raw materials Kopras could import. Despite old equipment, old methods and old formulas, she could still produce and convert Scotch masking tape in the little plant. "It was the best thing that ever happened to me," Kopras said. "I learned that you don't necessarily need sophisticated tools, but you do need a lot of ingenuity. We made the company stronger financially than it had been, in spite of the economic and political tumult around us." The assignment gave Kopras

firsthand experience with the environmental challenges of running a manufacturing plant in a developing country, a perspective that served her well when she became director, Corporate Safety, Environmental Technology and Safety Services and, now, manufacturing director, Occupational Health & Environmental Safety Division. Only a few months after Kopras' international assignment, two other women also were named to managing directorships.

Rosa Miller, now general manager, Surface Conditioning Division, says she was a "humble process engineer" at 3M when she talked with the vice president of 3M Latin America to find out how to pursue an international career. "I was in my 20s," Miller said. "I told him I wanted to run an international business some day. He mapped out what I needed to do. He probably doesn't remember, but he had an incredible influence on me." Following her "career map," Miller became a technical service representative offering product and technology training for 3M Health Care marketing and sales employees in Latin America, Africa and the Asia Pacific. Next, she took an

assignment to help grow 3M's hospital and dental businesses in Latin America and Africa.

Miller's chance to be a managing director surfaced in 1997. "The vice president of the region asked me if I wanted to settle in one place, the Philippines." Miller wanted a location in which she could "make a difference" and the Philippines fit her target. "I started my job in January 1998, when Asia was in an economic crisis. With monetary devaluation, 3M Philippines' sales had dropped from $100 million to $60 million." Miller focused on areas of growth potential, such as building the health care business in the country. She worked on skill development for the sales staff and started a reward and recognition program to improve employee morale. She was satisfied—she had the challenging assignment she had sought more than 20 years earlier when she called on that 3M vice president for career advice. His name was L.D. DeSimone, who became 3M's chairman of the board and CEO before retiring in 2001.

Several factors led to the stepped-up pace. In some countries, such as Brazil, economic barriers had fallen. The same was true in Eastern Europe. In other parts of the world, new trade agreements had transformed the economic landscape. And, in some emerging economies, industrialization was happening more quickly. "In the past," Baukol said, "countries first developed by exploiting their natural resources. Next, the national infrastructure was built, including roads and utilities. After that came industry and technology and finally a full-blown consumer economy. All that took many years and 3M could grow along with the economies. Now everything happens quickly and 3M has to be ready to do business immediately." That was particularly true because other multinational companies were 3M's key customers.

As expectations of 3M International Operations grew, investment in research and development (R&D) kept pace. Of 3M's 6,500 scientists, approximately 2,200 are now located outside the United States. On average, the company spends 6.5 cents of every sales dollar on R&D in operations around the world.

Thirty-eight international companies have manufacturing operations, while 29 have laboratories to help support 3M business plans. Their work includes technical service and support, manufacturing support and product modifications. Full-service laboratories exist in some of the international companies, such as Japan, the United Kingdom, Belgium and Germany. All international companies provide technical support to their customers through local technical service engineers backed by the international laboratories, just as regional laboratories provide technical support in the United States.

"Technical innovation simply could not happen without active information sharing among the labs," said Geoff Nicholson, retired staff vice president, Corporate and Technical Planning and International Technical Operations. A high-strength adhesive tape used for bonding baseplates designed to attach rearview mirrors to auto windshields was created at Sumitomo 3M in Japan and first used in the United Kingdom. A pharmaceuticals lab in the United Kingdom developed a new breath-activated aerosol device for asthma sufferers, but they struggled with designing the mechanism. 3M's lab in Germany had the expertise in plastics and moldings. "Together they developed an incredible product," said Nicholson. "It's up to us to create the kind of environment that will make this collaboration happen all over the world."

> **Community Impact and Turbulent Times**

3M employees have reason to be proud of their company's international impact. For each job 3M creates in a country of the world, three to 10 people are supported by that job. 3M donates funds for local education, health, arts programs and disaster relief. Not only is 3M successful, it is well-respected. In a 1990s survey in Japan, for example, 3M was named the third most-respected company in that country. 3M has won kudos for its environmental work in several countries including Korea, Taiwan and Germany.

1 Scientists in the United Kingdom were among the 80 scientists from the U.K. and the United States who worked for seven years to develop the first CFC-free asthma inhaler. **2** 3M telecommunications products helped Singapore build its fiber optics infrastructure in the mid-1990s.

Countries of the Asia Pacific region especially appreciated 3M's historic "staying power" when a dramatic economic downturn smacked the region in 1997 and 1998. In the United States, Wall Street suggested that 3M should reduce its risk and step back from the region. But Chairman of the Board and CEO DeSimone stood firm. He was proven right. Referring to the tough economic conditions at the time, Baukol observed, "There's an old adage that says 'It's better to be poor and healthy than rich and sick.' Right now, we need to make sure we stay healthy. If we can continue to supply our customers and give them the products and service they need; if we preserve our margins, balance sheet and market share; if we continue to treat our employees well, we'll be even more competitive going forward." 3M International weathered that difficult period and did better than just "holding its own." In addition, 3M's presence in 64 countries by 2001 gave the company a strong foundation that could offset regional downturns.

"People outside 3M frequently tell me how amazed they are by our ability to deal with turbulence," Baukol said. "It's rewarding to hear that, but it's not surprising. We are accustomed to our strengths, because we live with them every day."

time-tested truths

- 3M International Operations aren't intended to be "cookie cutter" duplicates of 3M's U.S. operations.

- 3M International flourished when it became an equal, integrated partner with 3M U.S.A.

- A long-held, international growth credo often is still true— FIDO (First In Defeats Others).

- 3M's global growth was a business-driven decision fueled by the knowledge that 95 percent of the world's population lives outside the United States.

- 3M's long-standing financial strength has allowed the company to take the "long view" in international expansion, regardless of economic volatility and political uncertainty.

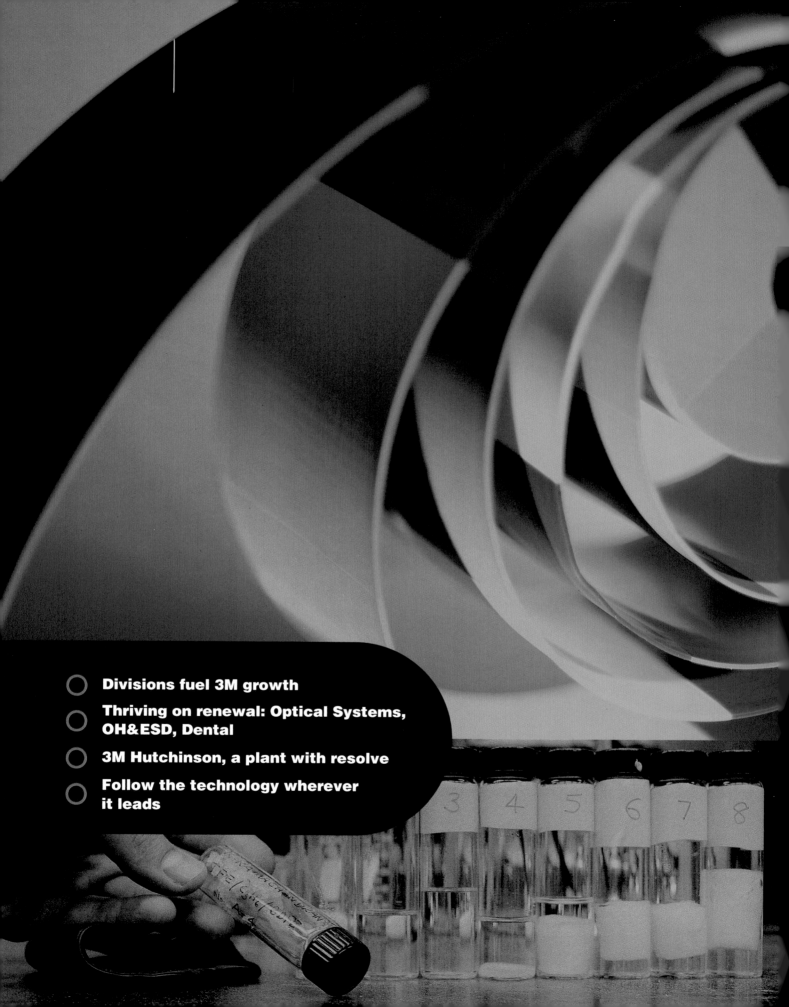

- Divisions fuel 3M growth
- Thriving on renewal: Optical Systems, OH&ESD, Dental
- 3M Hutchinson, a plant with resolve
- Follow the technology wherever it leads

Divide and Grow—
Follow the Technology

William McKnight had a revolutionary idea in 1948. It was
an idea uncommon to American business, but one that would
ignite growth, diversification and innovation for decades
to come. McKnight restructured 3M by creating divisions—
individual profit centers that had the power, autonomy
and resources to run independently. McKnight believed
that this divisional approach would keep 3M's businesses closer and more responsive to customers while
being a strong motivator for employees. The timing
was perfect. 3M had grown significantly during its
first 40 years. By the end of World War II, new

demands for products, people and diversification had set the stage for the company's rapid growth.

"Mr. McKnight wanted to keep the divisions small and focused on satisfying customers and giving people a chance to be entrepreneurial," said Dick Lidstad, retired vice president, Human Resources. "What we did was follow our technologies wherever they led us and leverage them into new businesses. Mr. McKnight didn't want bureaucracy to slow us down."

But, it wasn't a free-for-all environment. McKnight made sure that 3M remained strongly centralized in a few core functions—engineering, research and development, finance and human resources. A manager from each of these three areas was assigned to a division's operating committee to ensure consistent practices throughout the company. In their book, "In Search of Excellence," authors Tom Peters and Robert Waterman said 3M operated with simultaneous "loose-tight" properties—loose when entrepreneurial action mattered and tight when corporate consistency was the key.

> **Count on Change**
McKnight's decision to organize the company into divisions crafted a climate of perpetual change. As a division grew, it reached a size where it tended to spend too much of its time on established products and markets and less time on new products and businesses. That's when McKnight's "divide and grow" philosophy took over—new businesses were spun off and given new management teams. The results were gratifying.

"Almost without exception, that new unit began growing at a faster rate," said Lew Lehr, retired 3M chairman of the board and CEO, and—earlier in his career—a beneficiary of this philosophy when he launched the embryonic medical products unit.

When the new business was separated, the established division had to find new products and markets to meet its growth objectives to make up for contributions from the business that became independent. Observers of the phenomenon called it "renewal." As each small program was successful, it progressed in ever increasing sizes to: a project, a department and then a division. Diversification accelerated.

The examples are legion. When Magnetic Recording Materials was spun off from the Electrical Products Division, it grew to become its own division and then spawned a spate of divisions. A copying machine project for Thermo-Fax copiers grew to become the Office Equipment Division. A new venture in printing products turned into several divisions that became the Graphic Arts Group. The Occupational Health and Environmental Safety Division was a spin-off from the Retail Tape Division. Personal Care Products stepped out from the Tape Group. 3M's huge Reflective Products Division eventually was divided into four separate divisions.

To create never-before-seen products for new markets, McKnight also established a New Products Department in 1940 and, although it had different names over the decades including New Business Ventures, it had essentially the same charter. More recently, 3M

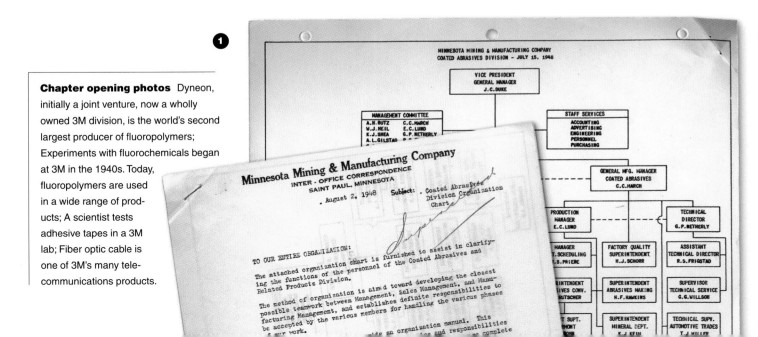

Chapter opening photos Dyneon, initially a joint venture, now a wholly owned 3M division, is the world's second largest producer of fluoropolymers; Experiments with fluorochemicals began at 3M in the 1940s. Today, fluoropolymers are used in a wide range of products; A scientist tests adhesive tapes in a 3M lab; Fiber optic cable is one of 3M's many telecommunications products.

created a Corporate Enterprise Development program in 1996 to look years out to see trends and opportunities that could help 3M leverage its technologies into "white spaces"—those untapped markets that the company had not yet entered.

There were two other major organizational changes in the company's life, aimed at creating more renewal and innovation synergy. After the company's first formal strategic planning effort in 1981, 3M was divided into four business "sectors" based on related technologies. Each sector had its own research lab to give 3M

From top to bottom, 3M's management provides active, spirited encouragement for new venture generation. **> Harvard Business Review, 1980**

increased clout. Seventeen years later, in 1999, 3M was organized into six "market centers" to more closely align the company's core businesses with the markets they served. A "millennium study" that sparked those most recent changes reinforced the power of the divisional structure from a half century earlier. Looking back, observers agree that this was the single most important organizational decision in 3M's history. The divisional structure with its "divide and grow" imperative created a unique climate for renewal, corporate self examination and re-creation.

> **Optical Systems: A Near Death Experience**

Back in the 1960s, 3M had developed a microlouver technology—the ability to create the equivalent of a microscopic Venetian blind in a single piece of clear film. This film featured about 3,000 tiny "blinds" per foot that looked transparent from one angle and opaque from another. Surely this film had multiple uses, from window treatments and automatic teller machines to ski goggles and maybe even computer screens. Believing this was "a technology in search of a market," 3M's New Business Ventures Division spun it off to become the Industrial Optics unit in 1979. But, the business had a shaky start and only one customer, 3M's own Visual Products Division, which bought the film to reduce glare in the overhead projectors they manufactured.

When it was next "adopted" by 3M's large Traffic and Personal Safety Products Group, the little business limped along with what one observer called "a grab bag of optical technologies," the best being light control film applied to car dashboards to reduce windshield reflection. But, the film was too pricey for the auto industry, and Industrial Optics was losing millions of dollars a year by the 1980s. That's when Ron Mitsch, then group vice president, Traffic and Personal Safety Products Group, recruited Andy Wong to take on, what Mitsch called, an "exciting, stimulating and kind of risky" assignment.

Coming from a lab management background, Wong was eager to embrace the new challenge of being a business unit manager. And, what a challenge it was.

1 When the Coated Abrasives Division was formed in 1948, employees were sent this letter and organization chart explaining the new division's structure. **2** Raymond Chiu (left), advanced research specialist, and Vincent King, senior research specialist, both of the 3M Microreplication Technology Center, Plasma Display Panel Project, helped develop the microreplicated barrier-rib panel, the core component of plasma displays. This is one example of a white space project that taps into a new market for 3M.

With not enough sales, the cost of running the Optical Systems plant in Petaluma, California, was too high. On top of that, production of the finished microlouvered film involved six different manufacturing locations around the country. There were quality issues and delays in filling customer orders. Critical patents on the technology were expiring and lower priced competitive films were emerging from Japan. With less than two years left on the California plant's lease—and orders to shut the operation down—Wong went into high gear. ❶

What happened next was renewal at its best. The Industrial Optics team developed and filed patents on a lower cost, better film. With a vastly improved—and simplified—manufacturing process, the Petaluma plant began producing film using two-thirds fewer processing steps and many fewer and simpler raw materials. The plant staff reduced production costs by nearly 70 percent and cut manufacturing time from 12 weeks to less than three. "By doing all that, we were able to afford smaller scale equipment that could be dedicated to manufacturing our film in one location, not six," Wong said. The plant began meeting all the important performance criteria. In a vote of confidence, 3M management decided to buy the Petaluma plant when the lease expired, rather than shut it down. But, the fight for profitability was a long, difficult one because Industrial Optics, renamed Optical Systems in 1989, lacked a core business. The next three years were characterized by more financial losses, three rounds of downsizing, and frustrating experimentation with product improvements and new applications.

Finally, in 1991, Optical Systems identified privacy filters for office computing as an untapped and potentially huge business opportunity. "It took us three generations of privacy filters over a 15-month period before we hit upon the winning formula," Wong said. "We were taught a valuable lesson in perseverance." In July 1992, Optical Systems finally introduced a full line of anti-glare, anti-radiation and computer filters with and without the privacy protection feature that became the foundation for a fast growing business. About the same time, Optical Systems also discovered that another novel film—derived from a technology called microreplication—could enhance the brightness of liquid crystal displays used in laptop computers at a time when laptops were proliferating worldwide. The product idea had its start with Sanford Cobb, then senior product development specialist, who had received funding through a 3M Genesis Grant to explore this new type of film. Paul Guehler, who was then division vice president, Safety and Security Systems, in which Optical Systems had its "home," urged the group to pursue the idea quickly. "Japan, the home of major computer manufacturers, needed it," he said. "I encouraged them to make the investment and move fast." Optical Systems experimented with different types of brightness enhancement film (BEF) to satisfy the standards of every major manufacturer and successfully reached the marketplace first with its new film.

Optical Systems has five locations that support the manufacturing of our brightness enhancement film around the world—Japan, Taiwan, Korea, China and the United States. **> Marc Miller**

manufacturing director, Optical Systems

"The biggest challenge we had in manufacturing the film was cosmetic uniformity," said Marc Miller, manufacturing director, Optical Systems. "The product had 500 prisms per inch of width, and each prism was smaller than a human hair. That's a little over ten miles of prisms on each square yard of material. We started manufacturing our film on existing equipment in our Menomonie, Wisconsin, plant where 3M makes

Scotchlite Diamond Grade reflective sheeting. You can imagine the challenge we had using equipment to make highway signs visible at a couple thousand feet, versus making a film for an LCD viewed at a distance of 12 inches. We couldn't tolerate even the most minor defects or flaws." Once the immense market potential for the film was proven, 3M made a manufacturing investment. "We developed the improved manufacturing process in 1994 and 1995 on an accelerated timetable," said Miller. "Our customers' needs were almost as embryonic as our product was. As their requirements matured, we were able to keep even or a little ahead." Miller explained the manufacturing process was constantly being refined. "We had to meet the higher expectations of an industry that was changing yearly," said Miller. "We had a worldwide team focused on improving our processes as well as the cost of our product."

By 1994 Optical Systems had its first profitable year and between 1991 and 2000 the business grew nearly 50 times, from $10 million in sales to just under $500 million. The business became a full-fledged 3M division in 1998, and Wong was named division general manager (and, shortly thereafter, division vice president). It was the fastest growing business in 3M throughout the 1990s and is the unqualified industry leader with its products sold in almost 60 countries. During this tremendous growth spurt, the division consistently exceeded company targets with 90 percent of its global sales each year coming from products introduced within the most recent four years. "We're in a changing,

rapidly growing industry," said Terry Jones, former business director, Electronic Display Lighting, Optical Systems Division, now director, Touch Systems. "We've made a point of obsoleting our products with newer and better ones."

Among the eight, major display-related innovations cited by computer manufacturer Compaq as part of the successful development of laptop computers worldwide over a decade, Optical Systems produced two of them— 3M brightness enhancement film and 3M dual brightness enhancement film. Both are now marketed under the Vikuiti brand.

In recent times, Optical Systems entered the touch-screen market by combining two consecutive acquisitions—Dynapro in mid-2000 and MicroTouch in early 2001.

> **OH&ESD: Action Teams Transform a Division**

When Robert Hershock returned to St. Paul in 1982 after serving as managing director, 3M Switzerland, he became the new general manager, Occupational Health and Environmental Safety Division (OH&ESD). He discovered that the fast growing division had been depending primarily on two products: the 8500 dust mask, the first disposable, lightweight, effective mask ever seen when it was developed in 1961; and the 8710 industrial respirator that successfully matched new U.S. Occupational Safety and Health Act standards established in 1971. Together, those two products accounted for most of the division's sales and profits.

1 Kenichi Saito, product development engineer, Optical Systems Division, helped develop Vikuiti brightness enhancement film (BEF). **2** The first disposable, lightweight dust mask, introduced by OH&ESD in 1961, became a division mainstay.

2

8500
Non-toxic Particulate Mask

Clear Vision

Adjustable Nose Bridge

Stapled Elastic Strap

Easy Communications

Lightweight Non-woven Fiber Filter
90.6% effective against particulates with 96% of the particulates under 5 microns

Minimal Breathing Resistance

Maintenance-free Disposability

"But, OH&ESD was a 3M aberration," said Professor Anne Donnellon, in a case study developed for the Harvard Business School. "It suffered from a technology base that was incapable of sustaining its earlier growth. It had no potentially successful new products in development." Profits were generated, but there was minimal

> Bob came into our lab and said, 'We have terrific market share, but our market is shrinking. We have to broaden into other kinds of safety products.' He was a fantastic leader.
>
> **> David Braun** *retired 3M corporate scientist, Occupational Health and Environmental Safety Division*

investment in pace-setting new products. People worked in their isolated "silos" and they had not been encouraged to take the kinds of risks that might require substantial financing. "The division generated only 12 percent of its sales from products introduced in the past five years not the 25 percent goal established by the company overall," Donnellon said. "Bob Hershock knew the division had to make dramatic changes."

Hershock worked to change the division's culture. He asked senior managers to participate in a cultural audit and self assessment of their own leadership styles.

He shared his vision of an innovative division where employees could take risks and have a high degree of autonomy in their work. He described a division where communications flowed freely up, down and across the organization. Hershock asked his managers to consider what they could do to help him realize that vision.

Over the next two years, OH&ESD experimented with business development teams focused on charting new opportunities and products, but their progress wasn't producing the results the division needed. That's when Hershock explored a whole new approach called "cross-functional action teams." The goal was to transform the division from a complacent and risk-averse one to an innovative, flexible, daring organization. Creating the action teams meant significant restructuring of the division, Hershock said. "Change like this is a revolutionary process. You can't expect to move from one system to another without some complications."

The action teams were pivotal to success. The teams focused only on new products with high potential. People who led the teams were those with a demonstrated passion for the product not seniority. Team leaders recruited team members, but individuals could decide to join or not. Team membership was above and beyond each employee's own existing job. Each member had training in the interpersonal challenge of real team work and each team established its own goals, budgets and milestones. Hershock, who retired as vice president, Marketing, made sure that each action team had the support it needed, including a "senior sponsor"

1 OH&ESD developed a new line of particulate respirators in the 1990s designed to meet stringent, new regulations. Today, 3M is the global leader in respiratory protection. **2** 3M developed this mission logo for use during the first joint experimental program with NASA. **3** 3M scientists pack up for a 1988 launch of the Challenger shuttle on which 3M experiments were conducted.

Background: Dyneon fluoroelastomer raw gum

②

3M even followed its technologies into outer space. As early as 1958, Scotch audio tape brought a Christmas message of peace from U.S. President Dwight Eisenhower transmitted from an Atlas satellite orbiting Earth. In the late 1960s, the Apollo 7 mission made extensive use of 3M fluoroelastomers that could withstand high temperatures. Over time, 3M tapes, plastics, sealers, adhesives and ceramics were part of spacecraft construction and even protective clothing for astronauts.

But, the most significant space age assignment came in the mid-1980s, when 3M teamed up with the National Aeronautical and Space Administration (NASA) to begin long-range, basic research in space. The attraction was the near-zero gravity and high-vacuum environment that created conditions virtually impossible to duplicate on Earth. At the time, Les Krogh, senior vice president, Research and Development, now retired, believed that the agreement with NASA would put 3M in the middle of some of the most exciting research being done. "It brought 3M's worldwide technical community recognition as a company at the leading edge of technology," he said. The image was enhanced when 3M became the

first nonaerospace company to respond when U.S. President Ronald Reagan called for private sector involvement in a permanently manned space station.

3M's interest in microgravity research initially came as a surprise to NASA according to Chris Podsiadly, then director, 3M's Science Research Laboratory, now retired, the 3M team leader. "When we first approached NASA, they said, 'You've got to be kidding,'" Podsiadly remembered. "We convinced them we were one of the premier materials companies in the world and this space 'lab' would lead to new products. In nine months, we went from a blank page to a piece of space hardware that flew in the space shuttle." 3M successfully conducted experiments in space including growing perfect organic crystals and making organic optical compounds—both with high potential applications in the embryonic fiber optics industry. More experiments with polymers yielded new information and Podsiadly's original team of about seven people grew to more than 100.

While 3M's involvement with the program ended in the late 1980s, as public support of America's space program eroded, 3M was a beneficiary of the pioneering work. "This project increased 3M's worldwide visibility," Podsiadly said, "and— perhaps most importantly— people began to understand that 3M was a leader in many technical areas."

③

from the division's executive team. The sponsor ran interference when a team faced resource problems or political resistance. Teams met quarterly with Hershock in informal lunches to review their progress.

From 1986 to 1996, OH&ESD introduced 20 new products, and 10 out of the 11 products developed by the division's action teams—those with the highest potential—made it to market on time. Overall, the time involved in new product development was cut in half. By 1992, 30 percent of the division's sales came from products developed in the previous five years. Time to market ranged from four months to 24 months depending upon whether new manufacturing processes and equipment had to be invented. Quality in the division reached a new high. "We met every single one of our objectives," Hershock said. "We significantly reduced internal barriers to innovation . . . and pushed decision making down to include more levels than ever before. And, we could honestly say that we built a workplace culture that really energized the division for growth."

> Dental Products: Renewal From the Ground Up

Few companies have ever won the Malcolm Baldrige National Quality Award—the most coveted recognition for quality in American business. In 1997, 3M Dental Products Division joined this elite group. Bob Sossaman, a senior tool and die maker at 3M's Irvine, California, plant where dental products are manufactured, echoed his co-workers when he said, "It was like winning an Oscar. It confirms that—every day—each of us is making an important contribution to something great."

In the 1980s, 3M's dental business was 20 years old. It had established a strong niche in dental bonding adhesives and was the market leader. But, by the late 1980s, strong competition was eroding 3M's business and its patents were expiring. "New product flow was down to about zero, the division had product quality issues and the financials looked poor," said Charles Reich, who became division vice president in April

1990 and currently is executive vice president, Electro and Communications Market and Corporate Services. Dental products had become a fast paced industry, a lot like a consumer business. New products had to be introduced quickly or the competition would step in and fill the void. Consistent quality in dental products was not the industry norm. If 3M Dental could be synonymous with quality, that would give the division a decided marketplace advantage.

3M's chairman of the board and CEO, Allen Jacobson, had just introduced a new quality program called Q90s, patterned after the Baldrige Quality Award. The seven-step Baldrige process involved important business dimensions including leadership, product development, information systems, human resources, results measurement and customer satisfaction. Reich asked the quality manager of Dental Products, Duane Miller, to get details. "We weren't trying to win the award," Reich said. "What we wanted most was to know how the Baldrige process could work for us."

> I was planning to retire. But, when I heard what management wanted to do, I rethought my plans. I was convinced we could do it if we worked together. And, I wanted to be part of the process. **> Jim Peterson** *retired advanced technologist, Dental Products Division*

What happened next involved every one of the division's 700 employees. For the first time, strategic planning wasn't done by an isolated management group; instead, one-third of the employees were involved. Teamwork—especially focused on identifying problems and solving them to benefit customers—became a top priority. Dental Products teams learned to work together to significantly accelerate new product development and commercialization.

On the way to winning the Baldrige Award, the Dental Products Division re-created itself with astonishing results. From 1992 to 1997, there was a whopping 55 percent increase in productivity. Sales doubled, the division's customer base grew by 80 percent, distributors gave 3M high marks and 3M dental employee satisfaction results far exceeded those of their competitors.

. . . the culture of striving for excellence— continuous improvement in how we meet our customers' expectations—that's what matters to me. And, it matters very much.

> **Christelle Dufaut** *materials management coordinator,*
Dental Products Division Business Center, 3M France

When Reich moved on to become vice president of the Occupational Health and Environmental Safety Division in 1997, Fred Palensky succeeded him and took the long awaited phone call from the Baldrige Award committee. Dental Products had applied twice in eight years and the second attempt was successful. "Winning the Baldrige Award was a thrill. But, the bigger thrill was doing business in that environment," Palensky, now executive vice president, Specialty Material Markets and Corporate Services, said. "The business is on its way to being the dental supplier of choice to every customer." The division has continued to grow and its achievement has been an inspiration to others at 3M. "I hoped that we could get out there, do it and lead by example," said Reich. "I hoped we could have a positive impact on the company and we have."

In late 2001, the Dental Products Division combined with ESPE, a developer and manufacturer of dental products and delivery systems based in Munich, Germany. The combined businesses now operate as 3M ESPE, a division of 3M Health Care.

> **3M Hutchinson—A Resolve to Renew**

Just after World War II, the community leaders of Hutchinson, Minnesota, met to decide how best to use the local plant no longer needed by the U.S. government. Their search led them to St. Paul where they persuaded 3M to buy the empty plant. It was February 1947 when 3M began producing what had already become its famous Scotch cellophane tape.

It was a small factory; it grew, it grew and it kept on growing . . . > **Arnold Piepenburg** *one of the first 10 3M Hutchinson plant employees*

For nearly five decades, the 3M Hutchinson site added a wide variety of consumer, office, industrial and electrical tapes, even though a crippling fire in 1951 leveled the plant's warehouse and could have stalled the growth. By late 1956, with a newly built 78,000-square-foot plant adjacent to the existing one, 3M began making Scotch magnetic tape. One year later, the plant

1 In 1997, 3M Dental Products Division won the coveted Malcolm Baldrige Quality Award. **2** The Hutchinson plant held an open house in 1948, just a year after it first began manufacturing Scotch cellophane tape.

produced its first roll of commercial videotape. With the fast growth of 3M Magnetic Media Division's products, the plant expanded again with a 244,000-square-foot addition in 1966. Meanwhile, the neighboring 3M tape plant saw multiple additions. When Post-it notes were introduced nationwide in 1980, the 3M Hutchinson plant was selected to manufacture them. There were many more plant additions over the years as manufacturing at Hutchinson grew.

Deservedly proud of its accomplishments, the 3M Hutchinson plant also became the first 3M facility to earn ISO-9002 recognition for meeting tough global quality standards. Within four years of that milestone, however, the 3M Hutchinson plant had the most challenging assignment in its history. When 3M exited the consumer and professional videotape business in 1996, the plant lost most of the work on which it had come to depend. Doug Ward, now manufacturing director, Personal Care and Related Products Division, was plant manager when that occurred.

3M's goal was not to lay off a single employee involuntarily. Some senior employees took separation packages and retired early, losing what Jim Bauman, who succeeded Ward as plant manager, estimated to be 7,000 years of manufacturing experience. That loss made the transition even more challenging, Bauman said, but with the help of manufacturing executives at 3M Center in St. Paul, the 3M Hutchinson plant was able to add six new manufacturing lines. They included VHB (very high bond) tape for the aircraft industry, Post-it flags, Scotch pop-up tape strips, surface mount supplies and specialty media. The plant also opened a new tape development center focused on pharmaceutical and microabrasives applications. Employment at 3M Hutchinson stabilized at about 1,700 employees after 1995.

When 3M made the announcement, the whole city of Hutchinson held its breath. 3M people came out and said, "We'll do everything possible not to lay off employees." And, they did.

> **Linda Rosenow** *long-time 3M Hutchinson employee*

One of the plant's strengths was its "focused factories," a system employed at all 3M manufacturing facilities that divides the work into business groupings to serve 3M customers at the highest level. Each of these focused factories had its own production and support employees. When the transition occurred, the plant was reorganized into seven focused factories: stationery and office supplies; high-performance tapes; specialty coating and converting; specialty media; tape development for pharmaceuticals and microabrasives; vinyl and nonwovens; and surface mount supplies. Plant employees participated in process and business teams to identify, plan and implement ongoing plant improvements.

Today, 3M Hutchinson is the company's largest manufacturing operation—covering 1.3 million square feet, on 230 acres and serving 21 divisions. To provide

1-2 The 3M Hutchinson plant had to renew itself after 3M exited the videotape business in 1996. It added six new manufacturing lines, as well as a new tape development center, and is now 3M's largest manufacturing operation. Shown are the North (top) and South Buildings.

Following technology wherever it leads sometimes means challenging a company titan. That's what Casey Carlson, a 3M industrial designer, did when he and his team introduced a new tape delivery system, the Scotch pop-up tape strip dispenser, in April 1997. "Scotch Magic tape, introduced in 1960, was the crown jewel," said Carlson, "and the legacy was so strong that it almost prevented innovation." Developed in partnership with 3M Chemist Elmer Blackwell, who focused on the tape strips, the new product led to a line of desk-top and wrist-band dispensers that provide handy, pre-cut, two-inch pieces of Scotch brand tape. The innovation won both an IDEA Silver Award and a Design Plus Award at the prestigious Frankfurt Fair in Germany in 1997. It also was selected as a "Good Buy" winner by Good Housekeeping magazine that year, which praised it as a "better than ever version of products we already loved."

"The program laid the foundation for development of a new 'tape delivery system' that can encompass all of our major lines in stationery and office supplies: tape, Post-it flags and Post-it notes," Carlson said. But, the road to innovation wasn't easy.

Some worried that a new tape dispenser would "cannibalize" the crown jewel of transparent tapes. Dispensed in the traditional "snail," curved shape, the product had been around since the 1930s and its market share was high around the globe.

"When you own a business that big and legendary," Carlson said, "innovation doesn't seem as important as avoiding a mistake." Because a clear majority of tape sales occur in November and December, the major gift-giving months, Carlson focused on developing a tape system that made wrapping gifts easier. While Carlson heard discouraging words from people within 3M (and some called him an incorrigible maverick), he also had sponsors and champions, including 3M's CEO and chief executive officer, L.D. DeSimone. "When

I met with Desi, he said, 'I like what you're doing and I believe in it. But, don't get upset. There are a lot of ideas that don't make it and, if that happens, move on to the next good idea.'" Carlson stuck with his Scotch pop-up program and, in 1999, he was one of the first winners of 3M's prestigious Innovator Award. The award went to technical people for exemplary use of their 15 percent time. (It has since been combined with the Circle of Technical

Excellence.) Reluctantly, Carlson invited his family to the awards ceremony and they all came. "My sister came up to me and said, 'I've been observing people, and you just don't fit.' But, that's the point, I said, when you watch the videos that feature award winners, none of these people fits a mold. We're kindred spirits." And, that's a good thing for 3M.

a sense of the plant's scale, in a single year, it produces nearly one billion molded parts used in 3M's transparent tape business and 5.5 million miles of transparent tape—enough to circle the earth 235 times. It is a proud plant. People who work there point to a strong safety record, extensive training programs for employees, high productivity, clean, neat surroundings and employee volunteerism in the community.

> **Follow the Technology Wherever it Leads**

At the heart of renewal are new applications of technologies. People call this "uninhibited research for uninhabited markets" at 3M, and the philosophy means following technology wherever it leads, often into new product areas never imagined. 3M's experimentation with fluorochemicals back in the mid-1940s is a prime example. Without knowing how the technology would be applied, 3M bought key fluorochemical patents from a Penn State University professor in 1944. Although she worked on developing a rubber material that could resist deterioration from jet aircraft fuel, Patsy Sherman, then a 3M lab technician, happened upon a totally different use for the compound that became the successful Scotchgard fabric protector in 1956. Experimentation

continued in a category of fluoropolymer compositions called fluoroelastomers.

That early work led to high tech applications for the military and aerospace, but the products were costly, said Bob Brullo, who joined 3M as a product development engineer in 1973. "Les Krogh, who later retired as senior vice president, Research and Development, was then vice president of the Commercial Chemicals Division," said Brullo. "We were trying to decide what to do with this little elastomer business. Les said, 'We're either going to get serious or get out of it.' The materials were ahead of their time and DuPont dominated the business. We decided to pick and choose where we were going to fight. We found exploitable, vulnerable niches where we could go in, develop new technologies and establish strong customer relationships. We came out of nowhere and became a player; DuPont couldn't ignore us anymore." 3M's new key customers were the manufacturers of O-rings for a myriad of uses. Since the late 1970s, the business has grown in double digits annually.

Looking for ways to expand its customer base, 3M sought out the automotive industry. "We started calling on GM, Ford and Chrysler with the idea of understand-

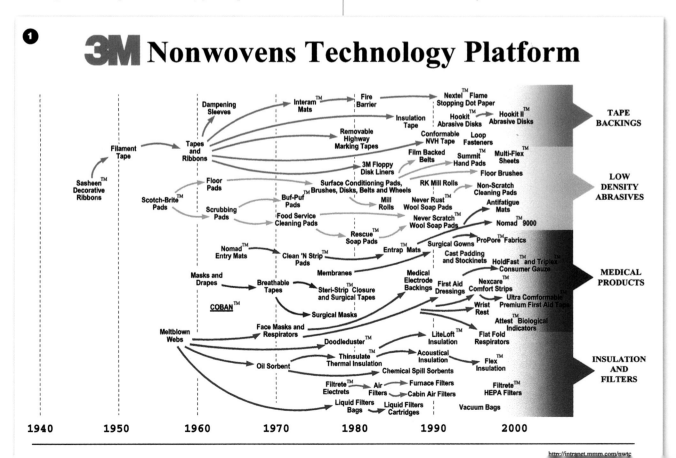

❶ **3M Nonwovens Technology Platform**

http://intranet.mmm.com/nwtc

ing their end-user requirements," said Brullo. "We developed products to meet those specific needs." Not long afterward, Brullo filled a small box with 3M's automotive parts samples and headed to Europe, at the encouragement of George Hegg, an executive with extensive experience in 3M's international business.

"I went from country to country working with our local 3M employees, calling on fabricators and end-users, explaining what our materials were and what they could do. We had to position ourselves as a raw material solution provider because we sold only the base polymer and proprietary curing agents not the finished parts. The next year it was Asia." Over time, Brullo upgraded his "sample box" to a fishing lure box that nicely accommodated his array of fuel line hoses, O-rings, oil seals for engines, engine valve seals, little rubber molded "elbows" for crank case ventilation and other prosaic pieces and parts made from 3M's Fluorel fluoroelastomers. From a 5 percent market share in 1978, Brullo said 3M's share in this high potential niche grew to about 55 percent in the United States by the late 1980s.

"We were a very small part of 3M's chemical business," said Brullo, "but we operated like a little, entrepreneurial company. We focused on offering innovative technologies and a very fast response time to our customers. We had a tremendous amount of freedom to do what we had to do. We also knew how to circumvent the bureaucracy when we had to. It was about 1993 when we caught up to DuPont globally and passed them." Brullo credits cross functional teamwork and strategic alliances with the success of the business.

"Sid Leahy was our group vice president," Brullo said. "He urged us to start building alliances outside the company that could lead to codevelopment projects." Experimentation followed with several alliances; some worked, others didn't. There were lessons learned, but out of these relationships came technology and product gains and the recognition that 3M should team up with a "big player" to leverage its applications know-how and technological expertise to the broader fluoropolymer industry. Along the way, the group won two Golden Step awards for their commercialization of major new products in 1982 and 1986.

1 This Nonwovens Technology Platform vividly demonstrates how 3M follows technology wherever it leads, into areas never imagined when the technology was first developed. Starting with ribbon in the 1940s, hundreds of products using nonwoven technology have since been developed in almost every area of 3M. **2** Dyneon is associated with a wide array of products ranging from nonstick coatings on cookware to seals used in space exploration. Dyneon, now a 3M division, is the second largest producer of fluoropolymers in the world. **3** Raw materials used in the production of Dyneon products.

The ultimate outcome of this search for the ideal alliance was a 3M partnership with German chemicals giant Hoechst A.G., formed in 1996 to sell a line of high performance rubber and plastic resin products. The joint venture, named Dyneon L.L.C., tested a business paradigm back in St. Paul— historically, people believed that whatever 3M took to market should be developed within the company's walls. When 3M and Hoechst embarked on this enterprise involving 600 employees, both companies were generating about $150 million in annual revenues on their fluoroelastomer products. Together, the pair quickly generated a 16 percent sales gain. The companies focused on a resin called THV that retained its flexibility at very low temperatures.

"Given our position in automotive," Brullo said, "we knew where to find new applications for THV." In short order, the material lined the filler tubes of auto gas tanks to limit the escape of vapors, helping car manufacturers comply with U.S. Clean Air Act laws. THV also was an ideal film for covering greenhouses. It was a natural for fiber optic tubing used to pipe light into areas where accompanying heat might be dangerous—in a chemical plant, for example. The new applications kept multiplying. "The combination of Hoechst's manufacturing capabilities and 3M's applications and marketing expertise means we'll be able to bring products to market faster than ever before," Brullo told a Twin Cities

business reporter in 1997. Brullo didn't stop there. In 1998, another joint venture, called Alventia L.L.C., was formed with the Belgian chemical giant Solvay A.A. The agreement allowed a key 3M raw materials plant in Decatur, Alabama, to use Solvay's proprietary technology. The end product was cost effective and available to both companies. Today, the Dyneon brand name is associated with a wide array of products found in such diverse uses as nonstick coatings on cookware to seals used in space exploration. 3M purchased Hoechst's interest in the joint venture at the end of 1999 and Dyneon is now the world's second largest producer of fluoropolymers. Brullo, now managing director, 3M United Kingdom-Ireland Region, was Dyneon's first vice president and general manager.

> **Telecom—Classic 3M at its Best**

With a four-page business plan, Wayne Bollmeier, division vice president, Electrical Products Division, set two young "intrepreneurs" loose in 1968. They were Red Carter, product sales manager, Electronic Products Division, and Gary Pint, then product manager, Telecom Division, both now retired. "Telecommunications and electronics were together at first under Wayne," Pint recalled. The start-up of what later became 3M Telecom—about an $800 million business in 2000— began with what Pint called "an incredibly simple plan"

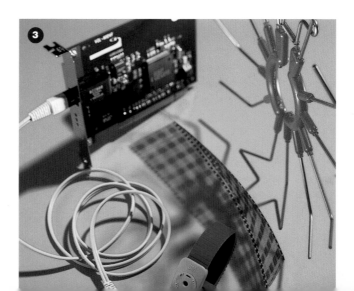

1-3 3M is a leading supplier of connecting, splicing, insulating and protective products for the electronics, telecommunications and electrical markets.

written by the two men. "It was classic 3M at its best," Pint recalled. "We had high-level sponsorship in Wayne, who trusted us and welcomed new ideas. He encouraged us to look at how 3M could build a market focus on communications and electronics combined."

At the time, the businesses were worth no more than $4 million. "We had connectors and insulating products and tapes and splice closures for the electrical industry," said Pint, who went on to become group vice president, Telecom Systems. "We had technology breakthroughs in connecting small gauge wires for electronics and telecommunications. We had splicing plastic that was insulated for telephone cables and something new— flat ribbon cables with multiconductor connectors that could be used in the emerging computer industry. But, this was the 1960s and there wasn't much computer business. We figured we could cover the market with 18 to 20 sales reps, four sales managers and a small staff in St. Paul with a little bit dedicated to R&D."

Carter and Pint asked Bollmeier for about $1 million

in project funding and he agreed to the plan on April 1, 1968, recalled Pint. "He left us alone," said Pint. "After about nine months, he came to us and asked, 'How long is it going to take to prove that what we did was right?' I said, 'By the end of this year, we'll have $6 million to $10 million in business and we'll be off and running.' Wayne believed in the business and he put up the money. The market was dynamic; it had a lot of unknowns, but he trusted us and believed 3M had a big opportunity."

By following the technology wherever it led, that embryonic start led to a huge business. From originally offering a few tapes and simple copper connectors, the 3M telecommunications business has expanded into about 5,000 products across several markets by applying the many innovative technologies available. In addition to inventing one of the first multiple copper splicing systems and the first multiple fiber mechanical splicing system, 3M products help deliver transmission signals to people's homes through the switches that send those signals.

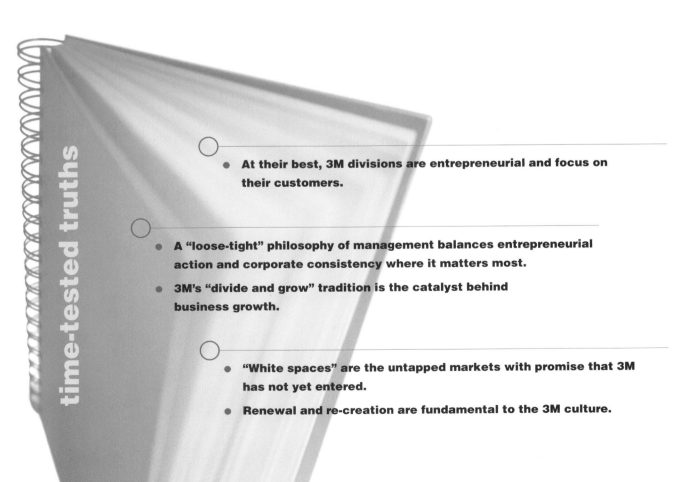

time-tested truths

- At their best, 3M divisions are entrepreneurial and focus on their customers.

- A "loose-tight" philosophy of management balances entrepreneurial action and corporate consistency where it matters most.
- 3M's "divide and grow" tradition is the catalyst behind business growth.

- "White spaces" are the untapped markets with promise that 3M has not yet entered.
- Renewal and re-creation are fundamental to the 3M culture.

- Pollution Prevention Pays
- Long-term investment in South Africa, Asia Pacific
- An enduring culture around the globe
- Good corporate citizenship

Grand Opening

BigBang₂

12/11/99

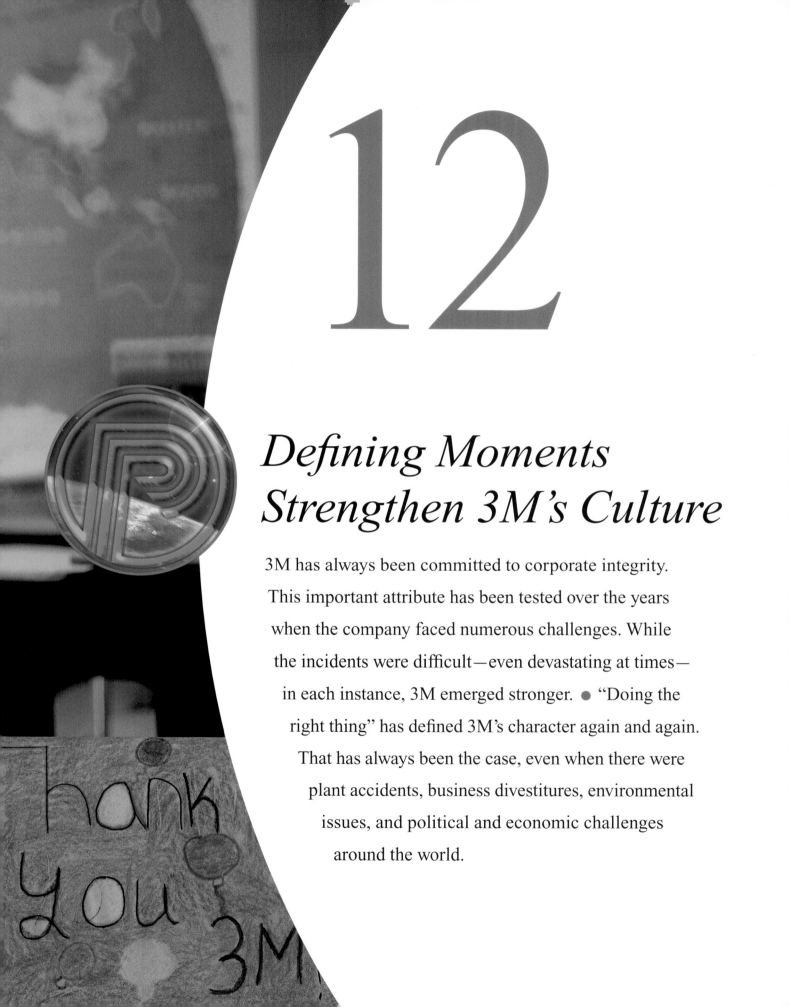

12

Defining Moments Strengthen 3M's Culture

3M has always been committed to corporate integrity. This important attribute has been tested over the years when the company faced numerous challenges. While the incidents were difficult—even devastating at times— in each instance, 3M emerged stronger. ● "Doing the right thing" has defined 3M's character again and again. That has always been the case, even when there were plant accidents, business divestitures, environmental issues, and political and economic challenges around the world.

Corporate core attributes and values combine to influence decisions—big and small, day after day. They establish the guidelines for how a company and its people will act. Over time, 3M's decisions and practices have underscored a commitment to "doing the right thing"—not the easy, expeditious or less costly thing.

> The Day "the Mining" Blew Up

At 8:20 a.m. on Thursday, February 8, 1951, a massive gas explosion rocked three 3M buildings at the corner of Arcade and Fauquier Streets on St. Paul's East Side. About 4,000 3M employees had just reported for work. The explosion started in Building 12, a six-story structure where minerals were crushed and treated in ovens heated with butane. The blast swept through underground tunnels and damaged a neighboring tape packing plant as well as 3M's main office building. Fifteen people died and 49 others were injured in St. Paul's worst disaster. Two sides of the minerals building were blown out and employees were pinned under falling floors, walls and ceilings.

"Mobilizing its forces quickly," the *St. Paul Dispatch* newspaper reported, "the company assigned one man to each victim's family to work with them as long as necessary. A $25,000 emergency fund was set up to pay for taxi fares to hospitals, baby sitters, transportation of relatives from out of town, telegrams to survivors, funeral costs and whatever else was needed."

3M also created an emergency aid committee. "The idea was to help families re-establish themselves," Ivan Lawrence, vice president, Personnel, told the *Dispatch*. "We were determined not to make them dependents, but to help keep them on an even keel and restore their lives as close as possible to what they were before the explosions."

The company quickly made sure that workers' compensation and insurance payments, as well as company benefits, were paid to the survivors. 3M also contacted the U.S. Office of Social Security to speed up payments. Since the day after the blast was a payday, a special paymaster's window was created to distribute wages on time.

Damage to 3M property totaled about $1 million but settling that claim was a distant second to caring for 3M people and their families. "The company just took care of people," said John Pitblado, branch sales manager, Los Angeles, at the time. Pitblado later retired as president, U.S. Operations.

> Pollution Prevention Pays and Pays and . . .

The 1970s would prove to be a massive test of 3M's corporate culture and resolve. That was when environmentalists and the federal government took aim at long-standing, approved environmental practices used by American companies. When Rachel Carson's book, "Silent Spring," was published in 1962, it began to raise the nation's collective awareness to the dangers of water pollution. Millions of people across the country marched in the country's first Earth Day in 1970 to call attention to environmental concerns. And, Congress passed the Clean Water Act.

Chapter opening photos 3M Visiting Wizards share their enthusiasm for science with children at area events; 3M helped fund the new Science Museum of Minnesota and has had a relationship with the museum for many years; Elementary students, like this one, write thank you notes for the school supplies they received through a program developed by 3M, known as Stuff for Schools; The Pollution Prevention Pays (3P) program began in 1975 with a goal of reducing the source of pollution in 3M products and processes, while saving the company money.

After the Clean Water Act was passed, 3M realized it needed to address all three parts of the environmental equation: air, water and waste. For 3M, the biggest issue by far was air emissions because hundreds of the company's products required solvents during manufacturing. In many cases, the only way to eliminate solvents was by developing completely new manufacturing methods that did not require their use. The search was on for alternatives.

Technical people were encouraged to eliminate or replace the solvents that they had used for decades. The company devoted more than $1 million annually to R&D efforts relating to just this issue. Because 3M recognized the benefits of pollution prevention early, it soon was viewed as a leader in this arena.

3M's leadership was due, in part, to the 1960 hiring of its first Ph.D. engineer who specialized in what was then called "sanitary engineering." Joe Ling came to Minnesota from China in 1948 to earn an advanced degree. Ling wanted to focus on municipal engineering, but there was no such program at the University of Minnesota. His advisors encouraged him to design the first degree in sanitary engineering, and Ling ran up 120 course credits instead of the required 72. "My advisors were so proud of their new major that they kept asking me to take more courses," he joked.

Ling and his wife, Rose, returned to China to help their country cope with its primitive conditions, but the Communists had taken over the country prior to their return. The Lings were treated well in their homeland, but the climate was oppressive. "My wife and I had many special privileges . . . But, this was not our China," Ling said. "Everyone was suspicious of everyone else. Everyone carried a notebook. Everyone was afraid to speak." The Lings left China for the United States and Joe Ling joined 3M.

"Like most American companies, 3M was just beginning to grapple with water issues," Ling said, "water for air conditioning, water for boilers, water sources for manufacturing and handling wastewater. 3M had lots of chemical engineers but only one environmental engineer, me." Unlike other companies, 3M, under Ling's direction, chose to adopt environmental policies that far exceeded the letter of the law. In 1966, Ling and fellow 3M engineer Charles Kiester, who later retired as senior vice president, Engineering, Manufacturing and Logistics, presented a paper to the 21st Industrial Waste Conference and advocated a carefully planned waste reduction program in addition to a waste disposal system.

When Ling appeared before Congress as it was crafting its first clean water bill, he advocated "a total environment concept" that focused on more than water alone. He explained to Congress that it would be counterproductive to mandate a zero-pollutant discharge into the nation's streams because moving to this level would create more pollution elsewhere than it would eliminate.

At 3M, Ling authored a comprehensive program in 1975 that he called Pollution Prevention Pays (3P). The goal was to eliminate or reduce sources of pollution in 3M products and processes rather than clean it up later.

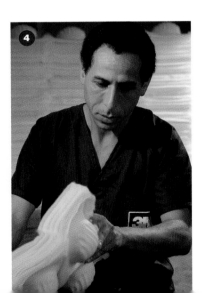

1 Rescuers rush an injured employee from the scene of a 1951 gas explosion at the 3M Minerals Building. **2** An early Pollution Prevention Pays (3P) brochure. **3** Tom Baltutis tests water samples at the 3M Cottage Grove, Minnesota, plant. **4** 3M employees in Argentina recycle waste that results from the manufacturing of respirators.

The third P—Pays—was a critical element. Ling believed that without a pay back there was no real incentive to change products or processes that were easy to use and worked well, even if they contained pollutants. Ling's ideas were radical for the era, but he caught the ear of Ray Herzog, then 3M's chairman of the board and CEO. Both men shared the philosophy that it would cost less to reduce or eliminate pollution at the source—rather than trying to clean it up afterward. When Herzog gave Ling the okay to proceed with 3P, it became one of the first environmental programs of its kind in the world launched by a major manufacturing company.

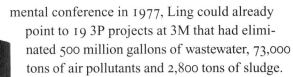

One early example was striking. 3M engineers replaced a proven, solvent-based manufacturing process with a water-based system for applying adhesive to Scotch Magic tape. That change eliminated millions of pounds of air discharges and significantly reduced pollution-control costs.

With savings like that, Ling quickly gained a wide audience for his approach. When he spoke to an environ-

We had a commitment to continuously reduce our impact on the environment. The world is a very small place and pollution doesn't respect national boundaries. **> Joe Ling** *retired vice president, Environmental Engineering and Pollution Control*

mental conference in 1977, Ling could already point to 19 3P projects at 3M that had eliminated 500 million gallons of wastewater, 73,000 tons of air pollutants and 2,800 tons of sludge.

By 1985, when Bob Bringer succeeded Ling as vice president, Environmental Engineering and Pollution Control, he estimated that the 3P program had saved the company $420 million—a conservative estimate because the sum was based only on first-year results from 2,261 3P projects. Together, these projects had reduced

According to our chairman of the board and CEO, Allen Jacobson, all new air pollution control installations will be judged not by return on investment but by their technical acceptability and environmental benefit. **> Bob Bringer** *retired staff vice president, Environmental Technology and Services*

air pollutants by 121,072 tons, water pollutants by 14,550 tons, sludge and solid waste by 314,000 tons, and wastewater by 1.6 billion gallons worldwide.

Taking an even stronger stand in 1987, 3M's Operations Committee, the senior leadership of the company, approved 3P Plus, a voluntary plan with a clear message: "With or without cost savings, we will spend what is necessary to protect the environment." A major investment of $150 million gave teeth to the message.

1 3M's innovative 3P program was a winner of a 1996 Presidential Award for Sustainable Development.
2 A system developed by 3M engineers reclaims more than 95 percent of a solvent used at the 3M Greenville, South Carolina, facility.

Over the years, 3M's focus on the environment also began to embrace the company's long-standing worldwide effort to reduce workplace injuries and illness as well as a pragmatic belief in sustainable development—producing products with fewer environmental, health and safety effects. By 2000, the project that Ling started in 1975 had saved 3M more than $850 million and prevented 1.7 billion pounds of pollution through 4,750 programs. Between 1990 and 2000, the company has reduced its volatile organic air emissions by 88 percent, cut its manufacturing releases to water by 82 percent and reduced its solid waste by 24 percent.

One unanticipated off shoot of the environmental program has been the development of new products that were only possible because of the company's new solventless processes. Film polymers in paper-thin sheets

Sustainable development meets the needs of the present generation without compromising the needs of future generations. > **Joe Ling**

that transmit and reflect light are among many technologies that have emerged. These brilliantly colored mirrors produced from polymers might never have been created if the process had involved solvents. By not using solvents, technical employees have often found it easier to get products developed and out the door.

3M received the first annual Gold Medal for Corporate Environmental Achievement given by the World Environment Center and America's Corporate Conscience Award from the Council on Economic Priorities; the 3P program won the first U.S. President's Sustainable Development Award; and, in Germany, 3M was ranked second in the world for "eco-performance" among the 50 largest chemical using companies.

> ### An Unpopular Decision Proven Right

"To a growing number of multinational corporations, South Africa is like a piece of flypaper," one business reporter observed in 1978. "It can hardly be overlooked. It tends to be pesky and it certainly is sticky."

3M had been in South Africa for 20 years when a small, but vocal, group of shareholders pressured the company to stop doing business there because the country was segregated and run by a white minority in a system called "apartheid." Many American companies left South Africa in the mid-1970s and others heard the same resolution posed at their annual meetings. "It's a complex question," Robert Adams, retired vice president, Research and Development, and chair of the company's Corporate Social Responsibility Committee, said in answering an angry shareholder at 3M's annual meeting in May 1978. "We certainly share the views of the proponents to eliminate racism in South Africa, but we differ on how it should be done."

3M was among the first 12 American companies to adopt the Sullivan Principles in 1977, a voluntary code in which the companies pledged to practice fair and equal employment practices as well as contribute to the

3 3M created an education and training center in South Africa to speed minority advancement in the company. **4** For more than a decade, 3M South Africa's Health Care business sponsored a program known as Move to Mobility that provides guide dogs, wheelchairs, walking sticks and mobility instructors to help people in rural areas.

By the early 1980s, there were concerns about 3M's concentration of all its corporate offices in Minnesota with no significant locations elsewhere. 3M leaders also believed that Minnesota's business climate discouraged expansion within the state. After 80 years in Minnesota, 3M began to look at new potential locations for some of its businesses.

Austin, Texas, looked appealing for 3M's new research and development campus. "The governor of Texas believed that the 'new Texas' should focus on technology, rather than our traditional industries, agriculture and oil," said Russell Bridges, who worked with Governor Mark White and later joined 3M. "3M wasn't having great success getting people from warmer climates to relocate to Minnesota and the engineering schools at the University of Texas [Austin] and Texas A&M had a lot to offer."

After considering 22 different cities in America's "sun belt," Austin was chosen. "3M wanted to create a combination of the Texas culture and the 3M culture," said Larry Joines, now retired, a 3M employee since 1952, who handled community relations. Austin was considered a sanctuary for people who wanted a more informal lifestyle. Locals saw it as one of the friendliest and prettiest cities in Texas with the highest level of education—given

the large number of college and university professors based there, plus the "brain trusts" of Motorola, Texas Instruments, IBM and Dell.

3M moved businesses involved in industries such as telecommunications, electronics, semiconductors, fiber optics, electrical transmission and distribution, and corrosion protection to Austin. Some were native St. Paul businesses, others had been acquisitions, such as the California-native Dynatel Corp. or the Austin-based APC Industries, both in product niches of the growing telecommunications business.

Bob Backlund, now retired, a 3M employee since 1953 in plant operations and management, participated in the design of the 1.7 million-square-foot center with nine interconnecting buildings on 158 acres. The labs were all on the same level with walkways and informal seating areas designed to spark spontaneous conversation and idea sharing. A huge open atrium created with 3M fresnel lenses captured light and brought it into the building. Interior colors of green, yellow, red and turquoise gave the spaces visual energy. A pioneering, holistic wellness program called Lifestyle 2000 had its start there. The center had high-speed communications lines and sophisticated videoconferencing equipment to help shrink the distance to St. Paul and other 3M locations. "Austin was designed to be an incubator for innova-

tion, a place where we could pilot new ideas and test them," said Backlund. "Because it was smaller, it was easier to start and try new things."

Ed Scharlau, who specialized in helping 3M families relocate to new cities and countries, was the first 3Mer to move his family to Austin in 1984. "The challenge in Austin was to move people and keep them whole as much as possible," he said. If a 3M employee was considering the move, the first step was a three-day, fact finding trip to Austin with a welcome reception, tour of the city and dinner with 3M Austin's leadership. Families learned about the housing market, schools and cultural attractions. Because the country was in an economic recession and mortgage rates were high, 3M helped ease financing costs. If employees didn't want the burden of selling their homes, 3M offered to purchase them.

A special program helped spouses find new jobs and volunteer opportunities. A 3M "friends club" offered recommendations for baby sitters, lawn services and orthodontists.

progress of black South Africans in the workplace and community.

3M South Africa was one of the first companies to integrate its workplace, even though local laws required segregation. The company's first full-scale cafeteria built for employees in the mid-1970s was also integrated— another radical step. To help speed the advancement of blacks into higher level jobs, 3M South Africa created its own education and training center in 1978.

By the mid-1980s, most American companies had bowed to shareholder pressure, but 3M was among the few that stayed in South Africa. "We believed that our aggressive effort to help blacks would ultimately prove more effective than pulling out of the country and forsaking our 1,250 employees there," Jim Thwaits, retired president, International Operations, said. "By withdrawing, we would have eliminated an opportunity to influence change."

Donn Osmon, now retired, then vice president, Marketing and Public Affairs, was assigned to coordinate the company's activities in South Africa during this controversial era. "We had boycotts against us, and we started to lose some business. The losses grew when customers withheld their orders because of our decision to stay," he said. "Our employees needed reassurance that we weren't going to leave. I met with church groups opposing our position. It wasn't pleasant, but at least they could understand our side when we said our employees had full careers in South Africa and most had their pensions built up. How could we walk away and dump them?"

Osmon remembered several highly lucrative offers made by large local companies to buy 3M South Africa, but the 3M Board of Directors' answer was "No thanks." "The whole decision boiled down to the economic welfare of our employees and their families."

3M was among 52 major American companies, including Kodak, General Motors, Control Data, Honeywell, Coca-Cola and Ford, that signed ads in South African newspapers in 1985 pledging to "play an active role" in ending apartheid.

Ultimately, 3M was proven right when South Africa gained its independence from apartheid in 1994 and a large number of companies that had left the country

returned. When that occurred, 3M was in the top 1 percent of South African wage payers; the percent of people of color in management had increased to 12 percent; and the company's goal was to increase that number even more. By 2001, nearly 40 percent of all managers and professionals were people of color. By staying put, 3M South Africa became known for fair and equal treatment and for supporting the emergence of a new society.

> **Thinking Long-Term**

This same willingness to remain when times were tough served 3M well in the Asia Pacific Region when a dramatic economic downturn in that region and depreciating currencies hit the company hard in 1997 and 1998. For more than 40 years, 3M had operated in the region and it had strong market positions. The region represented $2.6 billion in sales and 34 percent of 3M's total international revenues in 1997. As months passed, however, it became apparent that the economic weakness in Asia was deeper and more widespread than anyone expected.

Our goal is to be sustainable in countries that have a meltdown. It takes rigorous attention and action. We know how to do it and we do it well. Our employees and our customers in those countries value the fact that we'll be around. > **Ron Baukol** *retired executive vice president, International Operations*

Wall Street was impatient with 3M's performance and some observers suggested that the company should reduce its vulnerability and step back from Asia. But, Chairman of the Board and Chief Executive Officer L.D. DeSimone stood firm. "We have the ability to withstand difficult periods and we must," he said in 1999. "It was a steep, weighty problem for us, but we demonstrated that this company takes a long-term view. We're part of the Asian economies and we're tough enough to go through a rough period and come out stronger."

*Background: Volition
multimode fiber optic cable*

'Sorry, Mr. Ordway, Your Nametag has Expired'

For 30 years, Jerry Cederholm has had a glimpse of 3M's culture from a unique vantage point. As a security guard, Cederholm has walked the halls of 3M at all hours of the day and night. He's fielded phone calls; reported leaky roofs; shut off Bunsen burners; responded to alarms; and greeted executives, politicians, entertainers and athletes visiting 3M Center in St. Paul.

In recent years, Cederholm has been the first 3M employee most visitors to 3M Center meet. In hot or cold weather, he works in the guard shack greeting those who ask to park in the visitors' lot that is surrounded by the four administrative buildings.

Cederholm has noticed the quirks in 3M's culture of innovation. "I really respect the scientists," he said. "Some of them are a bit eccentric. I remember one fellow who kept his black dial phone long after we had push button phones installed in the labs. He had a corner cubicle that was piled high with papers. He must have crawled over a table to leave his office."

3M is still a family company, Cederholm said, but its size is challenging. "There's so much diversity—in products, in the number of projects the company's involved in, with people taking assignments all over the world," he said. But, even with all the change, the McKnight influence is palpable. "His spirit is still here," Cederholm said. "McKnight and 3M are synonymous. It feels like he might come in any day and look over my shoulder. I know we're operating in a changing world, but I don't

think 3M should ever stray from McKnight's values."

Comedian Red Skelton was Cederholm's favorite celebrity visitor. "He came for an anniversary event and took an informal walk around 3M Center," Cederholm said. "He was telling jokes and people were buckled over with laughter. He kept shaking employees' hands and saying 'thank you.'" Governors, city mayors, Olympians, President Gerald Ford, NASCAR drivers, even professional wrestlers have been guests at 3M.

Then there was the distinguished man wearing a suit and walking fast to a meeting. Cederholm was new to the company and he noticed the man's

nametag had expired. Cederholm politely but sternly asked the man to wait, while Cederholm called the front desk at 3M Center to confirm his decision. "I told Dorothy Fisher his name was John Ordway," said Cederholm, a native of Wisconsin who then had little knowledge of 3M's history. "She said, 'For crying out loud, let him in! He's on the board and he owns half of 3M.' Mr. Ordway was so nice about it; he never made an issue of it. He promised he'd get a new ID, too."

> **At its Heart, a Strong Culture**

In 3M's most challenging times, the company's culture has been tested and remained strong. The 1951 plant explosion brought out 3M's compassion for its employees and their families. When 3M was criticized for harming the environment, the company became a leader

McKnight did not want the evolution and expansion of the company to depend only on himself. He wanted to create an organization that would continually self-mutate from within, impelled forward by employees exercising their individual initiative. > **James Collins and Jerry Porras** *authors of "Built to Last"*

in pollution prevention. The company chose to be part of the solution, rather than a contributor to the growing, global problem. 3M believed it could also be part of a solution in South Africa and it did not bow to considerable public and shareholder pressure to leave the country. By remaining there, 3M put its South African employees and their families first. Similarly, when a steep economic downturn plagued Asia, 3M remained committed to being a long-term participant in the economy of that region.

William McKnight imagined a "flat" organization decades before the concept was a popular business model. His philosophy led to tenets of the 3M culture that employees and observers of the company repeat like a mantra: minimal hierarchy, intentional informality, strong support for creativity and innovation. People are trusted to make the right decisions on their own and they're rewarded for taking initiative. Challenging lead-

You can walk into a 3M plant anywhere in the world and you know it's 3M. Each plant has its own local habits and customs, but at the end of the day, people share the same belief in McKnight's principles. > **Neal Kurzejeski** *who has spent more than 20 years in 3M manufacturing*

ership is welcomed. When 3M employees show potential, they can expect broad responsibilities and multiple, varied assignments in their careers. The most effective leaders within 3M understand the value of teamwork, they promote openness and cooperation, and they actively share information and knowledge. Remarkably, whether a 3M employee is based in Finland, Japan, France, the United States or 60 other countries around the world, they share the same values with their colleagues oceans away. Some observers have said that this shared belief system—combined with cultural diversity—comes from international assignments that move people out of their home countries.

3M promotes a close-knit, caring, family-like atmosphere. Given its considerable size, this description may seem like a contradiction, but it is not. 3M tries to hire people for a career not just a job along a path of many corporate jobs. In fact, even in an era of "job-hopping," 3M's turnover rate is among the lowest of America's

Although 3M's leaders could never predict where the company would go in the future, they had little doubt that it would go far. It became a ticking, whirring, clicking, clattering clock with a myriad of tangible mechanisms well aligned to stimulate continual evolutionary progress.

> **James Collins and Jerry Porras**

Fortune 500 companies. From its early days, 3M demonstrated loyalty to its employees. In the depths of the Great Depression during the 1930s in America, 3M was able to avoid laying people off, when most other companies did.

The company gives its employees opportunities for career development and a variety of assignments that broaden them. Similarly, for decades, the company has had a promote-from-within policy that gives people with ambition a wide range of job choices.

When Edgar Ober, president, started profit sharing in 1916, and McKnight instituted a pension plan for employees in 1930 and an employee stock purchase plan in 1950, they were ahead of their time on all three counts. McKnight was convinced that 3M employees

Background: Scotchlite Diamond Grade reflective sheeting

were much more likely to be loyal and spend their careers with the company if they had a tangible stake in the organization. Equally important, McKnight and the leaders who followed him believed that people needed to be recognized for their contributions. That's why the company has a plethora of award programs that honor individual, as well as team, initiative and success.

People who have benefited from 3M's culture have moved a number of times and worked their way up. I'm one of them. > **Ken Bothof** *plant manager,*

3M Nevada, Missouri, plant

As the 3M work force changed and life demands on employees and their families increased over the decades of the 20th century, the company worked to be attentive to those changes. 3M was one of the first companies in Minnesota to start an Employee Assistance Program, in 1972. And, in the 1980s, the company focused on how more women and minorities could advance their careers and become leaders.

When economic recessions rocked American companies, 3M gave employees whose jobs were eliminated time to find a new job within 3M. And, if that effort was unsuccessful, they were offered outplacement services and a severance package. By the 1990s, when two-career couples and care for elderly parents became more common, 3M created a Work and Family Department to offer support and education focused on child care, long-term care, elder care, insurance options and a survivor support program for employees who lost loved ones.

> Good Corporate Citizenship

Raised on a small, South Dakota farm and the son of a community activist father, McKnight had a strong belief in giving. He made sure that his company was a solid corporate citizen and that it supported worthy local causes. McKnight also believed that 3M's community involvement would make its employees feel proud of their company and more connected to its broader goals.

In 1953, 3M was one of the first companies in Minnesota to create a corporate foundation. This formal commitment to community giving ensured that the money would be there for years to come, regardless of economic fluctuations in the marketplace. Along with cash contributions to education, health and human services, 3M has given numerous product donations each year and put great emphasis on employee volunteerism. In fact, a recent study of 3M volunteerism by the University of Minnesota Carlson School of

Mr. McKnight was a man with a golden heart. He felt very fortunate about what happened in his career and he wanted to give that benefit back. > **Don Larson** *retired president, 3M Foundation*

and Community Affairs

1 Denise Loving, 3M information analyst, is one of the many 3M employees who tutors students at St. Paul area schools.
2 Frank Junghans, a retired 3M chemical engineer, donates his time and skills to Habitat for Humanity through 3M Community Action Retired Employee Services (3M CARES).

Management found that more than 50 percent of the company's employees give volunteer time in a year and the dollar value of these gifts of time and energy exceeds $70 million.

Half of the foundation's cash funding remains in Minnesota with the focus on education, human services, arts and the environment. In the educational arena, funding is directed primarily toward higher education, particularly at colleges and universities where 3M recruits new employees.

3

We have a responsibility to be a good citizen wherever 3M operates. > Harry Heltzer

retired chairman of the board and CEO

One key beneficiary has been the University of Minnesota. 3M supports three endowed chairs at "the U." In addition, in anticipation of the Century of Innovation celebration, 3M contributed $15 million to the university to help support its future development. The money is designated to programs that enhance teaching and learning.

Half of the Foundation's giving involves disaster relief and matching gifts tied to employee contributions and volunteerism. The remaining 50 percent focuses on geographic areas of the United States where 3M has a

significant presence, for example, Austin, Texas, and Detroit, Michigan. 3M's corporate giving emphasizes its long and deep relationships in communities. The company's involvement with the Minnesota Historical Society (MHS) began in the late 1970s when Marshall Hatfield, a research chemist, was pursuing a personal history project. He discovered that some of the oldest items in the society's collection were captured on eroding glass plate negatives. Hatfield put the MHS in touch with experts at 3M who knew how to preserve them. That chance encounter ultimately

We needed to raise $14 million from the community and 3M's gift was like the Good Housekeeping Seal of Approval. > Nina Archabal

director, Minnesota Historical Society

led Hatfield to become president of the MHS board in 1994. Later a $1 million "anchor gift" from 3M helped fund construction of a new Minnesota History Center in St. Paul.

MHS is the second largest holder of corporate archives in the United States and 3M gave MHS a $500,000 grant to preserve and maintain 3M's historical

5

3 Each year 3M presents the Community Volunteer Award to employees who donate time to area charitable organizations. **4** 3M recently contributed $15 million to the University of Minnesota, so that students like these two will find teaching and learning enhanced. **5** A study done by the university's Carlson School of Management found that more than 50 percent of 3M employees volunteer every year.

collection. Since 1998, 3M has sponsored an annual National History Day at the MHS, a program that encourages as many as 25,000 Minnesota children, grades 6 to 12, to research and make presentations on science, technology and invention.

3M also has a relationship with the Science Museum of Minnesota that spans more than 25 years. Along with an annual gift of $120,000 beginning in 1993, 3M ❶ contributed $2.5 million to the new Science Museum perched on the Mississippi River Bluff in St. Paul that opened in December 1999. Volunteer Bob Barton, creator of 3M's Visiting Wizards, has worked with the museum for 25 years. Other 3M volunteers help with research on exhibits and new programs, technical training for museum staff and the preservation of artifacts. Still other volunteers have served on the museum board including 3M executives Paul Guehler, Bill Coyne, George Allen, Bob Adams and Ron Mitsch. 3M's product contributions to the museum have included Panaflex banners, multimedia and overhead projectors, Post-it notes with the museum logo, Interam wrap used during building construction, Nomad floor mats and maintenance supplies.

We had a last-minute request during construction. It was just wonderful being able to call 3M and ask, 'Can we get some help?' and the answer would always be, 'We'll go to work on it.'

> **James Peterson** *president, Science Museum of Minnesota*

In 3M's plant communities, the spirit of giving really shines. "We're a company of people who care about our communities," said Barbara Kaufmann, manager, 3M Foundation, Education Contributions. "We've always believed in being good citizens and looking out for the places from where we come. We want to work for good schools, healthy and safe communities." Each 3M plant

has a budget for community involvement and local employees help decide which causes to support.

At 3M's Nevada, Missouri, manufacturing plant with approximately 600 employees, the contributions from the plant and its employees account for $41,000, about one-third of the community's total United Way budget.

With about 1,000 employees and three separate plants, 3M Decatur, Alabama, is the largest employer in the area. The plants accounted for $121,225 to United Way in 2000, a combination of employee pledges, retiree contributions, a $35,000 corporate contribution, and a golf tournament that netted $9,766.

We think of ourselves as a 3M family in our small town. The spouse of one of our people on the production floor could easily be the Sunday school teacher or scout leader for my children. Many of our employees are community volunteers. > **Larry Johnson** *plant manager, 3M Knoxville, Iowa, plant*

"Because we hire locally, we've worked with our community college to identify the skills people need to succeed in a job at 3M," said Jim King, retired Decatur site manager. "Since 1992, the college has made a major effort to help us with production training, and we have people from our plant working on degrees in electrical and mechanical technology. The college is expanding its coursework and we're getting the training support we need." King is proud of the lives that his employees have outside the plant. "Sandra Klack is a production employee," he said, "and she's won 3M's national Community Volunteer Award two years in a row for helping teen-agers at risk."

1 3M organized the first Stuff for School Program in 1995. By 2001, the program had expanded and provided supplies to more than 14,000 students in 29 St. Paul public schools.

Over the years, 3M's penchant for giving has increased. 3M's cash contributions grew from $249,000 in 1953—the first year of the 3M Foundation—to $22 million in 2001. Product donations also have steadily risen to more than $20 million annually over more recent years. Early in 2002, 3M was awarded the Points of Light Foundation's Award for Excellence in Corporate Community Service in recognition of 50 years of volunteer service by 3M employees.

3M employees have always been willing to rise to a pressing need, including the aftermath of terrorist attacks on New York City and the Pentagon in Washington, D.C., on September 11, 2001. 3M employees from New York City and New Jersey assisted rescue workers at "ground zero," the site of the collapse of the World Trade Center's twin towers. John Becker, senior account representative, Occupational Health and Environmental Safety Division, slept in his van near the site so he could help rescue workers.

By September 13, 3M teams were in place in New York City and Washington, D.C., to support the rescue workers. "Our mission was to get the proper respirator products to the right people in the shortest time," said Dirk Edmiston, regional sales manager. Behind that simple statement was an all out effort on the East Coast as well as St. Paul and manufacturing plants in Aberdeen, South Dakota, and Valley, Nebraska. 3M donated more than 65,000 respirators to rescue workers at both disaster sites."

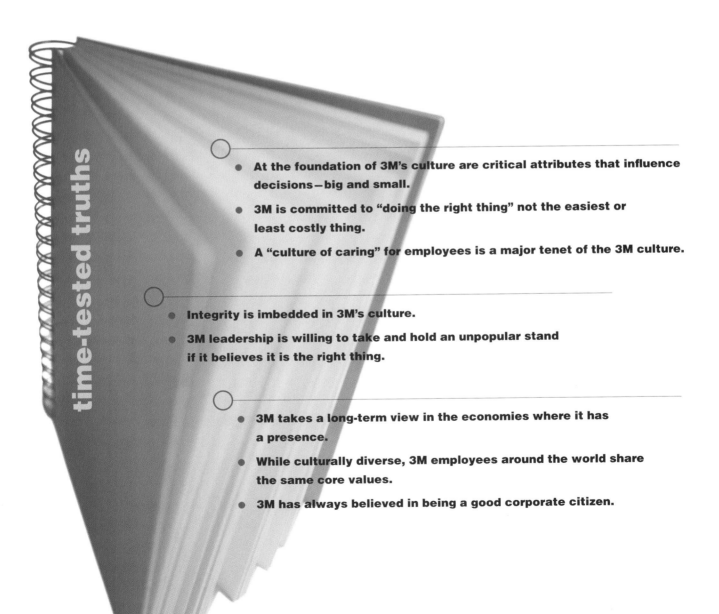

time-tested truths

- At the foundation of 3M's culture are critical attributes that influence decisions—big and small.
- 3M is committed to "doing the right thing" not the easiest or least costly thing.
- A "culture of caring" for employees is a major tenet of the 3M culture.

- Integrity is imbedded in 3M's culture.
- 3M leadership is willing to take and hold an unpopular stand if it believes it is the right thing.

- 3M takes a long-term view in the economies where it has a presence.
- While culturally diverse, 3M employees around the world share the same core values.
- 3M has always believed in being a good corporate citizen.

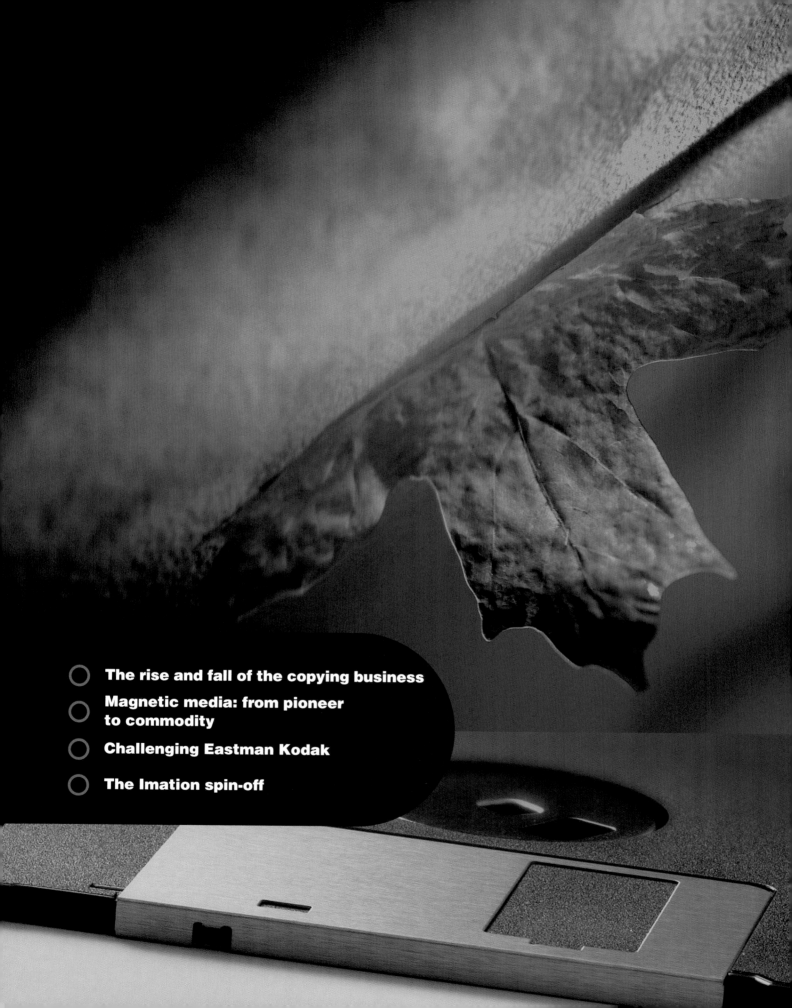

13

A Culture of Change

Long before "reinvention" became a buzzword of American business, 3M already had made change a central part of its corporate culture. Many say the company's success over the years is linked to its ability to change as 3M, its products and the world marketplace evolves. In fact, when the company greeted the new century in 2000, more than half the businesses that were 3M staples 20 years before had disappeared from the corporate portfolio. ● On the surface, eliminating a product, a project, even a division or more, might seem an admission of failure in business. But, that analysis would be superficial and incomplete. Over the years, 3M has worked to make its own products obsolete before its competition does—or the protection of crucial patents expires. 3M also has acquired companies with an eye on strengthening a core business. Some of these acquisitions have succeeded, while others failed to yield the expected product synergy or financial returns. For example, 3M acquired National Outdoor Advertising in 1947 (later called National Ad), believing that billboards would be natural venues for miles of Scotchlite reflective sheeting. Years later, even though National Ad produced strong revenues, the real goal—strong product synergy—hadn't materialized, so, in 1997, 3M sold the business.

In 1999, 3M sold its cardiovascular and orthopedic surgical products businesses valued at approximately $200 million when it became clear that 3M had no competitive advantage in an industry that favored suppliers with broad, deep product lines. In many cases, even though a business is exited, it leaves behind technological know-how that is valuable years later.

> 3M has an organic, living nature. Pruning is the natural, though difficult part of continuous revitalization. Meanwhile, new technology platforms become the seeds of future growth.
>
> **> L.D. DeSimone** *retired chairman of the board and chief executive officer*

3M even has shed businesses in industries it actually created when those ventures matured or changed so much that they no longer fit 3M or delivered the returns they once did. New competition often has been a factor in these tough decisions. For example, Xerox plain paper copying ultimately eclipsed 3M Thermo-Fax copiers, the first dry copying system in the world. 3M invented magnetic audio and video recording in 1947 and led the industry for decades before the business

> Yes, there were mistakes made. You work with human beings and you're going to make mistakes. **> Ken Schoen** *retired executive vice president, 3M Information and Imaging Technologies Sector*

became a low-price, low-margin commodity product in the 1980s. 3M also invented the world's fastest, high-speed, digital fax machine, but the product was ahead of its time, and 3M chose not to capitalize on the idea, believing that consumer acceptance would be slow.

In virtually every case, a product or business is shed when it no longer meets the rigorous financial expectations established in 1923 when William McKnight set annual sales growth at 10 percent and profit targets at 25 percent.

Chapter opening photos Carl Miller's "Eureka!" came after he viewed a leaf melting into a snowbank, which demonstrated differential heat absorption and led to the invention of thermography and 3M's Thermo-Fax business; Imation floppy diskette; Scotch recording tape No. 101A.

1 National Outdoor Advertising seemed like a natural outlet for Scotchlite reflective sheeting.

The decision to eliminate a product or business always involves soul-searching and loss for 3M decision-makers and employees alike. In making these decisions, 3M reflects an element of its culture dating back to 1902, when optimism and a can-do spirit prevailed over potentially fatal crises that threatened the very existence of the company.

Alex Cirillo Jr., vice president, Commercial Graphics Division, calls it the "MacGyver culture of 3M" (based on a 1980s' American television show): "We've always believed that we can take what's at hand—baling wire, this and that—and make something out of it, no matter what," he said. "We believe this in the beginning of projects, during projects and at the end of projects. We do everything possible to make something work before it's cut loose. This is a good thing, not a bad thing."

We need to have winning technologies, winning products and winning business positions.
And, if we don't, we have to take tough action.

> **John Benson** executive vice president, 3M Health Care Markets

Some observers have criticized 3M for the amount of time it takes to make a decision about "shedding" a business. The company kept National Ad in the fold for nearly 50 years. Some say the very existence of Duplicating Products (home of Thermo-Fax copiers) was questioned well before it departed 3M in 1985. The same observation was made a decade later when 3M decided to spin off its data-storage and imaging-systems businesses (with historical roots in magnetic recording and photography).

Of all the businesses 3M has shed over its 100 years, the two, seminal decisions that people point to as most significant involved the sale of 3M's Duplicating Products business to Harris Corporation in Atlanta, Georgia, and the spin-off of 3M's data-storage and imaging-systems businesses in 1995 creating a new company called Imation in Oakdale, Minnesota, near 3M headquarters. The two decisions have several elements in common—both involved businesses that 3M created and, in fact, ranked number one in the marketplace for decades. They were "homegrown" businesses—largely created within 3M and commercialized and built with the energy of many internal sponsors and champions. The businesses were risky because the products were based on pioneering technologies. They not only changed the basis of competition; they also created all new, global industries. The businesses were highly profitable for decades, and they represented a significant share of the company's total annual revenues. They also produced many of 3M's next generation of leaders.

Deciding to shed these businesses also set major precedents. Until the sale of the Duplicating Products Division to Harris, 700 employees never had left 3M at once. While they were guaranteed jobs at the new company, they no longer were part of 3M.

Even more difficult was the spin-off of 3M's data-storage and imaging-systems businesses, when 11,000

2 Bob Dwan and Groucho Marx, of "You Bet Your Life," listened to a recording on Scotch audiotape.
3 Magnetic recording and photography products eventually led to data-storage and imaging products in the 1980s and 1990s.

employees left to form a new company. At the same time, another 5,000 jobs were eliminated worldwide.

Both decisions occurred in a 10-year time span when the nature and pace of business changed dramatically in the United States and worldwide. A recession began in the early 1980s, followed by voracious corporate acquisitions in the mid-1980s; then a stunning market "correction" in 1987 led to another recession in America, financial losses, layoffs and a new term introduced to the corporate lexicon, "downsizing." Many companies, including 3M, faced hard choices. While some areas remained profitable, they didn't meet the company's financial objectives. 3M's decision to sell the Duplicating Products Division prepared the company for the most wrenching decision in its history, a decade later.

<blockquote>> The Long Rise—and Ultimate Fall—of Thermo-Fax Copiers</blockquote>

When mechanical engineering student Carl Kuhrmeyer graduated from the University of Minnesota in 1949, even this ambitious grad didn't see himself occupying an executive office next to William McKnight 25 years later. But, that's what happened, after Kuhrmeyer, at

❶

age 38, became the youngest general manager of a 3M division that created a brand new industry and generated $1 billion in annual revenues by 1980.

The story of the invention and commercialization of Thermo-Fax copiers is a classic 3M innovation model: create a product never seen before using new technology, grow that business through aggressive sales and distribution, lead the market for decades, exit the business when it has reached the end of its most profitable life cycle, harvest technological know-how and apply it to new products.

In retrospect, some believe that 3M should have committed more research and development (R&D) dollars to "obsolete" its copiers and stay ahead of the competition that ultimately surfaced. Others have suggested that 3M's undisputed leadership led the company to underrate the impact of competition. Whether these perspectives are accurate or not, Thermo-Fax copiers and the line of duplicating products that it spawned produced major, sustained profits over decades, accelerated 3M's international growth and proved that the company could successfully make and sell a product combining hardware (a copying machine) and a consumable product (coated paper). But, like most breakthroughs at 3M, the path wasn't easy or straight.

Copying a document in the 1940s meant putting pen to paper, typing the document using carbon paper or creating 15–20 copies on the mimeograph or Ditto machine, a process that produced less than perfect copies.

Thermo-Fax
BRAND
Copying Products

But, that all changed when Carl Miller, a scientist in 3M Central Research Laboratories, discovered the process that became Thermo-Fax copiers in 1948. 3M's New Products Division in the fabled Benz Building landed the assignment to transform his invention into a saleable product. There were about five projects being explored at the time including an offset plate for printing and a fluorochemical project that led to Scotchgard fabric protector eight years later.

"We had to fight to get enough money to develop the Thermo-Fax machine," Kuhrmeyer recalled, "because no one was sure of the market. 'Why do you want to do this; where's the market?,' they asked. We said, 'We think people are going to want to make copies of things and it's hard to do it today.' We thought, here's a chance to broaden 3M's product line beyond tapes and adhesives into something new and really make a mark on the world."

The development of Thermo-Fax copiers into a commercially viable product took a decade and an investment of about $1 million. Kuhrmeyer and a team of chemists and engineers worked closely with Miller to create the first desktop copying machine, called the Model 17 Secretary, in 1951. They overcame three, key technical obstacles. First, they needed a consistent, high-energy light source to shine across a sheet of paper. They went to General Electric for that invention. Second, they needed to build a reflector that would concentrate light into a narrow beam that crossed the paper's surface. Finally, they had to create a mechanism

that positioned the original document and copy sheet like mirror images. In addition to Miller's Thermo-Fax process, the company's patents covered each of these three elements of the new copier.

Around 1955, sales took off, and the Duplicating Products Division was born, with Ray Herzog, later named chairman and CEO, as its general manager and relentless champion. The division stayed in the Benz Building on the East Side of downtown St. Paul, where people knew they were breaking new ground. "We were separate," Kuhrmeyer said, "so we were independent. We had freedom to do what we needed to do. That was good because we were in a new business, very different from tape, abrasives or reflective sheeting. We were plowing new ground and building thousands of copying machines a month. Making a coated product like tape or abrasives is quite different than making a piece of hardware. We had to hire different kinds of people to get the job done, and we built factories that were different from anything else in 3M."

Through the 1950s and 1960s, Duplicating Products grew rapidly, because the Thermo-Fax machine had no real competition. While Xerox had surfaced by this time, their plain-paper copier was, "bigger than a piano," cumbersome and had a nasty habit of catching on fire, according to Dick Lidstad, retired 3M vice president, Human Resources, who began his 3M career in the Copying Products Division. The Xerox product was much more expensive at $5,000 per unit, compared to a $400 Thermo-Fax copier that used a specially coated

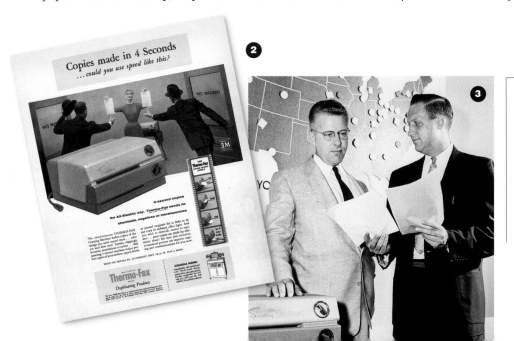

1 A 1955 advertisement for Thermo-Fax copiers.
2 A 1956 advertisement extolled the efficiency of the four-second copies.
3 Ray Herzog (right) and E.F. Boverman mapped out the market for new office products in the 1950s.

paper sold by 3M. To counter the cost issue, Xerox leased its machines and made money by charging about ½ cent for every copy a customer made.

The easily portable Thermo-Fax machine, dubbed "the down the street machine" by 3M sales representatives, had broad appeal inside and outside the United States. "Copying was a prime mover in helping us establish our foreign ventures," recalled Maynard Patterson, a leading architect of 3M's global expansion. "That was especially true in the 1960s when copying products' sales were going wild and so was 3M's international growth."

In fact, the first Thermo-Fax copier was introduced to Europe in 1955, only a few years after its United States debut. "The Thermo-Fax machine was a product that we could sell in almost any country or city of the world," said Kuhrmeyer. "After opening an office to sell copying products, 3M then could introduce tapes and abrasives."

3M was the undisputed world leader in copying from 1955 to 1970. In addition to copiers, the division introduced the first overhead projector (the Thermo-Fax copier was the only one on the market that also made transparencies). By 1965, the division introduced a dual spectrum dry copying process that produced an improved image, followed by a color copier in 1969.

By 1970, Xerox was nipping at 3M's heels. It had developed smaller, faster, more reliable machines. Japanese competitors had begun licensing xerography and making their own copy machines. Xerox also had targeted the larger volume markets, while 3M had focused on smaller markets, such as schools. In Kuhrmeyer's opinion, the power shift occurred when Xerox could tout permanent, plain-paper copies and 3M could not. Before long, other competitors, including Kodak and IBM, were pursuing the fast growing, lucrative copying business. By this time, Kurhmeyer was vice president of 3M's largest division—Duplicating Products.

> 3M was the market leader in tapes and abrasives in the United States, but in other countries there were local competitors that led the category. With copying machines, we won the business and the world beat a path to our door. That success generated cash flow 3M needed to invest in global growth. **> Ron Mitsch**
>
> *retired vice chairman of the board and executive vice president*

It wasn't until the mid-1970s that 3M introduced a copier that could compete with Xerox. "It took many millions of dollars to come out with a plain-paper copy product and we were late," said Kuhrmeyer. "We had been making about a 30 percent profit on our coated-paper copiers. When a product is pulling in revenues like that, it takes remarkable judgment to admit that your product might, in fact, be obsolete." In retrospect, Kuhrmeyer and others say that 3M should have purchased the Xerox technology when it had the chance 20 years earlier.

1 3M copying products were sold around the world. In 1970, a 3M employee trained distributor employees to service a 3M copier in Dakar, Senegal.

We were trying desperately to develop another thermography product that would compete with xerography. We introduced a lot of machines with a lot of different technologies. It was like searching for the Holy Grail. **> Dick Lidstad**

retired vice president, Human Resources

3M's dual-spectrum product competed head to head with Xerox until the late 1970s, when the competition finally pulled ahead for good.

"There is a life cycle for every product and that is one of the hardest things for management to recognize," said Kuhrmeyer. By 1980, 3M was no longer the market leader and Duplicating Products was not producing the 25 percent operating profit expected of established divisions. This was adversely affecting other parts of 3M's operations.

"There was pressure to find a solution," recalled Lidstad who, by 1983, was general manager of the Business Communication Products Division. While 3M had a foothold in the fax business, Lidstad told management that the Japanese "owned" the business and 3M had no unique product advantage.

One of the biggest mistakes the company made was not working with the people who began Xerox. We turned them down twice because their idea didn't fit our business model. 3M made most of its money selling sheets of coated paper. We couldn't imagine a copy machine business without consumables and only clicks on a copying machine counter. **> Ron Mitsch**

Lidstad hunted for a joint venture partner for the fax business so 3M could derive some benefit from its leadership but with no success. Meanwhile, the idea of a joint venture for Duplicating Products looked like a timely, pragmatic way for 3M to ease out of the business. The company struck a deal with its distributor,

Harris, in 1985, and, about three years later, 3M sold its share to Harris. About 700 3M employees joined their new employer. With the departure of Duplicating Products, another 1,200 3M employees found their jobs eliminated. To find new opportunities for these people, 3M created a company-wide early retirement package, allowing people age 55 or older to retire with enhanced benefits and a separation bonus. About 200 people took that option, while 1,000 found new positions at 3M.

Recognizing that we had lost our ability to compete and offer a distinctive and unique product was really hard for 3M. **> Dick Lidstad**

We'd built a tremendous business. The thought that we were now failing wasn't easy to take.

> Ralph Ebbott *retired vice president and treasurer*

"It was hard to accept," said Kuhrmeyer, "but you have to recognize reality. Every product has an end. There aren't too many products that continue for 50, 60, 70 years."

For decades, Thermo-Fax business and its "product progeny" had a mostly profitable and glorious ride.

> Magnetic: First a Pioneer, Then a Commodity

The fortunes of war, a singer's desire to prerecord his network radio show and 3M's commitment to a new research and development program all combined in the mid-1940s to revolutionize the recording industry. This fusion of seemingly unrelated events gave the world the first commercial magnetic sound recording tape, Scotch No. 100, in 1947.

In the 1890s, a Danish engineer, Valdemar Poulsen, had successfully invented a recording device that used wire to store magnetic impulses that could reproduce sound. For 50 years, others tried to refine this idea.

A major breakthrough came during World War II when U.S. Signal Corps officers monitoring late night German broadcasts realized the programs must have been prerecorded. But, how did they do it with such lifelike sound? The Germans had perfected a recording

Both our duplicating products and magnetic businesses were huge technical and business successes. In copying, we just didn't go to plain paper in time. We had a 50-year run in magnetic tapes, but the trouble was our technology was overcome by other types of recording media selling at lower cost and lower margins.

> **Paul Guehler** *senior vice president, Research and Development*

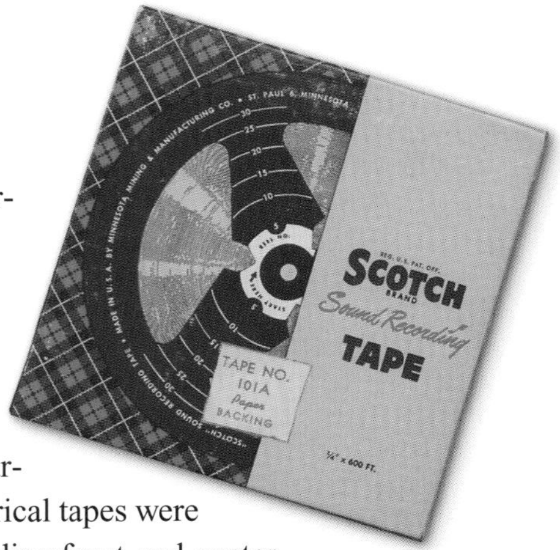
SCOTCH
Sound Recording
TAPE
TAPE NO. 101A
Paper Backing

machine called a Magnetophone that produced high-fidelity recordings on magnetic plastic tape, instead of wire, at a quality level never before heard.

The U.S. government was aware of this technology and 3M got its chance to experiment with making an even better magnetic tape in 1943: "We had our first exposure when the National Defense Research Committee asked us if we could produce magnetic oxide-coated acetate film and slit it in quarter-inch widths a mile long," said Hugh Tierney, vice president, Tape Research and Development and Manufacturing, at the time. "We claim to be coating experts and we certainly coat a lot of cellulose acetate film and we certainly slit a lot of film, so I thought, we ought to be able to do it. At least we ought to take a crack at it."

This new project surfaced when 3M's electrical tapes were major products demanding front-and-center focus: "We had to bootleg our work on magnetic tape because we were under pressure—and justifiably so—to take care of the ground we'd gained on competitors with our 60 different electrical tapes," Tierney, who retired as vice president, Reinforced Plastics Division, said. He kept the project going by announcing that Mel Hegdahl would be the "number one guy charged with the technical responsibility for helping to bring out this new product—magnetic tape." The 3M team used black iron oxide, refined from binders used in making sandpaper, and a gray, vinyl treated backing. It worked well, even though the 3M team had no machine on

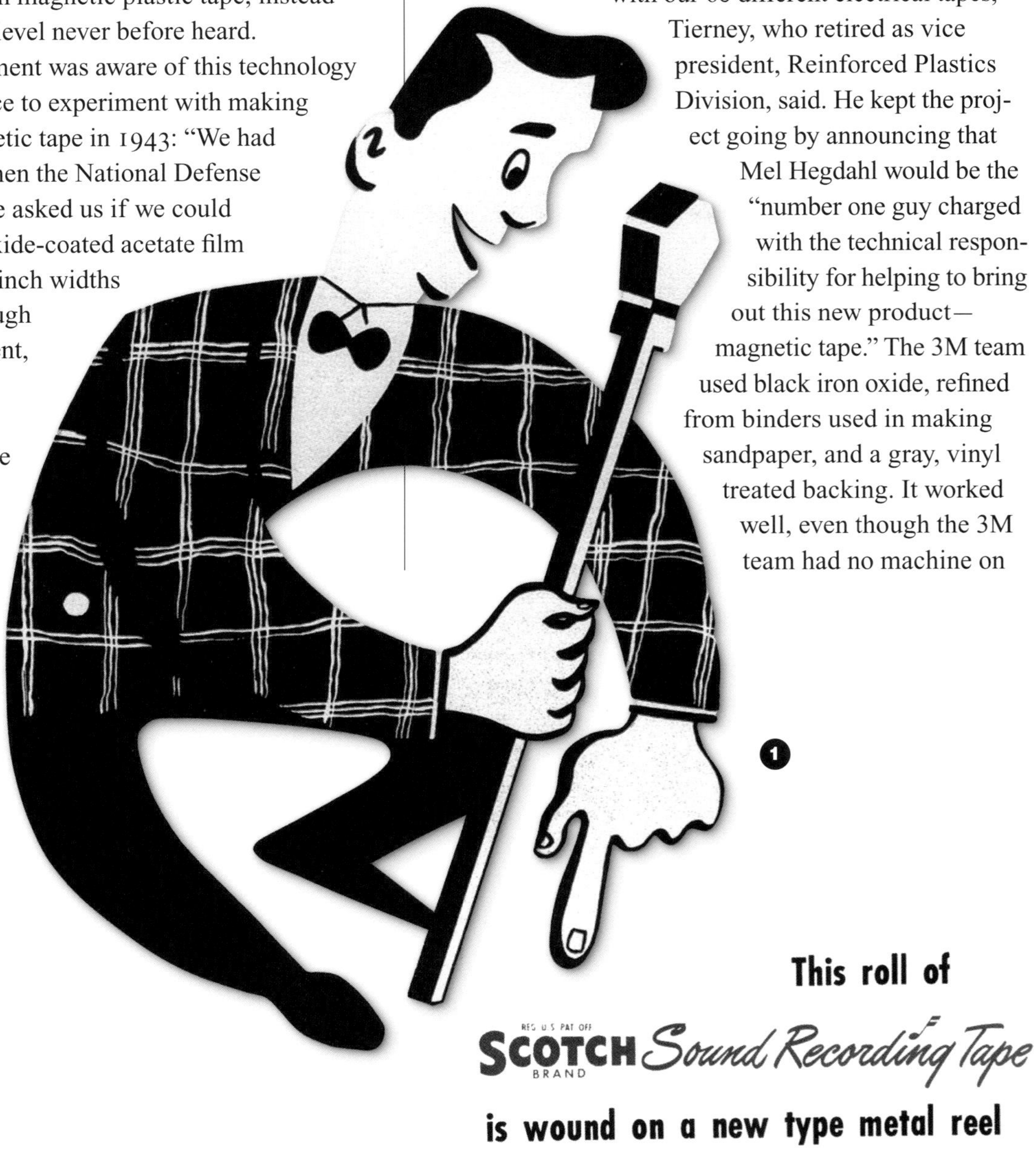
This roll of
SCOTCH Sound Recording Tape
BRAND
is wound on a new type metal reel

1

which to test samples. In addition, the backing solved coating and slitting challenges that were more difficult than any they'd ever encountered. Within a few months, 3M had already improved upon its first product.

About the same time the 3M team was inventing the world's first commercial magnetic tape, John Mullin, an electrical engineer who had served in the U.S. Signal Corps during the war, wowed his colleagues at a convention of radio engineers in 1946. After the war, Mullin had disassembled two German Magnetophones and mailed the pieces, along with 50 reels of tape, to his San Francisco home in 35 small packets. Mullin reassembled the machines, experimented with improving them, and unveiled audio tape recording to his stunned peers at the convention. Soon afterward, Bing Crosby, then America's most popular crooner, got wind of Mullin's demonstration and hired him to mastermind prerecording Crosby's weekly radio shows, a controversial step at the time. Crosby aired his first "Philco Hour" broadcast on 3M's magnetic tape in October 1947. Mullin soon joined 3M.

3M quickly "obsoleted" its own magnetic product with the far superior No. 111 recording tape that used red iron oxide. After its introduction in 1948, No. 111 became the international standard until the late 1960s.

3M had its pick of many potential markets and chose several: home recording, professional recording for radio, and record recording for making masters on tape instead of disks. Not wanting to get into the hardware business, 3M collaborated with recording machine manufacturers to create magnetic tape expressly for their equipment.

In 1955, 3M formed its Magnetic Products Division and, with audio recording tape a resounding success, work had already begun on videotape. As early as 1951, 3M produced a black and white video recording tape for Bing Crosby. A few years later, 3M developed a sophisticated "quadruplex" videotape for a brand new video recorder that Ampex Corporation was preparing to demonstrate for the Association of Radio and Television Broadcasters in Chicago. Ampex was using another company's magnetic tape that kept failing, putting the whole project in jeopardy.

We weren't always the smartest guys, but we were persistent. > **Hugh Tierney** *retired vice president, Reinforced Plastics Division*

Wilfred Wetzel, a 3M research scientist, heard the news only 24 hours before the public showing and huddled with tape binder scientist Melvin Sater in the 3M lab. Sater and his team worked nonstop for 20 hours and managed to make enough 2-inch-wide videotape for two sample rolls. After Wetzel had already boarded a plane for Chicago, a lab technician raced to the plane, passed the samples to the pilot on a message pole arming Wetzel for the meeting.

Sater's team had developed the tape without ever seeing the Ampex machine, and yet the result was

1 Whimsical artwork from a 1949 Scotch audiotape brochure cover.
2 Bing Crosby's successful recording of the "Philco Hour" introduced 3M products to the radio industry.
3 3M advertised its Wollensak sound equipment in 1962.

astounding: "photographic picture quality," one viewer gushed. The audience erupted in whistles, cheers and stamping feet. It took 50 years for phonograph recordings to evolve to spoken words and longer for good music reproduction. It also took 50 years before "talkie" motion pictures on film were available. 3M had progressed from inventing sound recording tape to high-fidelity video in just nine years.

From 1956 to the early 1980s, 3M produced a continuous stream of new products including open-reel audio and videotapes and tape cassettes, 8-track audiotape cartridges, magnetic tape for motion picture sound track mastering and computer tapes and diskettes. Videotape technology moved from a 22-pound roll of 2-inch-wide tape nearly a half-mile long used by broadcasters to video cassettes for home use. Consumer audiotape cassettes became small and compact, and the tape itself was only one-eighth-inch wide.

In 1983, when 3M won an Emmy award for pioneering the development of videotape, observers might have thought 3M's magnetic recording business was on top of the world. In fact, said Dick Hanson, who spent 25 years in 3M's Memory Technology Group, "by then, the whole magnetic media business was heavy in red ink." 3M had invented and "owned" the business with huge market shares and strong profits in the professional markets. 3M supplied all

I had product responsibility for what we called floppy disks when they were first on the market. We projected $100 million in sales for the disks and people said, what's your basis for speculating 20 to 30 percent growth? Nothing grows that fast. It turns out we underestimated it.

> **Dick Hanson** *retired director, Community Affairs, and vice president, 3M Foundation, formerly in the Magnetic Media business*

the television networks and companies specializing in instrumentation, from geophysical study to space exploration. Then magnetic tape became a consumer business and attracted competition from all over the world, primarily Japan. "The projected growth seemed too good to be true. We didn't have the capacity to produce fast enough to meet the explosive demand," said Alfred E. Smith, general manager, Magnetic Audio Visual Division, in the early 1980s. "We didn't move as quickly as our Japanese competition, and they invested a lot more in the business. We saw our operating margins cut in half, from roughly 20 percent down to 10 percent or lower. That diluted the rest of 3M's performance." Japan was particularly strong in the booming computer diskette business, as personal

1 3M won an Emmy in 1983 for its pioneering videotape. **2** In 1981, 3M celebrated the 25th anniversary of the introduction of videotape. **3** 3M Black Watch tape cartridges provided data centers with protection and readability for archival storage. **4** Floppy diskettes were another of 3M's many data storage products. **5** The 3M laser disk revolutionized information storage and retrieval in the 1980s.

computers became popular, and in the low-margin consumer audiocassette markets.

The computer business, later called "data storage," quickly became a commodity business with large-scale, automated production, multiple competitors, narrow margins and product offerings that were basically the same from company to company.

"If we were going to compete effectively in the industrial markets, we had to compete in consumer," said Smith. "We decided to do battle in the videocassette market. Our magnetic manufacturing processes became the best in the company; they had to be—we had the most competition. Data Storage introduced a new standard of manufacturing expertise to 3M."

"We put our best efforts toward being a world-class competitor," said Al Huber, retired sector vice president,

We had superior technology. We made magnetic media better than anyone else in the world, including the Japanese, but they were willing to accept a lesser profit. We thought we could be better technologically. Ultimately, we thought we could win. This drove the decision to spin off the business. We knew the new company (later called Imation) would have the best technology in the world. > **Charlton "Chuck" Dietz**

retired senior vice president, 3M Legal Affairs

Electronic and Information Technologies Sector. "3M invested heavily. We modernized existing plants, put in new plants and added the latest equipment in the United States, Europe and Japan. The end goal was to push the cost of manufacturing floppy disks, diskettes and videocassettes down to the lowest level possible. We succeeded in doing that in about four years. We could go toe to toe with the Japanese and do well."

Because 3M's traditional focus was in the industrial and professional markets, no one had strong background in the consumer arena. "Historically, our consumer experience was limited to products in which we had great strength, like Scotch brand tapes," said Huber. "We didn't have experience with distribution to the huge discounters like Target, Wal-Mart and the electronics superstores."

Competition for the consumer dollar was fierce in the 1980s and 1990s—TDK and Maxell were two well-known Japanese brands.

We kept trying to fix the same problem (with copying and magnetic) with the same solutions, so we ended up with the same answers. One of the positive sides of 3M is knowing what its core competencies are. The negative side is when we come across a business that's on the border of our core competencies, we still apply the traditional techniques. > **Fred Harris Jr.**

formerly division vice president, Audio and Video Products Division, now staff vice president, Community Affairs and Workforce Diversity

In the United States, the biggest audiotape competitor was Memorex, which promoted its product superiority in commercials featuring Ella Fitzgerald hitting a high note on tape and shattering glass. 3M struggled with quality issues, while the Japanese touted superior quality.

"By 1984 and 1985, our competition was investing heavily and taking an aggressive approach to winning market share," said Huber. "Frankly, we got behind the curve in competing with 'Japan, Incorporated.' It was a dog fight."

"After about four years, we were getting hammered," said Larry Thomason, then manufacturing director, Magnetic Media.

"We decided we had to look at where product prices and the cost of manufacturing were going. We examined every step of our process and made big changes." Through high-speed automation and major simplification of the whole manufacturing process, Thomason said magnetic media reduced its costs dramatically. For example, the manufacturing team reduced 3M's cost of producing a videocassette, including the tape itself,

It's sad that it's gone, but it served its purpose and had a good life. Video recording completely changed the television industry, and the computer business wouldn't have gotten off the ground without magnetic tape. > **Dennis Horsford** *retired*

product coordinator and marketing manager, Magnetic Media Division

from about $4 to 95 cents, even though the plastic cassette "shell" alone contained 36 different parts. "In most of our operations, we increased our production speed by more than two and a half times," Thomason said, "while ensuring high quality. We consolidated all of our magnetic manufacturing from four factories to one in Hutchinson, Minnesota, and we did it in 24 months."

Although 3M's magnetic media business earned awards for productivity improvements and topnotch

1 Scotch select series video-cassettes helped consumers pick the right one for the right use. The theme was: "choose them based on how you use them."

manufacturing, 3M was in a bind. While it sold its products for little or no profit, its competition sold their products for even less. Even though the consumer business had huge growth potential, 3M had little experience with a low-cost, low-profit-margin model.

The markings were clear—exit this business, even though 3M invented it. To stay in the "dog fight" meant 3M had to invest enormous amounts of money in order to remain the low-cost producer, with no assurance that profit margins ever would improve. "Exiting it was the right decision," Huber said.

> **Challenging the Giant**
In marked contrast to 3M's leadership in magnetic products, the company made a bold move in 1963 to face off with large, successful Eastman Kodak. Bert Cross, then 3M's president, believed that 3M's strong expertise in coating technology was a natural entrée into the photographic film business. To kick off this venture, in 1963 3M purchased Dynacolor, an American film processor and manufacturer, and a small French film manufacturer. Unfortunately, the 600-person French company was nearly bankrupt; its film product was substandard and 3M had agreed to build a movie film plant in India without the expertise it needed.

Kodak was head and shoulders above anyone else in the world. > **Ralph Ebbott** *retired vice president and treasurer and one of the first 3M employees to relocate to Ferrania*

Josef Kuhn, a multilingual 3M mechanical engineer, was appointed general manager of the stumbling French operation. He went in search of technical expertise to transform the French business into a viable manufacturer and build the plant in India, soon discovering that this business required far more resources than he first had imagined.

Kuhn, who later retired as senior vice president, Engineering, Quality and Manufacturing Services, and others from 3M learned about the availability of Ferrania, S.p.A. of Italy. "They had excellent technology for filmmaking and coating; better than we had. They also had a multilayer coating technology that we

lacked," said Kuhn. "Ultimately we learned a lot from Ferrania." Ferrania was a respected company with a major presence in Europe. 3M acquired Ferrania S.p.A. in 1964 in a stock purchase valued at $55 million. It was 3M's largest acquisition in its 62-year history. "They had technology and well-educated, good people but taking on Kodak was a big challenge and, in today's marketplace, perhaps insane," said Kuhn.

While 3M's coating expertise was a plus, the photographic business struggled with quality issues and effective marketing eluded them. Meanwhile, other new competitors entered the scene including Germany's Agfa, Britain's Illford and Japan's Fuji.

Ultimately, 3M's photographic business became the largest supplier of private label film to customers around the world, but the consumer business stayed with Kodak and the newest up-and-comer, Fuji. 3M even introduced the world's fastest daylight-balanced color transparency film in 1983 but chose not to invest further in the business, especially when adaptation to digital photography would have required significant dollars. 3M actually made its greatest strides in medical X-ray films, including a high-speed film that cut down exposure time and a high light system that eliminated the need for a darkroom to load and process X-ray film.

Although 3M exited the photographic business in its restructuring and spin-off of businesses in later years, the Ferrania acquisition gave 3M a major presence in Italy. By 2000, 3M Italy ranked No. 4 in Europe and No. 5 in the world, after Japan, in total 3M business.

> **An Unprecedented Decision**
On November 14, 1995, 3M announced an unprecedented restructuring of the company. The leadership had decided to spin off its marginally profitable data-storage and imaging businesses into a new company and discontinue its audio and videotape businesses. That meant eliminating 5,000 jobs worldwide, mainly through attrition and early retirement programs. It meant finding new products that could replace major production that disappeared from the company's 400,000-square-foot manufacturing plant in Hutchinson, Minnesota. Approximately 11,000 3M employees joined the new company, soon named Imation.

How we went about this is unusual in business. We didn't give Imation a poor balance sheet. We gave them a balance sheet that looked very much like 3M's. 3M didn't need to get richer from the transaction. Our main concern was a clean break and a good start for the new company.

> L.D. DeSimone

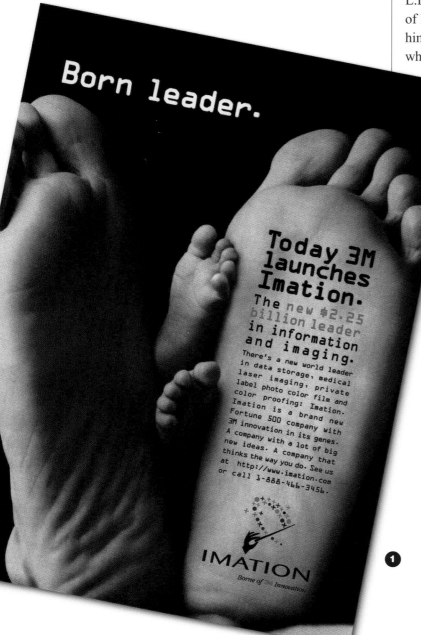

Imation, whose major products would be data cartridges, diskettes and optical disks, medical imaging, X-ray film and color proofing products, became a $2.25 billion publicly traded company on July 1, 1996. Bill Monahan, a 16-year 3M veteran, became Imation's new chief executive officer. Monahan's challenge was to create a nimble company that could keep pace with an ever changing market.

At 3M, the decision was painful but uniformly supported by upper management. Ultimately, 3M's chairman of the board and chief executive officer, L.D. DeSimone, sat at a table and polled every member of his management team. He asked each person to tell him what he or she thought of the spin-off idea and whether this was the best decision. They all agreed it was, knowing that 3M would not be the same company after the spin-off.

It was hard getting to the decision, not making it, said DeSimone. "I said, 'This is the best option we have' . . . there was no perfect option."

There was emotion behind this decision. The process went on for about two months with meetings almost daily. At the end, there was exhaustion, almost like the exhaustion you suffer with the loss of a parent. **> Kay Grenz** *vice president, Human Resources*

1 A 1996 advertisement announced the spin-off of 3M's data storage business into a new company, called Imation.

The spin-off was one of those reality checks, pointing out our need to stay competitive as a company . . . it was a wake up call—and a sobering one—for a lot of our employees.

> **John Benson** executive vice president, Health Care Markets

The decision was a shock and a loss for employees at all levels. At 3M, where people had come to believe that they were guaranteed a "job for life," the spin-off proved this assumption wrong. It was Lidstad's role as vice president of Human Resources at that time to see that 3M people who had to leave made a safe landing. He had learned much from the sale of Duplicating Products 10 years earlier.

"It was a joyless process to tell people the reason was that we just couldn't be successful in the business and that they had to leave the company, knowing that they didn't want to leave," said Lidstad.

"Our policy has always been to be honest with people," said Lidstad. "Tell them as much as you can and do it very well." 3M created a "transition center" not only for 3M employees affected by the spin-off, but also for anyone in 3M who wanted information, support and counseling. It gave employees an opportunity to deal with the loss, and it gave them a chance to consider all their job options. It also offered financial and retirement planning. "I think people viewed that as important and timely assistance," Lidstad said. "We also offered employee assistance for people going through the grieving process. For many employees, it was like a death in the family."

time-tested truths

- Shedding a product, project or division can be healthy; it is sometimes a necessary part of a growing, changing company.
- There's time to win and a time to cut your losses: know the difference.
- Decisions to sell or exit a business require courage, clear heads and compassionate follow through.
- Even if a business is sold, valuable expertise and technology often remain in the company.
- When the marketplace and the margins change, re-visit your business goals.
- Good ideas can come from outside 3M; be wary of "not-invented-here" blind spots.

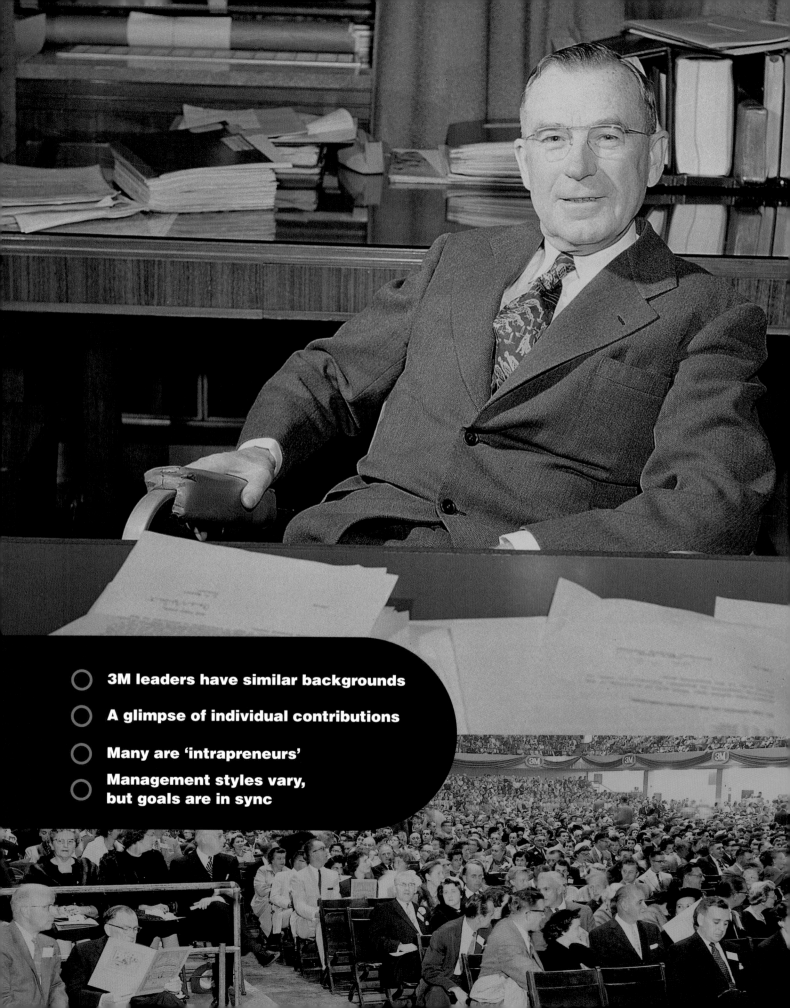

- 3M leaders have similar backgrounds

- A glimpse of individual contributions

- Many are 'intrapreneurs'

- Management styles vary, but goals are in sync

14

3M Leaders—The Right Choice at the Right Time

Bert Cross played a mean banjo and never went to college. William McKnight carried his own luggage and wore mended suits. Ray Herzog was a high school coach and science teacher. Lew Lehr grew up in a little Nebraska town and worked on nearby farms during summer vacations. ● The 13 men who became the leaders of 3M in its first 100 years were largely Midwestern, middle class, hard workers. Most came to 3M with technical training; all built their business careers at the company; and none felt fully prepared for the opportunities that came their way. But, that didn't keep them from tackling new assignments with gusto.

"The leaders of 3M were common people with modest beginnings," said John Pitblado, who joined 3M at age 28 and retired several decades later as president, U.S. Operations. "They were willing to work hard and they were curious. Nobody tried to climb the social ladder in St. Paul. We didn't have lunch at the downtown Minnesota Club; our headquarters were out in the sticks."

3M people have been willing to challenge their leaders over the years. "The company is like a caring family, although we didn't always feel that 'father knew best,'" said Ralph Ebbott, who spent his career in finance and accounting and retired as vice president and treasurer. "The CEO was always very much in charge, but we felt we could openly disagree with him."

Until 2001, when W. James McNerney, Jr., from General Electric, was named 3M's 8th chairman of the board and 13th senior executive, every one of the leaders came from within 3M. Starting with McKnight, they all spent years in the trenches of research and development (R&D), sales, manufacturing, international and division operations.

The leadership and personal styles of these top executives varied. Those who worked directly or indirectly for them agree that each was the right choice for the times. In his own way, each fostered innovation and growth. All of these men had one basic similarity, observers recall. They all stood tall in tough times.

We all buy equipment from the same vendors and raw materials from the same people. We buy the same computers and software. We listen to the same consultants. We hire from the same schools. So what's the difference? It's people. Plain and simple. This company relies on people.

> **Charles Kiester** *retired senior vice president, Engineering, Manufacturing and Logistics*

After Henry Bryan, Edgar Ober, Lucius Ordway and McKnight shepherded 3M as the company's presidents from 1902 through 1929, seven men followed them as leaders of the company. McKnight served as chairman of the board from 1949–1966, while Richard Carlton (1949–53); Herbert Buetow (1953–63); and Bert Cross (1963–66) ran day-to-day operations as president.

> **Carlton: Father of 3M Research**

With his bachelor of science in engineering, Richard P. Carlton, hired in 1921, was the first technical person with a college degree. Carlton is credited with creating the company's first lab with quality measures and standards and, within a few years, he was coordinating research, engineering, manufacturing and new product development. Carlton contributed many of his own patentable ideas to 3M including a new adhesive binder using safer, synthetic resin; a flexible and durable abrasive disc to grind curved surfaces on cars; and a process

Chapter opening photos William McKnight introduced the company's first pension plan in 1930; A 1950s annual shareholders meeting; Illustration of 3M's modest beginnings in Two Harbors, Minnesota; A sketch of 3M leaders, A.G. Bush and Richard Carlton.

for electrocoating sandpaper, giving it more cutting power. By the 1940s, the versatile Carlton had added labor relations to his responsibilities. In 1949, at age 56, Carlton became 3M's fifth president, serving until ill health forced him to resign in 1953 just a few weeks before his death.

Carlton was a man who nurtured innovation, rejected the notion that only people with degrees could come up with the best ideas, fostered knowledge sharing and served as a mentor to many. When Maynard Patterson became general manager of 3M Canada, Carlton gave him "ground cover." "We anticipated some trouble because all 3M business in Canada was to be done through this new, little company," said Patterson, who later retired as group vice president, International Division. "'If you ever have any trouble,' Carlton told me, 'pick up the phone and call.' He gave me wide scope to do what I felt had to be done."

"Dick Carlton called a meeting of all the lab people, including the flunkies like me without college degrees," said Don Douglas, who retired as 3M's vice president, Reflective Products. Carlton addressed the educated: "You all know that if you put this and this together, you'll get this," Carlton said. "But, you take Don Douglas, he doesn't know any better, and he'll put this

and this together and he'll get something entirely different." A move at that time to hire only people with college degrees for technical jobs fizzled.

Carlton created a technical policy committee in the 1940s that became a forerunner to 3M's Technical Council and Technical Forum in which, even today, ideas are freely shared company-wide. John Pearson, a Carlton Society member, served on that committee. "That effort was the first intended to 'institutionalize' a culture of innovation at 3M," he said. "Dick was a strong proponent of getting people involved so they didn't become isolated islands. On Saturday mornings, we brought our lab notebooks up-to-date and we talked with people from other labs. We'd sit down, tackle problems and pick each other's brains. Carlton encouraged that." It isn't surprising that the Carlton Society, named after him, honors 3M technical employees whose careers exemplify innovative research that led to patentable products.

Carlton created 3M's Central Research Laboratory with a broad imperative for experimentation as well as for conducting research to support the company's division labs.

"Carlton set the tone for all the labs," said Les Krogh, retired senior vice president, Research and Development. "He was an idea man and he had a huge tolerance for

1 Henry Bryan, a 3M founder, served as the company's first president. 2 Edgar Ober served as 3M president for 21 years. 3 Lucius Ordway's substantial investments carried 3M through its early years; he served as president from 1906–1909. 4 William McKnight, hired as an assistant book-keeper in 1907, served as president from 1929–1949 and chairman from 1949–66. 5 Richard Carlton served as president from 1949–1953.

experimentation." While working on ways to create electrostatic coating for sandpaper, two young lab technicians, who had spare time, cut out paper dolls and put them in the coating apparatus. "Who should come along but Mr. Carlton," Krogh remembered. "He said, 'Hi, fellows, how're you doing?' He looked at the dolls, which were coated beautifully, and he said, 'I think you've got it.' He never said a word about the paper dolls."

Richard Carlton was the first to stress the importance of investing a significant percentage of earnings back into research. He won the support of 3M's senior leaders. That investment had a domino effect; it produced marketable products that created an explosion on 3M's bottom line. **> Don Larson**

retired president, 3M Foundation, who joined 3M as a production employee

Lew Lehr, who later became a chairman, credits Carlton with envisioning 3M's Health Care business—a venture that started small and, under Lehr's direction, grew to be a major 3M market center and revenue producer.

> **Buetow: The Quiet 'Mirror' of McKnight**

If ever there was an unsung leader at 3M, it was Buetow. He stood in the long shadow cast by McKnight. Buetow was an administrative powerhouse and a businessman with heart. When a February 8, 1951, explosion shredded the six-story 3M minerals building, killing 15 people and injuring 49 others, Buetow was there. A manager expressed his concern about 3M customers, lamenting, "This'll put us weeks behind schedule." Buetow countered, "Let's take care of our people first; then we'll worry about schedules."

During his tenure as president from 1953 to 1963, Buetow led major growth initiatives. 3M's embryonic international business was expanding fast; plants and facilities in the United States were multiplying; new business opportunities sprouted like spring wheat. When asked in 1957 how big 3M wanted to be, Buetow said, "Size is not so much an objective as it is a result. We will continue to grow in direct proportion to the ambitions of people who want a better future, both for themselves and for others whose condition can be improved through 3M products, services and know-how. To

1 The Carlton Award, named for President Richard Carlton, is given to technical employees who demonstrate innovation and collaborative research. **2** Under Herb Buetow's watch in 1951, a gas explosion roared through the 3M minerals building, killing 15 and injuring 49 others. **3** Buetow, 3M's president from 1953–1963, had a reputation for fair play, sound judgment and meeting challenging assignments. **4** A 1955 executive meeting at 3M's Wonewok Conference Center.

do less than our best at solving problems and filling needs would limit our growth . . . I don't believe any of us wants that."

By the time Buetow became president, 3M had a "vertical organization" in which divisions and international subsidiaries had a strong measure of autonomy. This plan was based on McKnight's notion that 3M would "divide and grow" by creating entrepreneurial businesses led by people who were in charge of their own product and profit destinies. It was a creative approach when McKnight envisioned it in 1948. Peter Drucker, the guru of management theory, told McKnight it was a bad idea. Never mind, McKnight did it anyway, and Buetow inherited a stable of ambitious 3M people with an entrepreneurial bias.

Buetow was particularly strong in finance and that solid oversight of the company's assets made it possible for 3M to generate enough cash to finance its own ambitious expansion in the years Buetow was president. "His focus was on the financial and administrative areas that he knew well," said Wally Forman, retired executive director, Compensation, Benefits and Organization. "Herb Buetow had three organization charts in his center desk drawer. Chart 1 represented the present organization, chart 2 was a proposal and chart 3 reflected what the ultimate organization should look like. Whenever anyone came to him with a proposal, he'd lean back in his chair and pull the desk drawer out far enough so that he could see chart 1 and chart 2 to make comparisons. The day Bert Cross became president, we went to his

office to congratulate him and he asked, 'Where are my 1–2–3 charts?' "

Buetow also appreciated the need for a skilled sales team. "He helped strengthen sales and marketing with the help of A.G. Bush, who had been hired by McKnight," said Don Larson, retired president, 3M Foundation. "He sold top management on the need for

> Herb Buetow learned everything he knew from William McKnight. They had the same philosophies. Herb put trust in people. When he gave you an assignment, he expected it to be done right and on time. > **James Klein** *retired manager, International Customs and Trade Affairs*

a corporate aircraft at a time when we had many things cooking and we needed to save time. He was instrumental in creating Wonewok Conference Center near Park Rapids, Minnesota, because he believed in creating a place away from the office to share ideas and to dream."

Buetow was a low-key, quiet man by nature and leadership style. He loved classical music and, upon his retirement, the company endowed the Buetow Music Chapel at Concordia College in St. Paul in his honor. Buetow died in 1972 at age 73.

> Cross: The Entrepreneur as CEO

Bert Cross started his career at 3M in 1926 as a lab technician, advancing to manufacturing manager, Adhesives Division, five years later. Cross soon distinguished himself as a risk-taker and champion for a seemingly profitless product—Scotchlite reflective sheeting. While it was a large profit generator in later years, when Cross was manager, New Products, in 1945, the product's future was uncertain.

Here's one of the things I liked about 3M. Sure, you had a boss and you were theoretically working for him, but Bert Cross and Harry Heltzer always made me feel like I was on the same team working with them—not for them.

> **Don Douglas** *retired vice president, Reflective Products Division*

Young Harry Heltzer, a metallurgical engineer by training, came up with the idea of using glass beads to reflect light. He made his first beads by pouring molten glass out a window of the 3M minerals building and collecting the shattered glass six stories below. But, turning the glass bead idea into a commercial success was costly and 3M's first product—center striping for roads—didn't reflect enough and it couldn't withstand the rigors of traffic

and weather. Another embryonic product designed to make street and highway signs more visible wasn't much better.

Phil Palmquist, a pioneer in reflective technology, had been told to stop working on the project and go back to working on coated abrasives, a proven money-

One of the most significant factors in creating the 3M of today was reflective products. The technology led to all of our light management applications. They represent about 25 percent of the company's total sales. > **Paul Guehler**

senior vice president, Research and Development

maker for 3M. Instead, Palmquist returned to the 3M lab about four nights a week from 7 p.m. to 11 p.m. and successfully created a reflective product that was 100 times brighter than white paint. Cross became the product's champion.

"It took us eight long, dry years to finally make 5 cents in profits from Scotchlite sheeting—or at least to get the bookkeepers to agree that we made some money," Cross said. Sales for Scotchlite reflective sheeting were $3,500 in 1938, the first year; $10,500 in the second; $16,000

SEPTEMBER 15, 1964 / FIFTY CENTS

FORBES

①

PRESIDENT BERT CROSS

in the third; and $33,000 in the fourth. World War II gave Scotchlite sheeting a huge boost because the military ordered it for blackout markings on aircraft landing strips and along tank trails.

Under Cross' leadership, the market for reflective sheeting grew dramatically and, in 1948, he was named vice president and general manager of the new Reflective Products Division.

After his success with reflective products, Cross brought his classic entrepreneurial thinking to Graphic and Printing Products—the fertile ground that created 3M's Thermo-Fax copiers and revolutionized copying. Later, he would imagine still another new business for 3M Photographic Products.

Cross was a researcher at heart and, when he retired from 3M in 1970, he had 18 patents to his name.

Only Cross' exterior was gruff. "On the surface, he appeared to be hard as nails," said Don Hambleton, who worked in administrative support during the 1960s and retired as assistant secretary, Finance. "But, when you got to know him, he had a heart a lot bigger than most people realized." Cross had an authoritarian leadership style; he was a stern disciplinarian, and he expressed his opin-

ions in no uncertain terms. But, Cross also was an effective mentor—two men who reported directly to him, Heltzer and Ray Herzog, followed him as 3M CEOs. All three were considered "product pioneers" because they made their marks at 3M in new ventures that became major, revenue producing businesses.

Cross was a strong supporter of Clarence Sampair and Maynard Patterson, the "co-architects" of 3M International. During Cross' seven years as the company's top executive, from 1963 to 1970, 3M started 15 new international companies around the world.

After serving as president from 1963 to 1966, Cross was the first person to succeed McKnight as chairman of the board. While McKnight continued to serve as honorary chairman until 1973, Cross had the challenging distinction of following him in the top job. Cross died in 2001 at age 95.

1 The September 1964 issue of Forbes magazine featured Bert Cross on the cover. **2** Cross, pictured in 1971, was proud of the patent awarded on his own invention—the Plastiform magnetic hatband. **3** Cross' first paycheck in 1926 was for $27.50.

> Heltzer: Extending the Global Arena

When 22-year-old Heltzer knocked on 3M's door looking for work in 1933 in the depths of the Great Depression, he got a job unloading freight cars and feeding mineral crushers. "I started as close to the bottom as anyone could," Heltzer said. But, he had aspirations, and Sampair, then head of production, and Cross, then new products' champion, became Heltzer's role models. "I found people I had great respect for and I said, ultimately, 'I'd like to be in their jobs.' "

From the factory to sales to production management and finally group vice president managing multiple divisions and businesses, Heltzer's span of responsibility grew over 33 years, until he was named CEO in 1970 to succeed his role model Cross. The appointment came

as a big surprise to Heltzer: "I arrived home from a business trip and there was a note from Bert to come and see him," Heltzer remembered. "I went in and he said, 'Well, we've made our selection.' I was a candidate, but there were others, too. I said, kind of resigned, 'Well, that's fine.' Then Bert said, 'It's you' and I answered, 'You've got to be kidding!' "

A creative and persistent innovator himself, to this day Heltzer believes that no matter how large 3M becomes, the spirit of innovation will stay intact as long as people have the freedom to pursue their best ideas. "You have to gamble on people who are creative and willing to work hard with an appetite for challenge," he said. "If you keep enough ideas cooking, some will come along as products. Then, when you find you've got a breakthrough product, you pour as much effort, talent and money into it as you can. That was McKnight's philosophy and it continues to be a sound one."

On Heltzer's watch from 1970 to 1974, 3M added 13 new international companies, bringing the total outside the United States to 48. He was a strong proponent of overseas experience for 3M's future leaders, well before an offshore assignment was considered a career-maker. And, while these companies had broad autonomy and authority, Heltzer could see the importance of integrating 3M's international and domestic businesses so that both were operating with a one-company mindset, regardless of geography. That was a hard sell but, under Heltzer, this shift in thinking began.

Given his involvement with the origin and growth of reflective products, Heltzer was a strong advocate of maintaining solid, trusted relationships with government policymakers and regulators. "Legislation doesn't come as a result of one day or one hour or one period of time," Heltzer said. "It may take years before it's drawn and there has to be a continuing relationship to get our story across."

Heltzer was also a proponent of strategic acquisitions, even though the company's bias had always been to "grow its own" new ventures. "Not everything can be invented here, no matter how much we provide in the way of talent, imagination and dollars," Heltzer said in the early 1970s. "Sometimes an acquisition is the obvious answer."

As one who benefited from good mentors, Heltzer was supportive of new ideas, said Ray Richelsen, retired executive vice president, Transportation, Graphics and Safety Markets. "I was an engineer in Reflective Products and barely 30 years old. I remember walking into an Operations Committee meeting—it was like walking into a room full of gods. We were asking for money to make glass beads in a completely different way and here was Harry, the inventor of glass beads. When I finished, he said, 'Let me get this straight. You're going to make them wider; you're going to get the lead out; and you're going to make them for less cost?' I said, 'Yes, sir.' He said, 'I tried to do that for 15 years and couldn't get it done. Good luck, son.' The project was approved. What struck me about Harry was that he was so supportive."

When 3M was implicated in making illegal political contributions to national candidates, including the committee to re-elect President Richard Nixon, many at 3M regard Heltzer as standing tall in one of the company's biggest—and most publicized—challenges. "Whether or not he was personally involved, I don't know," said Richelsen. "But, he was the guy in charge and I remember he said in 1974, 'I'm going to resign because it happened while I was CEO and I'm going to take the blame for it.' That was a very classy move on his part."

Observers remember Heltzer's leadership style as outgoing, warm-hearted and gentlemanly. "Harry was like an old shoe, easy to approach and affable," said Ebbott, retired 3M vice president and treasurer. "He knew what he wanted and he wasn't a pushover, but he was very courtly in the way he went about things."

When Gordon Engdahl, retired vice president, Human Resources, went over budget on a capital expenditure, Heltzer took him to task. "He read me the riot act because I'd overspent and I admitted I had done exactly that," Engdahl said. That same evening in the parking garage, he came over and put his arm around me and said, 'Gordy, I just want you to know that talk was nothing personal.' He could differentiate between business and human relationships. He didn't want me to see it as a personal attack."

> ### Herzog: Stepping Up, Standing Tall

With Duplicating Products Division generating more than 20 percent of the company's revenues, Herzog— the man who built that business—rode his success to the CEO's office in 1974 after Heltzer's abrupt resignation. It probably was the most challenging moment in his career: Herzog briefly assumed three roles as CEO, president and chairman of the board. "He wore three hats and it was very hard," Herzog's wife, Jane, remembered. "He was exhausted all the time. The responsibility was unnerving, but he also believed he was up to it." Observers credit Herzog with helping the company regain its self-esteem after the political scandal.

"When Ray took over, there was no one else in the succession plan, so he had to take over everything," said John Ordway, long-time board member and grandson of 3M's early investor Lucius P. Ordway. "For two to three

1 Harry Heltzer, who played a key role in developing 3M's reflective products business, served as chairman and CEO from 1970 to 1974. **2** Ray Herzog, center, pictured at a management meeting in 1957, assumed the roles of CEO and board chair in 1975.

R. H. HERZOG

years, he ran the company, domestic, international, everything—with a couple vice presidents. It was tough. He led 3M with an iron fist and he had to do it. There were a lot of decisions to make because the company was growing fast."

Not long after becoming CEO, Herzog reflected on what it would take to move the $3 billion company forward: "If I could ask for anything," he said in 1975, "it would be for good people who are determined to be successful. I guess maybe I'm lucky, because it seems to me we've got them."

Herzog didn't set out to be a corporate leader at all. He taught high school math and science and coached the St. Croix Falls, Wisconsin, high school basketball team. Herzog met his future wife, Jane, while teaching in St. Croix Falls, her hometown. But, he realized the opportunities were better in business than in education so Herzog took a job as quality control analyst in 3M's main abrasives plant in 1942. "I don't think Ray ever aspired to be CEO," Jane Herzog said. "But, he would always grab another challenge. Competition is an integral part of 3M, I believe, and my husband was a great competitor, along with most of the others who climbed the corporate ladder."

Herzog had an affinity for numbers. He could pick up a sheet of figures and analyze it immediately. When new assignments surfaced, he gravitated toward the one with which he could do the most good, for example, new product development. Herzog was an advocate of new ideas. "Ray was charismatic; he had a keen business sense; and he exercised it rapidly," said Roger Appeldorn, retired 3M corporate scientist and a driving force behind 3M's important new microreplication technology.

"Ray had a complete perspective from product creation to market. When he saw an opportunity, he didn't hesitate to go ahead and do it," said Appeldorn. "He created BPSI, Business Products Sales Incorporated, and without that 3M never would have built the division into a billion-dollar business. When we came up with the prototype for a new overhead projector in January 1962, he told us he wanted to be in production by August. He'd show up in the lab unannounced and invite us to lunch or dinner. It was an impromptu recognition of our efforts and, when we talked about the project, he knew the details." Herzog practiced McKnight's philosophy of giving people latitude. "He allowed people to make mistakes and he didn't penalize them for mistakes that might even cost the company money," said Jane Herzog.

Although duplicating products had been Herzog's pride and joy, generating multimillion-dollar revenues for 3M over many years, he knew they would run their course and disappear, Appeldorn said. "The only thing we can do," Herzog told Appeldorn, "is create as many new businesses as we can because this Thermo-Fax business will die." This was a premonition that would come true in the early 1980s. "He knew this even before Xerox came on the scene," Appeldorn said. "He understood that every product has a life cycle and the cycle ultimately comes to an end."

In support of innovation with profitable results, Herzog created the Golden Step Award in 1972 to recognize people responsible for new business ventures that meet a high level of sales and profitability. Since then, more than 6,000 employees have won Golden Step awards as members of new product teams.

Herzog had a strong personality—authoritative and dynamic. Some described him as a "hard driver," while others called him the "Iron Duke." Herzog was willing to live with his decisions, whether popular or not. "Ray was tall, muscular and powerful looking," said Ebbott.

"When he made a decision, it was done. He was also the person who said work has to be fun and if it's not fun anymore it's time to move on."

"Ray was chairman of the board and CEO when I was involved in starting an Orthopedic Products Division at 3M," said Bill McLellan, retired staff vice president, 3M Corporate Services, Austin, Texas. "I remember going in for Operations Committee reviews, and my knees were shaking behind the podium. Ray was a tough guy and very astute. He did things that were important to the company, notably foster the growth of our copying business."

"Ray was disciplined and tough-minded," said Dick Lidstad, retired vice president, 3M Human Resources. "I liked him because he wasn't one who was taken with power. You knew he had power, but he didn't manhandle it. He was fond of saying, 'People only use about 5 percent of the authority they have and, at 3M, we're looking for people that use the other 95 percent.'

"In saying that, Ray was giving people permission to do things. He encouraged them to go out and follow their instincts."

Ray Herzog died in 1997 at age 82.

> ## Lehr: The Amiable Planner with Vision
When Herzog became CEO in 1974, he tapped Lewis Lehr, a chemical engineer, to become president of U.S. Operations. When Lehr was named 3M chairman of the board and CEO four years later, he already had earned universal respect and was favorably regarded by associates and employees alike.

Like Herzog and the other leaders who preceded him, Lehr came from a modest background. He was born in Elgin, Nebraska, and worked summers on farms during the Great Depression. Those years taught Lehr the value of work and all-out effort. Lettering in football and basketball, Lehr was class president and valedictorian. After serving in World War II under Gen. George Patton, Lehr earned his engineering degree at the University of Nebraska and, on a professor's advice, traveled to Minnesota in 1947 to find a job in the 3M Tape Division. Evenings, he attended law school because he had a keen

1 Ray Herzog (right) and Bing Crosby at the 1964 Beat Bing National Pro/Am Golf Tournament. **2** A 1984 issue of Nation's Business magazine featured Lew Lehr, 3M's chairman and chief executive officer.

LESSONS OF LEADERSHIP

PHOTO: STEVE WOIT—PICTURE GROUP

Keeping All The Lines Open

To run a multibillion-dollar corporation, 3M's Lewis Lehr believes, you must communicate.

By Del Marth

3M's Leaders

Henry S. Bryan *President 1902–1905*

Edgar B. Ober *President 1905–1906, 1909–1929*

Lucius P. Ordway *President 1906–1909*

William L. McKnight *President 1929–1949, COB 1949–1966*

Richard P. Carlton *President 1949–1953*

Herbert P. Buetow *President 1953–1963*

Bert S. Cross *President 1963–1966*

Bert S. Cross *COB and CEO 1966–1970*

Harry Heltzer *COB and CEO 1970–1974, COB 1974–1975*

Raymond H. Herzog *CEO 1974–1975, COB and CEO 1975–1979, COB 1979–1980*

Lewis W. Lehr *CEO 1979–1980, COB and CEO 1980–1986*

John M. Pitblado *President, U.S. Operations 1979–1981*

James A. Thwaits *President, International Operations 1975–1987*

Allen F. Jacobson *COB and CEO 1986–1991*

L.D. DeSimone *COB and CEO 1991–2001*

W. James McNerney, Jr. *COB and CEO 2001–*

COB = Chairman of the Board
CEO = Chief Executive Officer

interest in patent law. But, his life at 3M soon became too busy for him to continue law school.

In the 1940s, Lehr had a chance to try his hand at product development; his creativity and persistence ultimately spawned a new division. Three surgeons from the highly respected Cleveland Clinic asked 3M to develop an impermeable adhesive-backed plastic surgical drape to reduce the risk of infection during operations, and Carlton asked Lehr to conduct the clinical work. By 1948, the new surgical drape satisfied doctors, and it generated revenue for the first time.

The pioneering success of the new product was challenged when the drape shriveled in high temperatures during sterilization. Told to stop working on the project, cease manufacturing and unload the inventory, Lehr said "Yes, sir," but he waited until the factory had produced six months' worth of drapes. In his spare time, Lehr sold a government agency on the drapes; he showed his boss the receipt and convinced him to rescind his cease-and-desist order. On the heels of that shaky, entrepreneurial start came autoclave tape for hospital linens, surgical tapes, wound closures and nonwoven surgical masks in about a ten-year time span. By the time Lehr was named president, U.S. Operations, in 1975, 3M Health Care was producing 7 percent of 3M's global sales.

Lehr inherited a tough business environment in the 1970s when the economies of the United States and other major industrialized nations were suffering simultaneous recessions. At the same time, the United States

Background: Post-it note

1 From left: Bert Auger, R.C. Bertelsen and Lew Lehr worked on the packaging for surgical drapes in 1950. **2** 3M contributed products and technology to the U.S. space program in the 1960s and, later, 3M conducted research projects aboard several space shuttle missions.

faced an energy crisis and the cost of raw materials soared. 3M's earnings were off and savvy competitors with new technologies nipped at the company's heels.

Soon after Lehr was named chairman of the board and CEO in 1979, a Fortune magazine article offered insight into his nature: "Lehr is more cerebral than Herzog," the article noted. "He is generous with his time

Lew Lehr brought strategic planning to 3M. He was a visionary and he encouraged new business models. **> Ron Mitsch** *retired vice chairman of the board and executive vice president*

and easy-going . . . The unpretentious son of a haber-dasher, he walks the corridors chatting with underlings without striking fear in their hearts. He seems incapable of affectation. While Lehr was having his picture taken for this article, the photographer's glasses fell through a wire mesh. Lehr watched with interest as an engineer fished them out (with adhesive on a pole) . . . much the way children reclaim quarters from beneath grates. What kind of sticky stuff does 3M use on the end of its poles, Lehr was asked. 'I don't know,' he admitted amiably, 'Some kind of gunk.'"

The reorganization of 3M under Lehr's leadership as chairman of the board and CEO was a significant turning point. By 1980, the company had grown dramatically to about 40 business units organized among five business groups, each with different management and business goals. In some cases, sales representatives from 3M divisions were competing against each other by offering similar products to the same customers. When they met on this competitive turf, some 3M reps didn't even realize they represented the same company.

This duplication of effort moved Lehr to propose the first formal strategic planning process that 3M had undertaken in its eight decades. He established seven study committees of 3M senior management to examine what 3M could expect in the year 2000. The committees included research, international, community

Everybody said, 'You can't get this done in six months,' and he said, 'We're going to do it.' The process succeeded because 3M had the right leader doing it. **> Arlo Levi** *retired vice president and corporate secretary*

relations, manufacturing, sales and marketing, and human resources. Interestingly, each committee chair was selected because his committee's focus was not his own business specialty. Nor did 3M seek the help of an outside management consultant because Lehr believed it would take that firm six months to understand the company. "We'd all gone to industry meetings and then talked informally about how we'd reorganize 3M," Lehr reasoned. "We knew how to do it ourselves."

The committees did, however, conduct careful research with outside sources in modern business parlance, known as "benchmarking."

This "organic" approach to planning was effective, Lehr said. Those who had participated in the work from beginning to end were accepting of the results. The process was efficient, focused and took five months. From that planning came significant changes for 3M. The company was reorganized into four business "sectors" in which divisions with compatible technologies were grouped together. (Nearly 20 years later, in 2000, 3M would reorganize into six market centers focused on compatible or allied markets.)

In addition, because Central Research was being torn between long-range research and more immediate research needs requested by 3M divisions, "sector labs" were created. That meant that division labs would focus on shorter range research, up to seven years out;

> Lew Lehr took the lead in transforming 3M into a very quality-minded company. Historically, 3M cared about quality, but he understood that we had to have systems to ensure reliability and quality throughout our organization, rather than just inspecting the end quality of our products.
>
> > **Charles Reich** *executive vice president, Electro and*
>
> *Communications Markets and Corporate Services*

sector labs would handle a five- to 15-year span; and Central Research could return to its long-range research mission focused on new ideas and a time frame of 10 to 20 years.

The planning process also underscored the importance of continuing to integrate 3M's domestic and international functions while giving people working in the United States and outside the United States more chances for "cross training." In addition, because the

> To be a good manager, you have to like people, you must have a sense of humor, and you cannot fix your feet in concrete unless you're willing to crack the concrete once in a while to get your feet out. > **Lew Lehr** *retired chairman of the board and CEO*

company had grown dramatically, it became clear that 3M needed a more formal structure for identifying people with top potential and giving them the experience and opportunities to move into senior positions in 3M's heavily "promote from within" corporate culture. To achieve this, 3M created a Human Resources Policy Committee in 1982.

Given his own creative approach to starting and building 3M Health Care, Lehr was concerned about promoting a spirit of internal entrepreneurship. To help accomplish this, Lehr asked Gary Pint, then group vice president, Electrical Products Group, to chair the effort.

1 3M China Ltd. became the company's 53rd international subsidiary in 1985. **2** Lew Lehr was universally respected and favorably regarded by his associates and employees. **3** The Lewis W. Lehr Career Quality Achievement Award was first presented in 1996.

"Gary created subgroups in manufacturing, in our sales offices, in our plants," said Lehr. "He asked them all to develop guidelines for internal entrepreneurship and to determine how people should be recognized for being entrepreneurs inside the company. It was an awareness program designed to make people understand that even if they came from the tax department or the fire department, there was always room for doing things a better way." About the same time, the committee, with Lehr's full support, hired Gifford Pinchot, a well-known management consultant and author of the book "Intrapreneurship," to do his own assessment of 3M's intrapreneurship quotient. People inside 3M also began using Pinchot's apt term.

Lehr also is credited with seeing the huge potential in consumer products at a time when the company was still operating on a strong industrial products mindset. He put his full support behind Post-it notes when others inside the company were openly skep-

❸

Lew Lehr was a visionary and a terrific people person. He'd reach out to everyone. He won the respect of 3M employees, customers, other CEOs and people in government. **> Dave Powell**

vice president, Marketing

tical, and he backed an ambitious effort in magnetic products to compete with Japanese manufacturers for the fast growing consumer audiotape and videotape markets. He supported 3M's involvement with National Aeronautics and Space Agency (NASA), which involved conducting research in space and exploring materials science, and he backed increased spending in research and development. He was CEO when—after years of painstaking work—the People's Republic of China allowed 3M to establish the first company wholly owned by a foreign firm.

The usually amiable Lehr also was willing to take on Minnesota's governor in 1983 when the state adopted a "superfund law" that expanded corporations' liability for hazardous waste damages. On a broader level, Lehr became an outspoken critic of Minnesota's business climate. Not long afterward, Lehr announced the decision to invest in a major new research and development facility in Austin, Texas.

Before and after his retirement, Lehr was active in a large number of volunteer organizations, often serving in a leadership position. He felt strongly that contributing to society as a volunteer was a responsibility for every successful business person.

> **Jacobson: Disciplined, Cost-Conscious and Big-Hearted**

Like some of 3M's earlier chairmen, Allen Jacobson was a chemical engineer, but among all of 3M's leaders he knew the most about manufacturing, because he spent 18 years of his career in and around plants. While "Jake"—as he was nicknamed—spent his first three years in the 3M Tape Lab, he quickly moved into process engineering and manufacturing production, working as a technical assistant to plant managers in Hutchinson, Minnesota, and Bristol, Pennsylvania.

Jake came right out of the core of 3M's business. He was an engineer's engineer, very strong and all business. He loved the details, he was hard working and he was stern. But, behind it all, he had a sense of humor. **> Dick Lidstad**

retired vice president, Human Resources

Eight years after joining 3M, Jacobson showed enough promise to be named production superintendent at Bristol and, within four years, he became manager of the St. Paul Tape Plant. While he moved on to divisional leadership, management of 3M's international operations

The caption reads: Lewis W. Lehr / Career Quality Achievement Award

in Canada and Europe and later the industrial and consumer sector in the early 1980s, Jacobson didn't forget his roots in manufacturing when he became chairman of the board and CEO in 1986.

To outside observers, Jacobson had a style dramatically different from his predecessor, Lehr. In contrast to Lehr's personal warmth and salesmanship, Jacobson was seen as the analytical, tough-minded leader who focused on cost cutting and efficiencies in the second half of the 1980s as America—and the world—slid into a deep, long recession. Lehr told Jacobson that, among many qualities he admired in him, Jake was pleasantly "predictable."

If I were to describe my style of doing things, I'd say I was a hands-on manager who likes to have as much involvement as possible with 3M people. **> Allen Jacobson** *retired chairman of the board and CEO*

Jacobson took his role as sponsor seriously and considered it one of the high points of his career. "Some of the opportunities I was able to sponsor grew into divisions, such as Packaging Systems, Disposable Products, Converter Specialties and Automotive Specialties," he told a colleague in 1986. "The role of a sponsor is one of the most rewarding a manager can play."

The 1980s presented a new economic scenario, and

Jacobson was the right choice to steer around the shoals. Slower economic growth had become a worldwide phenomenon in that decade, and 3M could no longer bank on brisk business in one part of the world counteracting

I was new to my position in Environmental Engineering and Pollution Control and I brought a number of recommendations to the Operations Committee about things that I thought we needed to do. Jake got fully behind them, and he made the environmental commitment for the company. **> Bob Bringer** *retired staff vice president, Environmental Technology and Services*

slow business elsewhere. In addition, by this time the technological capabilities of companies in other countries had grown significantly. 3M had more and better competition and it was global in nature. The best way to win in this new climate was to be more productive and efficient, Jacobson believed. Even so, 3M would not cut back on its research and development spending; under Jacobson, investment in research and development steadily increased.

Jacobson is credited with creating the J35 program aimed at reducing three, key manufacturing areas by 35 percent. They were: the labor involved in producing a product; the cost of ensuring quality through better

1 Allen Jacobson, pictured in 1952, was 3M chairman and CEO from 1986–1991. 2 3M reached its first $10 billion year in 1988 while Allen Jacobson was at the helm. 3 Fortune magazine ranked 3M the second most admired corporation in America in 1986. 4 The April 10, 1989, issue of Business Week magazine focused on 3M Innovation.

engineering; and manufacturing "cycle time." "We had to make some basic changes," Jacobson said, "and we needed to give people time to make them. If you have to change a factory layout and install more automated equipment, you can't do that overnight. The program lasted five years and, because of it, we became a more competitive company."

Those efficiency gains were particularly important in helping 3M compete in lower margin product categories. And, when the U.S.

> Jake had a strong, engineering mind. The efficiencies were probably very visible to him, before others saw them. > **Don Larson**

recession reached 3M's door in 1991, observers credit Jacobson's cost-cutting program with helping the company weather the economic downturn better than most.

When Jacobson became chairman of the board and chief executive officer, 3M management already had decided to get out of its once highly prized office copying business. Seven hundred people joined the joint venture formed with Harris. It was Jacobson who insisted that approximately 1,200 other people displaced by the decision be helped to find jobs elsewhere in 3M or be given substantial early retirement packages. "In order to preserve our culture, I felt we had to treat people the way we would like to be treated," said Jacobson. "We put them on an unassigned list and did everything possible to find jobs inside 3M for them. I think that decision did a great deal to preserve our credibility with 3M employees."

During his tenure, Jacobson emphasized the importance of grooming future 3M leadership by encouraging people to take international assignments. Of the approximately 30 members of his Management Committee, 68 percent had 3M experience outside the United States. "That," Jacobson said, "was not the norm among American companies." Under Jacobson, 3M set a goal of generating 50 percent of the company's total revenues from outside the United States by 1992. Between 1987 and 1992, international revenues grew from just under $4 billion to $7 billion and reached the 50 percent goal. Jacobson also emphasized the importance of strong technical support worldwide not just in the United States.

> Allen Jacobson was very disciplined. He is the reason 3M made it into the 1990s successfully.
> **Paul Guehler**

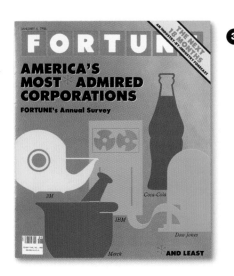

It was on Jacobson's watch that 3M reached its first $10 billion year in 1988. To mark the occasion in the United States, he announced that December 27 would be an extra holiday for all U.S. employees, and he encouraged the general managers of 3M's international companies to follow suit.

Jacobson, like other chairmen, was active in his community through his years at 3M. Well into his retirement, Jacobson, like Lehr, continued to volunteer his time.

> DeSimone: The Champion with Grit and Persistence

L.D. DeSimone was 21, a native of Montreal, Canada, and a chemical engineering graduate of McGill University when he joined 3M in Canada. Eager for challenges, DeSimone—nicknamed "Desi"—took technical positions in the United States, Canada, Australia and Brazil, all in a single year.

"Desi was a brash kid who was running around the world," Jim Thwaits, then 3M president, International Operations, told a newspaper reporter in 1989. "But, he was very innovative and smart." When he was sent to Brazil in 1965, DeSimone was given responsibility for all manufacturing there within three years. It was a mixed blessing because tough import restrictions meant that neither equipment nor raw goods were available for many 3M products. DeSimone and his employees jury-rigged machines and scrounged for alternative materials to make products ranging from surgical masks and respirators to abrasives.

Thwaits said that DeSimone's success in Brazil demonstrated that he understood all the steps taken along the production path. The assignment also involved traveling to remote places. Thwaits remembers when bad weather forced him, DeSimone and other 3M managers to take refuge in a remote Costa Rican hotel, sleeping six to a room with an open shower and toilet in the corner. DeSimone's adaptability in that incident and over the years showed Thwaits that, in his words, "Desi wasn't a stuffed shirt."

DeSimone's leadership at 3M will be remembered for his empathy for people, his commitment to innovation and his willingness to make hard decisions and weather tough economic times.

When he became 3M's chairman of the board and chief executive officer in November 1991, DeSimone was about five years younger—at age 55—than most of his predecessors. His tenure lasted a full decade until his retirement shortly before he was 65. In the company's first century, no one, with the exception of McKnight, served longer as chairman of the board and CEO.

DeSimone inherited a company threatened by a deep recession in 1991. Observers credit him with recognizing that 3M could not "save its way out of crisis," said Appeldorn. "He said we had to get back to creating new products and developing new businesses. We had to regain our intrapreneurial edge. He did it by leading by example. He acted as a champion for a lot of little businesses. For example, he kept our Industrial Optics business alive when it had been formally killed a couple

1 In 1995, 27 percent of 3M's sales came from products introduced within the previous four years. 2 DeSimone, pictured in 1995, served as chairman and CEO from 1991–2001.

times. He was able to keep little projects moving and funded so they didn't get lost. Desi was a champion like Herzog and Heltzer—only more so. To a great extent, I think Desi developed the intrapreneurial CEO management style at 3M."

Under DeSimone's leadership, 3M inaugurated the Pacing Plus Program that singled out the most promising new products and business ventures and rewarded them with additional corporate resources, attention and accelerated effort to bring them to market. One look at the major revenue producers for 3M in its centennial year illustrates the power of DeSimone's idea. Many of those now successful ventures were Pacing Plus Programs in the 1990s.

But, one venture that didn't make it was 3M's once successful information and imaging business, a sector that DeSimone was asked to lead in 1989. When he accepted the responsibility, the business was the least

What's important is what we're doing now and how we're preparing for the future. Principles don't change. Values don't change, but our surroundings change. We have a saying, 'If you want to be comfortable with the future, you better be part of creating it.' > **L.D. DeSimone** *quoted in*

Corporate Report magazine when he was named Executive of the Year

profitable of 3M's four sectors, despite improved earnings in the highly competitive markets of consumer videotapes and computer diskettes. The huge sector produced a mind-boggling array of products, from magnetic tapes to laser imagers and advanced color-proofing systems. As a sector manager, DeSimone's challenge was to cut costs, while not sacrificing research on new products. Lehr called it "a fine balance."

While DeSimone and his sector were able to make major gains in profitability, the business still fell short of historical 3M expectations, and DeSimone's even-handed approach to decision-making became clear. "The business has been providing a good portion of the earnings increase of 3M," DeSimone told a business reporter in 1989, "but it still doesn't provide the quality

Desi will be remembered years from now as one of the most thoughtful leaders of our company. He didn't make a decision without considering every potential ramification and, for him, the number one consideration was employees. I know, because I saw this first hand. > **Kay Grenz**

vice president, Human Resources

of earnings that 3M averages . . . and that's the crux of the thing."

It was DeSimone who put his own personal and emotional investment in the business aside and polled his management team in late 1994. Carving out 3M's memory and imaging businesses and cutting them loose meant that 20 percent of the company's revenues would disappear. Strategically, if both businesses were to grow, they needed to be combined in a single unit. That ultimately became a new company called Imation.

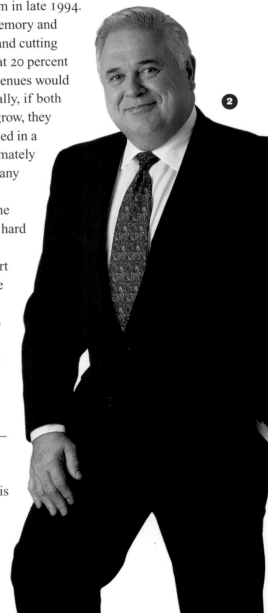

DeSimone had the courage to make the hard decision about what had been a major part of 3M. Some say the decision came too late, but virtually no one questions the reason for it—or the courage required to make it. This was a wrenching choice, one that DeSimone— who focused on the impact of decisions on people—felt to his bones.

When the economy of the Pacific

Desi's tenure as chairman was the longest since William McKnight's. The leaders he singled out, the decisions he made and the technology he supported are important to 3M today and will continue to be vital in 3M's future. He embodied the culture of 3M—multicultural, multilingual, multidisciplinary. He has been all of those things and more. **> Bill Coyne** *retired senior vice president, Research and Development*

Rim went into a tailspin in the late 1990s, its impact on 3M's performance was significant. Though he was criticized by Wall Street, DeSimone stayed the course, believing that the company's long-term investment in that region would pay off. Rather than back away from business interests there, 3M held firm and the decision continues to pay off.

Desi's legacy will be a strong, almost dominating, attitude toward the environment. **> Alex Cirillo**

division vice president, Commercial Graphics Division

DeSimone will also be remembered for his belief that business has a key role in sustaining the planet's environmental resources. He co-authored a book with Frank Popoff, chairman, Dow Chemical Company, called "Eco-Efficiency" that outlines how business has a major stake in sustainable development. The book makes a case for eco-efficiency and its direct rewards for business including enhanced productivity, better access to capital and new product and business opportunities.

> McNerney: Focus on Global Competitiveness
As 3M moved into the 21st century, it named its first chairman of the board and chief executive officer from outside the company. W. James McNerney, Jr. took over the company's reins on January 1, 2001. A native of Providence, Rhode Island, McNerney came to 3M from General Electric (GE), where he last served as president and chief executive officer of General Electric Aircraft

Engines in Cincinnati, Ohio. He had been at GE for 19 years before joining 3M.

Shortly after his appointment, McNerney and the 3M management team launched a number of initiatives to drive growth and performance in the midst of one of the toughest postwar manufacturing recessions. Rejuvenating volume growth, improving quality and driving efficiency were the immediate objectives.

Six Sigma, the company's primary initiative, presented a new, data-driven pathway to process improvement. Nearly every employee is involved in this quest for improvements in costs, cash and growth that will benefit 3M, its customers and its suppliers.

3M Acceleration is focused on faster and more effective commercialization of new products. This initiative provides a process to prioritize research and development investments and to make sure that the very best high priority and high potential opportunities are fully funded and commercialized.

The Sourcing initiative not only helped the company overcome a challenging economic environment, it set the stage for long-term improvement of 3M's financial performance.

eProductivity is helping 3M take better advantage of the Web to increase speed, enhance customer service and build customer relationships. This initiative uses the latest technologies both to drive down cost and accelerate growth.

In 2001, the management team, under McNerney's guidance, also fundamentally changed the dynamics of leadership development at 3M. These advances were based on 3M's deep-rooted respect for an individual's personal ownership over his or her own development as a leader and were designed to give each person both the freedom and the tools to make a difference for the company.

"First, we established what we expect from our leaders and put programs in place to further their development," McNerney said. "Second, we formed the 3M Leadership Development Institute to foster the attainment of these critical leadership attributes. Third, we

1 W. James McNerney, Jr., named CEO in 2001, was the first 3M leader recruited from outside the company.

changed the focus of our employee assessment and compensation system to better motivate, reward and recognize our very best contributors. And fourth, we are making the most of our 'global brains'—facilitating the international transfer of knowledge, best practices and people to advance 3M's already powerful global capabilities.

"This renewed focus on leadership development motivates and encourages everyone to reach their full potential," he said. "When we raise the game of every individual and every team, we raise the game of the entire company."

McNerney said he continues to be impressed by the vast technological, market and geographic power of 3M. In fact, in 2002, the company's official name was changed from Minnesota Mining and Manufacturing to 3M Company to fully capitalize on the power of the brand.

"We will continue to invest in successful technology platforms, and our rich culture of innovation will always be the springboard for new products. At the same time, we are infusing that culture with new energy and aggressively pursuing multiple avenues for growth to complement and leverage 3M's historical organic growth engine."

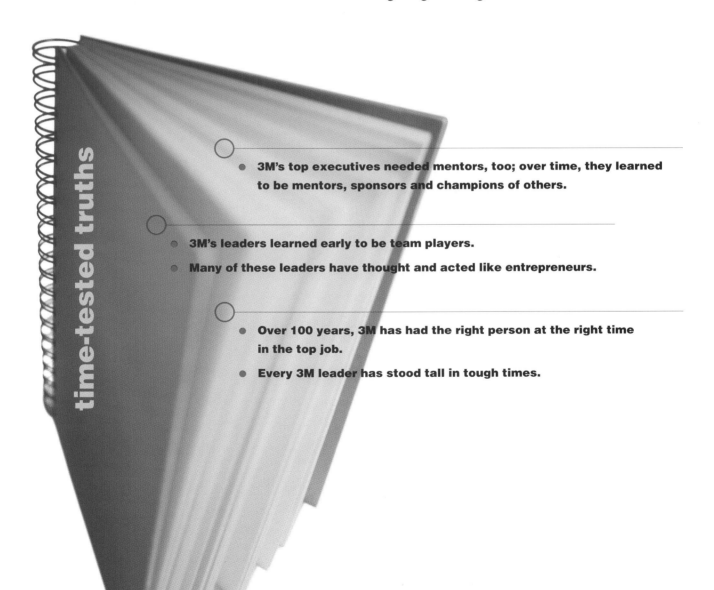

time-tested truths

- 3M's top executives needed mentors, too; over time, they learned to be mentors, sponsors and champions of others.

- 3M's leaders learned early to be team players.
- Many of these leaders have thought and acted like entrepreneurs.

- Over 100 years, 3M has had the right person at the right time in the top job.
- Every 3M leader has stood tall in tough times.

Acknowledgments

This book is a compilation of 3M voices, memories, facts and experiences from the company's first 100 years. In the course of three years, more than 250 employees, retirees, customers, board members, journalists, business scholars and other observers of 3M were interviewed for this book. They told us stories we've heard before, as well as new ones that may surprise readers of this book. Countless others contributed photos, memorabilia, research support and feedback on the manuscript. The Minnesota Historical Society, which houses the 3M archives, was most helpful in providing both research materials and many of the images used in this book. Our thanks to them all.

3M Trademarks *(Partial Listing)*

Active™	Lacelon™	Safety-Walk™	Tartan Turf™
Aldara™	Littmann™	Sasheen™	Tattoo™
Aseptex™	Magic™	Scotch®	Tegaderm™
Black Watch™	Magnetic™	Scotchban™	Thermo-Fax™
Buf-Puf™	Microfoam™	Scotch-Brite™	Thinsulate™
Colorquartz™	Micropore™	Scotchcal™	3M™
Command™	Minitran™	Scotchcast™	Three-M-Ite™
Controltac™	Mistlon™	Scotchgard™	Transpore™
Diamond Grade™	Nexcare™	Scotchkote™	Tri-M-Ite™
Durapore™	Nextel™	Scotchlite™	Trizact™
DuraPrep™	Nomad™	Scotchlok™	Unitek™
Dyneon™	Novec™	Scotchmate™	VHB™
Elek-Tro-Cut™	O-Cel-O™	Scotchshield™	Vikuiti™
Filtrete™	Panaflex™	Skimmit™	Volition™
Fluorel™	Plastiform™	Steri-Strip™	Wetordry™
Imperial™	Post-it®	Stikit™	
Interam™	Reston™	Tambocor™	
Isotak™	Retsul™	Tartan Track™